The Critical Lawyers' Handbook

Law and Social Theory

Series editor PETER FITZPATRICK,
Professor of Law and Social Theory, University of Kent

This series brings social theory to bear on law in a variety of
perspectives, including critical theory, feminism and
postmodernism. It aims to be at the intellectual forefront of the
study of law but also addresses traditional areas of legal
scholarship.

Other titles in the series:

THE CRITICAL LAWYERS' HANDBOOK

Edited by
Ian Grigg-Spall and Paddy Ireland

Pluto Press

London • Concord, Mass

First published in 1992 by
Pluto Press, 345 Archway Road,
London N6 5AA
and 141 Old Bedford Road,
Concord MA 01742, USA

British Library Cataloguing in Publication Data
A catalogue record for this book is available from the British Library

ISBN 0 7453 0508 3 hb
ISBN 0 7453 0509 1 pb

Library of Congress Cataloging in Publication Data
The Critical lawyers' handbook / edited by Ian Grigg-Spall and Paddy
    Ireland.
        p.   cm. – (Law and social theory)
    Includes bibliographical references.
    ISBN 0-7453-0508-3 (cloth). – ISBN 0-7453-0509-1 (pbk.)
    1. Critical legal studies.   I. Grigg-Spall, Ian.   II. Ireland,
Paddy.   III. Series.
    K235.C753   1992
    340'.115–dc20   91-46155
                                                                    CIP

Typeset in 9.25/10.75 Stone by
Stanford Desktop Publishing Services, Milton Keynes
Printed and bound in the United Kingdom
by Billing and Sons Ltd, Worcester

Contents

3: Critical Legal Practice

4: Critical Lawyers' Groups

5: An Alternative Guide to Solicitors' Firms and Bar Chambers

Acknowledgements

Except in the 'mist-enveloped' regions of modern bourgeois ideological individualism all commodities are the products of collective labour. This book is no exception. Tracing the myriad relationships of labour which lie behind its production would be a fascinating and awe-inspiring task – from lumberjacks to computer assemblers, from parents to fax operators, from childcarers to coffee pickers, from roadsweepers to lorry drivers, from all the living writers to all the dead writers of past generations on whom we stand. They all deserve recognition. Of the contributions of some, however, we are able to make particular mention. Freda Vincent, who in coping with over 30 articles on different disks with different formats now dreams in WordPerfect 5.1; Peter Fitzpatrick, our Series Editor, who still wakes with the words 'word length' and 'price' on his lips; Sarah Carter, our law librarian, who assiduously checked all references (once again discovering the ineptitudes of mere academics); Joanne Conaghan for 'grinning and bearing' the occupation of 'her' computer; the CLGs in Coventry, Warwick, Cambridge and Kent who commented upon early drafts; the Kent Law School for its financial support; Anne Beech, Linda Etchart and Monica Ali at Pluto for their efficiency in bringing this project to fruition; all our authors who are patiently waiting for *CLH 2*; and Beth, Charlotte, Holly, Joanne, Nell and Patrick for their conversation, hugs and smiles.

Finally, in the vein of 'collective labour as the private property of an alienated other', we would like to thank Pantheon Books Inc., a division of Random House Inc., for its kind permission to publish David Kairys's and Duncan Kennedy's articles from the *Politics of Law: A Progressive Critique*, and *Law and Critique* for their permission regarding the NCLG interview.

Introduction

This handbook is published as part of Pluto's new legal series Law and Social Theory. This series brings social theory to bear on law from a variety of perspectives, including critical theory, feminism and postmodernism. It also aims to address critically traditional areas of legal education. These objectives are reflected in this handbook.

This series is supportive of what has come to be called the critical legal studies movement, sharing with this movement a deep dissatisfaction with the dominant 'black-letter' approach of traditional legal education with its emphasis on the exposition of legal rules abstracted from their social, political and economic context. The critical movement rejects this expository tradition, on the grounds that any study or practice of law must examine the complex role of law within social structures. In avoiding such issues, the dominant tradition deliberately projects law as autonomous and politically neutral. In the words of the formative statement of the British Critical Legal Conference:

> The central focus of the critical legal approach is to explore the manner in which legal doctrine, legal education and the practices of legal institutions work to buttress and support a pervasive system of oppressive non-egalitarian relations. Critical theory works to develop radical alternatives, and to explore and debate the role of law in the creation of social, economic and political relations that will advance human emancipation.

In short, law generally acts to consolidate and maintain an extensive system of class, gender and racial oppression. Critical lawyers seek a theory and practice that makes the overcoming of such oppression a central political task.

One of the objectives of the handbook and the series is, therefore, to provide 'active supplements' to traditional legal texts and practices: 'supplements' both in the sense of providing information about how legal subjects and practices came to be constituted, how their key bodies of knowledge were formed, and how these legal knowledges interweave with dominant social, political and economic ideas; and in the sense of Derrida's 'dangerous supplements' wherein those elements which have been suppressed, disregarded or marginalised in the constitution and development of legal subjects are explored. These absent elements are dangerous because they have to be hidden or demoted for the subject to exist as it does. To restore them is to go to the constitutive core of the subject.

The handbook and the series also explore the important differences which have emerged in the critical movement. In the areas of critical legal theory and education these differences have come to be characterised as the divisions between the American critical legal studies movement committed to trashing; those committed to critique, who draw heavily on Marxist theory, feminism and the critical social theory of the Frankfurt school; and the postmodernists, influenced by the works of Foucault, Lyotard, Baudrillard and Derrida (for examples of each of these, see Kairys, Thomson, and Douzinas and Warrington in Chapter 1). These debates continue in the pages of various journals and publications and the contributions to this handbook reflect, in many ways, the current position in this engagement. The editors hope that the forthcoming critical supplements will provide a new medium for this debate.

In order to clarify the issues involved our authors were asked to indicate the contribution of their perspective to an understanding of law as an exercise of oppressive power and to the development of a political strategy for social transformation. As a way of highlighting the tensions within the movement, we have prefaced sections of the book with our original brief to authors, leaving it to our readers to judge the validity of the original objective and the success or failure of our contributors in grappling with these issues.

The handbook further identifies a crucial issue which has been generally avoided in the debate, namely the absence of any self-reflection, or (if you like) critique, of the educational and teaching practices of law schools. As Duncan Kennedy argues (in Chapter 2), traditional legal education is both a training *in* subordination and a training *for* subordination. 'Black-letter' doctrinal teaching trains students to accept not only the notion of law as a complex of neutral, impartial rules, but also as a set of legitimate hierarchies of authority – the teacher substituting for the judge as the high priest or priestess of truth. This training in and for subordination to law, judges, courts and the professional hierarchy attempts to destroy all critical thought so as to produce an alienated and subordinated person 'fit to practice'. The critical legal studies movement has, on the whole, failed to take seriously the question of what changes in teaching and educational practices are necessary to the establishment of critical theory and education in law schools. What teaching practices will foster the development of politically active, critical law students, rather than produce a new alienated form of education albeit one in radical guise? In this respect we hope that this handbook and the other critical supplements in the series will enable students to free themselves from law's established authorities and hierarchies and approach their studies in a more intellectually independent and open manner.

In the area of legal practice, it is not surprising that the arguments fiercely fought out in the academic domain about approach and perspective have not explicitly received the same attention. The time demands of practice offer little opportunity for practitioners to stand back, contemplate and articulate their thoughts on the nature of critical legal practice and how it might relate to the wider issues raised by critical legal theory. The contributions of practitioners to this handbook are, therefore, particularly welcomed and will, we hope, help to provide a basis for developing an interchange between practitioners, academics and law students. Very little has been done towards theorising the nature of critical legal practice although this is clearly crucial to the critical enterprise as a whole. In our view, a critique of orthodox practice is not sufficient; a substantive discussion of the possibilities and limits of a critical practice is essential (see Economides and Hansen, and John Fitzpatrick in Chapter 3). As in legal education, the organisational structures of law centres, solicitors' practices and Bar chambers have received little or no attention, although some law centres and certain Bar chambers have gone through agonising, and in some cases destructive, debate on this issue (see Watkinson in Chapter 3). We must recognise that structural changes are crucial to the creation of a new generation of critical lawyers. The old traditional forms must be discarded and new critical working relationships developed. On this matter we have a long way to go.

Finally, in our view, the achievement of any of the above changes in legal education and legal practice requires some form of organisation which brings together students, critical legal academics and practitioners. The critical movement in Britain has, until recently, failed to create such a structure. The formation, in the last few years, of Critical Lawyers' Groups in a number of university and polytechnic law departments has provided a basis for remedying this failure and producing pressure for change. Chapter 4 contains a brief account of the present organisation and activities of CLGs and seeks to encourage both their formation and the active participation within them of practitioners as well as of students and academics. One of the successes of existing CLGs thus far has been the active involvement of many practitioners as speakers at meetings. Chapter Five is a further move in this direction, attempting to identify practitioners who may be willing to be associated with local CLGs and CLACs, and providing an alternative guide to firms and chambers for students seeking placements and training.

We would like to thank all of our contributors for their enthusiastic and active cooperation and look forward to their participation in CLG debates in law departments around the country.

1
Critical Legal Theory

The philosophers have only interpreted the world ... the point,
however, is to change it.

> (Karl Marx, 'Theses on Feuerbach',
> *Selected Works of Marx and Engels*, 1973, p. 15)

Historically, the process by which the bourgeoisie became in the
course of the eighteenth century the politically dominant class was
masked by the establishment of an explicit, coded and formally
egalitarian framework made possible by the organisation of a parlia-
mentary, representative regime. But the development and generalisation of disciplinary mechanisms constituted the other dark side of these
processes. The general juridical form that guaranteed a system of
rights that were egalitarian in principle, was supported by these tiny,
everyday physical mechanisms, by all those systems of micro-power
that are essentially non-egalitarian and asymmetrical that we call the
disciplines.

> (Michel Foucault, *Discipline and Punish*, 1979 p. 222)

One must start by knowing what is going on, by freeing oneself from
the mystified delusions embedded in our consciousness by the liberal
legal world view.

> (Alan D. Freeman, 'Truth and Mystification in Legal Scholarship',
> *Yale Law Journal*, 1981, vol. 90 p. 1229)

The Enlightenment is dead, Marxism is dead, the working class is
dead ... and the author does not feel very well either.

> (N. Smith, *Uneven Development*, 1984, p. iii)

Foreword: Critical Approaches to Law Who Needs Legal Theory?

Alan Thomson

Among law students and practitioners, even radical practitioners, theory tends to have a bad name. Many, reflecting on their experience of jurisprudence or theory courses, come to the conclusion that theorising about law is little more than the self-indulgent pastime of a few academics, harmless in itself, but largely irrelevant because it has no impact on the real world. The dominant view appears to be that legal theory and legal practice are extreme poles, with substantive or 'black-letter' law (which is seen as a good deal closer to the practice pole) in between. From this it follows that if one is concerned to change the world in practice a radical lawyer is better advised to master such things as housing law, the legal aid provisions or labour law than to bother with legal theory. How often are we told that to be an effective radical lawyer one must first (and last?) be a good lawyer – an attitude we should note which assumes that law is merely a neutral tool which the good may use to do good even though the bad use it to oppress.

This view of theory as marginal, a mere optional extra for those with intellectual pretensions, may not be an unfair characterisation of many traditional jurisprudence courses and writings, though as I will suggest they are far from simply harmless. One of the main thrusts of the critical legal studies movement, committed as it is to changing the world and rejecting any idea of pure theory out there, is that theory does matter in practice in the real world, for the simple reason that the 'reality' of the real world is sustained in large measure by leaving unchallenged the implicit theories which constitute it as real. In other words the more we treat what passes for the real world and the facts of life as the only possible world and the only possible facts, then the more that acquiring the skills and knowledge on which that world works and which make it what it is (such as lawyers' skills and knowledge of substantive law) will appear as the only things worth bothering about. Conversely, the more we recognise the artificiality of the 'real' world, in the sense of it being an artifact, and the mere orthodoxy of 'the facts of life' (Berger and Luckmann, 1967), the more we are forced to recognise that not only do we sustain this world by playing by its rules, but also that it is not 'black-letter' law but theory which has the capacity to affect practice in more than a marginal way. Quite simply it is only if we adopt a more or less conservative ('realistic') view of the real world and of legal practice, and do not question its implicit theory, that legal theory will appear as irrelevant. One thing critical legal theorists are not is conservative, for their aim is not to support but to subvert the existing order of things, by disclosing by what and how it is supported and sustained.

Critical legal theory must, therefore, make explicit the implicit theory on which the existing legal rules, institutions and practices are based, with the aim of showing that since that theory cannot support what it claims it can, the world could be otherwise. This is particularly clear in the agenda of the American Critical Legal Conference. Moreover, it immediately distinguishes critical legal theory from traditional jurisprudence. While traditional jurisprudence claims to be able to reveal through pure reason a picture of an unchanging and universal unity beneath the manifest changeability and historical variability of laws, legal institutions and practices, and thus to establish a foundation in reason for actual legal systems, critical legal theory not only denies the possibility of discovering a universal foundation for law through pure reason, but sees the whole enterprise of jurisprudence (and this is what reveals it as not harmless) as operating to confer a spurious legitimacy on law and legal systems. Furthermore, by treating law as a discrete and distinct object, jurisprudence reinforces, as does the concept of 'black-letter' law, the idea of law as having an autonomous existence separated from politics, morality and everyday conversation. In denying this separation, along with the claims that would found law in reason, critical legal theory attempts to reconnect law with everyday political and moral argument, struggles and experiences, with all their attendant incoherences, uncertainties and indeterminancies. Most importantly, in rejecting a view of law as the expression of reason, critical legal theorists reveal, in different ways, law as the expression and medium of power. Against those who assert, whether they see themselves as conservative or progressive, that there is no need for theory because law is obvious, critical legal theorists assert that law is far from obvious primarily because its relation to power is not obvious. In short, the need for theory arises because the relationship of law and power is not self-evident – the practical point being that if we are to resist power it is a necessary, even if not a sufficient, condition that we first try to understand it.

The Diversity of Critical Legal Theory

While united in the importance they attach to theory as a means of realising in practice the better world to which they are committed, the critical legal theorists do not endorse a single theoretical position. Rather, as the pieces which follow illustrate, the movement consists of a plurality of approaches and strategies to get at the power in the law. Indeed many see in its denial of any single royal route to truth (contrary to the 'project' of jurisprudence), and in its celebration of diversity, its most liberating aspect. For it embraces not only grand theorising about the power relations behind the law but also micro-analyses of power in particular aspects of the legal process and of legal discourse. In what follows I attempt to identify in very broad brush-strokes some of its more influential approaches and strategies.

Trashing the Liberal Edifice

This approach, which has centrally informed the American Critical Legal Conference (see Kairys in this chapter), essentially involves showing, sometimes in very broad terms, sometimes in very particular areas, that the claims law makes cannot be sustained. For example, the claim that law is a means of resolving disputes which is politically neutral in that it does not reflect particular interests, or the claim that law consists of rules which form a clear and coherent system and which are capable of determining, without relying on external value preferences, answers to all but perhaps the most exceptional of hard cases.

The basic strategy is to take law and its claims seriously and, by trying to see if they add up, to reveal the fundamental weaknesses and contradictions in the whole edifice. More particularly the edifice, of which law is seen as a part, is generally identified as the liberal world view. This is based on the premise that it is possible to reconcile and coordinate the different purposes and interests of individuals in a social order which is just in the sense that it transcends relations of power, privileging no particular interests and grounding all obligations on consent. While this has been the promise of the West, finding expression in (inter alia) the rule of law, constitutionality and freedom of contract, again and again it is argued that that promise has not been fulfilled, not only because there is a gap between reality and the ideal, but because the ideal is fatally flawed in that it contains irreconcilable contradictions.

These contradictions, which in some versions are based on a fundamental contradiction between the individual and the social, are, it is argued, reflected at every level of the legal operation. For example, there is the endemic contradiction between deciding on the basis of rules and deciding by reference to standards, or the contradiction between assuming individual actions are based on will and intention and treating such actions as socially determined.

The point that those critical theorists adopting this approach make is that while in practice one pole of these contradictions tends to be privileged, the individual rules and free-will pole, the pull to the other is perennially present. Thus, the contradictions remain, revealing the promise of law to create a just social order as empty.

Politically such work has shown that if law cannot deliver on its promise to transcend power, it must be concealing power, and that the power of the law is, therefore, in large measure ideological, that is to say it makes social relations based on power appear legitimate and just because they appear to be beyond power. Practically this approach leads to two political strategies. First, arguing for shifting the emphasis in legal decision-making towards the unprivileged, more social pole. For example, emphasising the social responsibility of acting in good faith as opposed to ideas of individual entitlement in contract cases, or stressing the social determinants of behaviour in the criminal justice system. Secondly, seeking to engender real participation of the community as a whole in the decisions that affect them, for law, it is argued, only *appears* to be a way of avoiding making, on the basis of argument, the political and moral decisions that affect any community. Crudely, by seeking to expose the trick whereby liberal legality claims to have overcome social relations based on power, the American critical legal theorists claim to be contributing to resisting power. However, since they generally eschew presenting any theory of power to set against liberal theory (as opposed to showing how such a liberal theory of legality serves the interests of empirically powerful groups such as capitalists, men and whites), they largely remain within the democratic tradition of giving power to the people in some unspecified sense.

Structuralist Approaches

In contrast , what distinguishes what I call structuralist approaches is precisely that they *do* offer a theory of power relations. Thus, while largely accepting the critique of liberal legality as creating false appearances, structuralist critiques seek to go further, and to reveal theoretically the real power relations which those appearances conceal. In short, they claim that there are deep structures of power which theory can draw out and represent.

By far the most influential of such structuralist approaches to law have been Marxist critiques, though some versions of feminism adopt a broadly similar strategy. They are represented in this chapter by Fine and Picciotto, by Adelman and Foster, and are discussed in Bottomley. Broadly, this strategy uses a theoretically constructed map of the real power relations (for example class relations or patriarchy) in a particular society to explain the nature of the legal process, institutions and ideas in that society. Primarily this has taken two routes: first, by showing how dominant groups in society have gained control of and use the legal system to preserve their interests, and secondly, by showing how liberal legality, based on such ideas as equality before the law and individual rights, serves to legitimate inequality by sustaining a superficial and false ideology of equality. In more deterministic accounts this takes the form of showing for example how the ideology of liberal legality and the rule of law, as well as many more particular legal concepts (such as private property and freedom of contract), are the necessary and practically adequate appearances of social relations under capitalism: necessary in the sense that they function to preserve the dominant interests of capitalists or of men, and practically adequate in that they reflect the everyday processes such as market exchange and the marriage relationship which in practice sustain and reproduce existing power relations.

While I will leave the pieces to which I have referred to speak for themselves I might add that the great attraction of such accounts is that, potentially, they enable one to specify much more clearly a critical practice in relation to law. For example, if one accepts the view that liberal legality, bourgeois rights and ideas of equality before the law are mere humbug concealing the real relations of power in capitalism, namely the exploitative relations between capital and labour, at least one part of the agenda of a critical practising lawyer may look relatively clear. There is a real dilemma in using law to fight the system which (theory tells us) law maintains.

'Post' Approaches

Politically inspired largely by the perceived failure of Marxist socialism to deliver its promise of a society that overcomes exploitation, the last two decades have witnessed a growing doubt about the Marxist project and a growing feeling that it is infected with the same weakness as the liberal capitalist system it opposes, and of which, as the counter culture of capitalism, it is arguably a part.

That weakness is seen by many as the continuing faith, shared with its liberal protagonist, in the capacity of reason to realise progress. Thus, many argue that domination and exploitation are not the monopoly of any one theory, but are characteristic of all theories, especially those, such as Marxism, which make claims to truth on a grand scale. The reaction to this doubt, which questions the capacity of any theory, as a set of words or symbols, to represent reality and, therefore, to provide a foundation for a critique of law or anything else, has been complex and multifaceted.

Perhaps one of the most important early influences of this way of thinking in relation to law came from the writings of Michel Foucault. In his attempt to free us from a belief in deep underlying structures, Foucault argues that to conceive power as something which some possess and use to repress others is to fail to see that power is not just the localised possession of a few, but a ubiquitous feature of social life which it positively constitutes, including for example, us as individuals. In short, there is nothing which is not the effect of power, and no form of knowledge which is not also itself a form of power. Contrary to Marxism, there is no essential humanity, or 'us', to emancipate. The practical import of this is that, while power cannot therefore be overcome, we can use the resistances it engenders. The role of the theorist is, therefore, the modest one of exploring the microprocesses of power – operating in institutions such as the family, prison and schools – to reveal the possibilities of resistance. The piece by Fitzpatrick reflects this approach in its attempt, while recognising law as a form of power, to argue for an idea of law related to particular situations, which can operate as a form of resistance to the power of law as a whole.

While Foucault represents one reaction to the doubt of reason and the consequent suspicion of theory, particularly in its grander and more imperialist versions, that doubt is revealed in many other ways which impact on our understanding of law. First, following from a rejection of an idea of theory as something out there which can be taken off the shelf to decode the world and reveal its true structure, comes a rather different conception of theory, namely of theory as essentially reflexive, the product of reflection on lived experience, and an attempt to give voice to understandings which have been suppressed in large measure by the dominant grand narratives of truth. Feminist writing which argues for feminist theories of law, rather than merely fitting women into male theories, as discussed in Bottomley, exemplifies this approach, as does much writing on law in relation to racism and imperialism.

Secondly, rejoicing under the wilfully paradoxical label of post-modernism, and represented by the piece by Douzinas and Warrington, we find a position that seems to bring the discussion of theory full circle, for on one reading it is a theory that seeks to establish the impossibility of theory. Certainly a law student encountering much of this postmodern writing may be forgiven for thinking that he or she had stumbled upon some old-fashioned self-indulgent jurisprudential theorising joyfully celebrating its innocence in relation to the 'real' world. On another reading, however, such writing, by insistently demonstrating that no text can ever sustain the basis on which it makes a claim to truth, that all forms of thinking are constraints, and that all readings of texts are just that, namely particular readings (none of which can sustain a claim to be privileged as an authoritative reading), is essentially liberating. Certainly, by inviting us to read law and other texts anew to discover new and suppressed meanings opens up a brave new world of possibilities. While structuralist accounts such as Marxism have the capacity to liberate us from the 'real' world by showing us that it is merely the surface appearance of a deeper reality of power, a merely dictated orthodoxy, are we not more liberated when we recognise there is no orthodoxy at all and no privileged interpretation of reality? If words do not mean anything and only how we use them matters, everything is politics because everything is open. But is it? I leave it to you to read Douzinas and Warrington for yourself.

Critical Theory and Legal Practice

As many, including Economides and Hansen in this book, have pointed out, critical legal studies has dominantly been a movement in the academy and has largely failed to inform legal practice. In this section I want to explore briefly two questions: what use is theory in practice, and can legal practice, informed by critical legal theory, be progressive?

Let me begin by saying that critical theory cannot do what I suspect many busy radical practitioners would dearly like it to do, namely provide ready-made, off-the-peg answers to practical dilemmas, such as which areas of practice to concentrate on, or which strategies to adopt in particular cases. It can only indicate some of the wider implications and consequences of certain courses of action, and in particular reveal that, unless legal actions are seen in the context of larger political action, they may well be counter-productive, at least in the long term. It may enable the practitioner to keep the broader picture in sight, but it would be counter to the whole spirit of such theory to treat it as a source of answers as opposed to a resource which people in real situations may use to create reflectively their own particular answers. Indeed, a central argument of critical legal theory is that one of the most significant sources of domination and oppression is the belief that there is only one correct answer and objective truth. Certainly this is what the critical theorist seeks to dispel in the classroom.

More positively, what critical legal theory can do is demonstrate the possibilities. By disclosing the multitudinous operations of power in the law and legal process which sustain existing reality, one reveals that reality is only one possible world, thereby bringing other possibilities into view. For example, by trying to understand better (than those who defend it) the edifice of liberal legality, and thereby revealing its incoherences and contradictions, one acquires a means of resisting its arguments; by demonstrating how private property comes to be seen as natural, other forms of social relation become imaginable, and by showing that the official reading of any legal text, such as a case, is only one possible reading, one is freed to argue for other readings.

The great attraction of the postmodernist stance is that it apparently maximises those discovered possibilities. Under its wand all that is solid melts into air for it reveals that there are no truths in the way of anything. Nihilism becomes everythingism. While this liberation is clearly wonderfully exhilarating for a few academics (see the piece by Douzinas and Warrington), it is a good deal less clear that it is so for the rest of the world. Not only can it be taken as a charter for anything goes (Douzinas and Warrington see it as the new neutrality which favours no particular politics), it also rejects (as I cannot) the view that among the multitudinous forms of power which constitute our present reality there are certain *dominant* structures of power – most centrally, in my view, those of capitalism. Quite simply, while I do not believe that overcoming capitalism, or indeed making any other structural change, will overcome all forms of power and exploitation, there are nevertheless priorities in the choice of forms of power to resist now, and capitalism, along with male and racial oppression, is one of them.

Indeed in my view the structuralist versus postmodernist debate is largely phoney: one needs a structuralist analysis to resist and challenge the constituted dominant structures of power, but deploying such an analysis does not necessarily entail accepting that it is a privileged truth, or that it is not therefore a form of knowledge which is also a form of power. Just as using scientific knowledge, unless one is a committed metaphysician, does not imply that one accepts that the foundations of science are secure. On the one hand, postmodernism, which looks initially like the *most* liberating position, seems, because it explains too little, laughably impotent in the face of the realities as they are constituted by the dominant structures of power. On the other hand, postmodernism rightly warns us to be suspicious of trying to explain too much. More particularly, postmodernism leads us to recognise that to remain critical, critical legal theory must resist simply replacing the liberal theory it criticises with a theory of its own, which is complete, coherent and determinate. This means that liberal legality can be no more totally rejected than it can be totally accepted.

This brings me to my second question: whether, informed by critical legal theory, legal practice can be progressive. The dilemma here is whether critical legal theory, which goes beyond the sort of theorising called for by Hansen and Economides (namely identifying, in the sociolegal tradition, the broader consequences of adopting particular legal strategies), can justify using the law. For, as Kairys points out, critical legal theorists tend to see law as part of the problem and not part of the solution. On one view, best represented by certain Marxists, and until recently by a significant section of the trade union movement, law is such an integral part of the system of capitalist exploitation that to use it even for the immediate benefit of disadvantaged groups such as workers, women and the unemployed, is merely to perpetuate in the longer term the underlying system of exploitation which it seeks to justify (see Edie et al. in this book). For example, to struggle for employees' rights or women's rights, it is argued, merely reinforces a system which exploits people precisely by seeing them merely as bearers of rights rather than as real people with individual needs and experiences. There are numerous variants of this position. For example, the view that equal rights, because they are merely the expression of the surface appearance of capitalist production relations (that is, of exchange relations) conceal underlying oppression and exploitation; the view that rights thinking is essentially a male world view; the view that law itself is not the source of exploitation but merely hides the source of exploitation which lies elsewhere; the view that since law is so essentially uncertain and indeterminate any short term legal gain will be rapidly offset by the dominant groups changing the law, or the view that since law reduces people to isolated individuals it runs counter to the only possible basis for radical change, namely collective action.

Against this position is levelled the charge of utopianism, of passing up the chance of alleviating some suffering and exploitation now in the name of an uncertain possibility in an indefinite future. For those who identify themselves with the postmodernist banner, utopias are impossible dreams, and historically much suffering has been inflicted in their name. Further, they remind us that, just as in their critique of reason from the standpoint of reason, we can never escape the system of which we are a part, and there is no independent 'outside' from which liberal legality can be seen aright. Moreover, as Fine and Picciotto pragmatically point out in the context of the struggles of the labour movement, to simply refuse to play the legal game, while all the others are playing it for all they are worth, is to be clobbered by it. Similarly for women not to pursue the liberal goal of equal rights on the grounds that women's oppression involves much more is to reject a vital platform from which to struggle for that much more.

In different ways all the pieces in this chapter confront this dilemma, a dilemma which Bottomley, considering the situation of the feminist lawyer, aptly calls a double bind. All (except perhaps Foster and Adelman who press for a 'politics of abolition' in relation to law) recognise that in some cases law can be used progressively, while sharing the view that we have to reject what Peter Fitzpatrick calls the 'surpassing' dimension of law. This I interpret, following Lukacs (1968), as meaning not being mystified by the claims of law as a whole in either totally rejecting or totally accepting them.

In conclusion, in my view the primary role of critical legal theory, like Marcuse's idea of the role of art, is to continuously keep alive other readings of the world in the face of the deadening orthodoxy of 'reality'. That does not mean that, while it stands opposed to 'reality', critical theory is a theory against legal practice, for legal practice too can be a practice against 'reality'. Critical legal theory can contribute to make it such.

The Politics of Law: A Progressive Critique
David Kairys

We Americans turn over more of our society's disputes, decisions and concerns to courts and lawyers than does any other nation. Yet, in a society that places considerable value on democracy, courts would seem to have a peculiarly difficult problem justifying their power and maintaining their legitimacy. The judiciary is a non-majoritarian institution, whose guiding lights are neither popularly chosen nor even expected to express or implement the will of the people. Rather, its legitimacy rests on notions of honesty and fairness and, most importantly, on popular perceptions of the judicial decision-making process.

Basic to the popular perception of the judicial process is the notion of government by law, not people. Law is depicted as separate from – and above – politics, economics, culture or the values or preferences of judges. This separation is supposedly accomplished and ensured by a number of perceived attributes of the decision-making process, including judicial subservience to a Constitution, statutes and precedent; the quasi-scientific, objective nature of legal analysis, and the technical expertise of judges and lawyers.

Together, these attributes constitute a decision-making process in which 1) the law on a particular issue is pre-existing, clear, predictable and available to anyone with reasonable legal skills; 2) the facts relevant to disposition of a case are ascertained by objective hearing and evidentiary rules that reasonably ensure that the truth will emerge; 3) the result in a particular case is determined by a rather routine application of the law to the facts, and 4) except for the occasional bad judge, any reasonably competent and fair judge will reach the 'correct' decision.

Of course, there are significant segments of the Bar and trends in legal scholarship that repudiate this idealised model. The school of jurisprudence known as legal realism long ago exposed its falsity; and later jurisprudential developments, such as theories resting the legitimacy of law on the existence of widely shared values, at least implicitly recognise the social and political content of law. Moreover, concepts like public policy and social utility, while limited to certain notions of the public good, are generally acknowledged as appropriate considerations for judges, and it is commonly known that the particular judge assigned to a case has a significant bearing on the outcome.

But most of this thinking is either limited to law journals or compartmentalised, existing alongside and often presented as part of the idealised process. For example, balancing tests, where judges decide which of two or more conflicting policies or interests will predominate, are presented and applied as if there were objective and neutral answers, as if it were possible to perform such a balance independent of political, social and personal values which vary among our people and (to a lesser extent) among our judges.

Despite the various scholarly trends and the open consideration of social policy and utility, legal decisions are expressed and justified, and the courts (as well as their decisions) are depicted and discussed throughout society, in terms of the idealised process. The public perception – the crucial perception from the standpoint of legitimacy – is generally limited to the idealised model. One will often hear cynical views about the law, such as 'the system is fixed', but even such observations are usually meant to describe departures from, rather than characteristics of, the legal process. While this perception of the idealised model is not monolithic or static (at various times substantial segments of society have come to question the model), it has fairly consistently had more currency in the United States than in any other country.

Indeed, public debate over judicial decisions usually focuses on whether courts have deviated from the idealised model rather than on the substance of decisions or the nature and social significance of judicial power. Perceived deviations undermine the legitimacy and power of the courts, and are usually greeted with a variety of institutional and public challenges, including attacks by politicians and the press, proposals for statutory or constitutional change and, occasionally, threats or attempts to impeach judges.

While there is presently considerable dissatisfaction with the courts and their decisions from a variety of political perspectives, it is usually expressed in terms of this notion of deviation from the idealised model. Thus, the conservative criticism that the courts have overstepped their bounds – going beyond or outside legal reasoning and the idealised process – is now commonplace, as is the accompanying plea for judicial restraint to allow our 'democratic processes' to function.

The authors of this book are also dissatisfied, but the content and implications of our critique are very different. At this early stage there appear to be four basic elements of our evolving legal theory.

First, we reject the idealised model and the notion that a distinctly legal mode of reasoning or analysis characterises the legal process or even exists. The problem is not that courts deviate from legal reasoning. There is no legal reasoning in the sense of a legal methodology or process for reaching particular, correct results. There is a distinctly legal and quite elaborate system of discourse and body of knowledge, replete with its own language and conventions of argumentation, logic and even manners. In some ways these aspects of the law are so distinct and all-embracing as to amount to a separate culture, and for many lawyers the courthouse, the law firm, the language, the style, become a way of life.

But in terms of a method or process for decision-making – for determining correct rules, facts or results – the law provides only a wide and conflicting variety of stylised rationalisations from which courts pick and choose. Social and political judgements about the substance, parties and context of a case guide such choices, even when they are not the explicit or conscious basis of decision.

Judges are the often unknowing objects, as well as among the staunchest supporters, of the myth of legal reasoning. Decisions are predicated upon a complex mixture of social, political, institutional, experiential and personal factors; however, they are expressed and justified, and largely perceived by judges themselves, in terms of 'facts' that have been objectively determined and 'law' that has been objectively and rationally found and applied. One result is a judicial schizophrenia which permeates decisions, arguments, and banter among lawyers.

Secondly, we place fundamental importance on democracy, by which we mean popular participation in the decisions that shape our society and affect our lives. While there is a very real sense of powerlessness that pervades contemporary society, to blame this solely or even principally on the courts misses the point.

Those democratic processes that the courts are supposedly invading in the conservative view consist essentially of the right to vote and freedom of speech and association. Our society allows no democracy outside this public sphere of our lives. For example, the economic decisions that most crucially shape our society and affect our lives, on basic social issues such as the use of our resources, investment, the energy problem, and the work of our people, are regarded as private and are not made democratically or even by the government officials elected in the public sphere. The public/private split ideologically legitimises private – mainly corporate – dominance, masks the lack of real participation or democracy, and personalises the powerlessness it breeds.

The law plays a crucial role in this: the idealised model, the notion of technical expertise, and the notion of the law as neutral, objective and quasi-scientific lend legitimacy to the judicial process, which in turn lends a broader legitimacy to the social and power relations and ideology that are reflected, articulated and enforced by the courts. However, existing democratic processes do not provide meaningful choices or constitute meaningful mechanisms for popular control or input, which is perhaps why half our people do not vote. These processes – and the law – provide a false legitimacy to existing social and power relations.

The current and seemingly endless debate over judicial restraint or activism also misses the point. There is no coherent framework or principled resolution of this debate within the legal system, just as and because there is no legal reasoning. Rather, with very few exceptions, the pleas for judicial restraint and activism, sometimes unintentionally or unconsciously, mask a political direction and are wholly dependent on the historical and social contexts. If one favoured social security and restriction of child labour over maximisation of profits during the New Deal, one was for judicial restraint; if one favoured racial equality and justice over maintenance of white privilege and the historical oppression of black people in the 1960s, one was for judicial activism; if one favoured prohibition of abortions by choice in the 1980s, one was for judicial restraint. There is afoot these days a conservative brand of 'democracy' using, in part, the fashionable label of judicial restraint, that allows little or no room for popular participation or scrutiny. In this view, powerful (largely corporate) interests, the patriarchal, authoritarian family and, in selected areas, government officials are not to be interfered with, by the courts or by the people.

Thirdly, we reject the common characterisation of the law and the state as neutral, value-free arbiters, independent of and unaffected by social and economic relations, political forces and cultural phenomena. Traditional jurisprudence largely ignores social and historical reality, and masks the existence of social conflict and oppression with ideological myths about objectivity and neutrality. The dominant system of values has been declared value free; it then follows that all others suffer from bias and can be thoughtlessly dismissed.

Left thinking about the law and the state has long recognised this political content and lack of neutrality. However, there has been a tendency to oversimplify with analyses that often seek to seek an almost mystical, linear, causal chain that translates economics into law. For example, a common orthodox Marxist explanation is that law is a superstructural phenomenon that is mysteriously governed and determined by an underlying base of economic relations and/or instrumentally controlled by the ruling elite or class. But the law is not simply an armed receptacle for values and priorities determined elsewhere; it is part of a complex social totality in which it constitutes as well as is constituted, shapes as well as is shaped. Moreover, such analyses lose sight of the fact that the law consists of people-made decisions and doctrines, and the thought processes and modes of reconciling conflicting considerations of these people (judges) are not mystical, inevitable or very different from the rest of us. It is often difficult to resist dehumanisation of one's opponents and a blanket rejection of all people and institutions which constitute and symbolise a system one deeply wishes to transform.

However, judges are not robots that are – or need to be – mysteriously or conspiratorially controlled. Rather, they, like the rest of us, form values and prioritise conflicting considerations based on their experience, socialisation, political perspectives, self-perceptions, hopes, fears and a variety of other factors. The results are not, however, random. Their particular backgrounds, socialisation and experiences – in which law schools and the practice of largely commercial firms of law play an important role – result in a patterning, a consistency, in the ways they categorise, approach and resolve social and political conflicts. This is the great source of the law's power; it enforces, reflects, constitutes and legitimises dominant social and power relations without a need for or the appearance of control from outside and by means of social actors who largely believe in their own neutrality and the myth of legal reasoning.

Fourthly, while the law has many important functions, the legitimation function is crucial to an understanding of its doctrines, rationalisations, results and social role. The law's ultimate mechanism for control and enforcement is institutional violence, but it protects the dominant system of social and power relations against political and ideological as well as physical challenges. The law is a major vehicle for the maintenance of existing social and power relations by the consent or acquiescence of the lower and middle classes. The law's perceived legitimacy confers a broader legitimacy on a social system and ideology that, despite their claims to kinship with nature, science or God, are most fairly characterised by domination by a very small, mainly corporatised elite. This perceived legitimacy of the law is primarily based on notions of technical expertise and objectivity and the idealised model of the legal process – in short, as described above, on the distorted notion of government by law, not people. But it is also greatly enhanced by the reality, often ignored in orthodox left thinking, that the law is, on some occasions, just and sometimes serves to restrain the exercise of power.

A realistic, understandable approach to the law that explains its operation and social role must acknowledge the fundamental conflicts in society; the class, race and sex base of these conflicts; and the dominance of an ideology that is not natural, scientifically determined, or objective. The discretionary nature of court decisions, the importance of social and political judgements, and the dominance of the ideology of advanced capitalism characterise our judicial process far better than any notions of objectivity, expertise or science.

On Marxist Critiques of Law
Robert Fine and Sol Picciotto

The revival of Marxism in Western Europe in the 1960s and 1970s was a reaction against the failures both of a Stalinism, which supported the dogmas and tyrannies of state socialism, and of complacent liberalism, which ignored or tolerated the inequalities and oppressions of capitalism. Consequently Marxist critiques of law and the state have had a twofold dynamic, focusing on the limits both of bourgeois freedom in systems based on private property, and of 'socialist' freedom in systems based on state property.

The central question concerning the role of law in a class society is its apparent autonomy and neutrality. The social-democratic tradition idealised existing legality as an order into which any social content could be fitted, capitalist or socialist. This was expressed in Karl Renner's classic view that the forms of law do not change but only their functions (Bottomore & Goode, 1978; Renner, 1949). In this perspective, the rule of law could only be fully realised under socialism, since under capitalism it is distorted and corrupted by private interests. The transition to socialism means the democratisation of state institutions, particularly through the legislature, and the gradual extension of legal regulation into the private sphere through social legislation (especially through the nationalisation of industry, but also by welfare legislation on employment, social security, child protection, etc.).

This view of legal forms has been criticised by contemporary Marxists for its ahistorical idealisation of legal reasoning, procedures and remedies and its cursory acceptance of the administrative procedures of the state. The reasons for injustice are thought to lie not in the law but in inequalities of power in the economic and social spheres. This perspective has often lain behind research into law in society, which seeks to reveal the economic, political and other interests which prevent legal institutions working as they should. Its focus being on the shadow that falls between the real functioning of law and the ideal form of law itself, it tends to depict law as a functional instrument for social change.

Renner's positivistic theory was sharply criticised by the Soviet jurist, Evgeni Pashukanis, whose work in the 1920s represented an important attempt to apply the method of Marx's critique of political economy to jurisprudence (Beirne & Sharlet, 1980; Pashukanis, 1983; Sharlet, 1974). Pashukanis became influential in the 1970s and provided a fruitful starting point for analysis, especially of private law. He located law as a specifically capitalist form of regulation or control. He argued that law is based on exchange relations between owners of commodities each of whom appears as an abstract juridic subject and whose interrelationships are necessarily mediated by contract and other legal forms. As a historical form of control, what characterises law, according to Pashukanis, is abstraction, isolation, mutual indifference, the reproduction of substantive inequalities and the mystification of the rule of people as the rule of law. In his eyes, the transition to communism entails the withering away of bourgeois law; true community is beyond law.

This critique was fraught with theoretical and political problems. Since Pashukanis saw law as based on exchange relations and since he equated capitalism simply with the generalisation of exchange (rather than with exploitative relations of production which derive from the exchange of labour power), he could only conclude that all exchange was capitalist exchange and all law was bourgeois law. The result was a one-sided critique which excluded the possibility of socialist legality and neglected any question of democratising and socialising the law. This played into the hands of the evolving Stalinist regime, which deployed his theory of the primacy of technical regulation under socialism to justify the power of the bureaucracy and its disregard for legal constraints. Pashukanis and his theory were brutally dispatched by the chief prosecutor, Vishinsky, who condemned him as a member of 'a band of wreckers' and 'Trotsky–Bukharin fascist agents' (Arthur 1977; Beirne & Sharlet, 1980; Binns, 1980; Fine, 1984; Norrie, 1982; Redhead, 1978).

In the 1970s Marxist theories of law were also influenced by structuralist perspectives. According to structuralist Marxism, social relations are divided between the economic sphere of production, seen in the narrow sense as the immediate process of production or the labour process, and the sphere of reproduction which includes family, law and the state (Althusser, 1965, Poulantzas, 1978). Such theories present the economic sphere as 'dominant in the last instance' while emphasising the 'relative autonomy' of the legal, political and ideological superstructure. Relative autonomy, however, is itself seen either as functional to the reproduction of capitalist relations of production, in which case it is merely a working part of a larger whole, or the autonomy is stressed at the expense of any real connection to economic relations. This theory was criticised by Marxists for reifying the separation of economics and politics and the ultimate primacy of the economic as a natural feature of all social organisation. It appeared either as a refinement of the mechanistic base-superstructure model, or as a return to pluralist sociology (Clarke, 1982; Holloway & Picciotto, 1977 and 1978; Thompson, 1978). For such reasons, structuralism did not help to grasp the forms of class power embodied in law, relying instead on an ahistorical opposition between consent and coercion, which in its neglect of consensus-formation in authoritarian regimes failed to comprehend the force of right-wing populism.

Critical Marxism has argued that class relations should be seen as relations of production in a wider sense than economic determinism allows. Capitalist relations of production necessarily present themselves in both mediated and differentiated forms; the generalisation of commodity exchange and its transformation into capitalist production gives rise to the fragmentation of social life and the emergence of two apparently separate spheres of existence: economics and law. The sphere of economics is based on seemingly natural laws concerning the movement of things; people appear as bearers of commodities, subordinate to external economic forces and related to each other by money. In this 'objective' sphere relations are mediated by money and everything has its price, determined by market forces. The juridico-political sphere, on the other hand, appears to be based on the seemingly natural qualities of human individuals. In this 'subjective' domain individuals appear as free agents and things as dependent on their will. Private property appears as the materialisation of free will, individuals take the form of juridic subjects, relations between individuals are mediated by seemingly impersonal laws of their own making, and the state appears as the articulation of the general will. It is a world of juridic subjects and free citizens whose intersubjectivity is based on reciprocal rights and duties. The social origins of juridic forms are as concealed as those of economics (Sayer, 1987, and Grigg-Spall and Ireland in this book).

For critical Marxism, the fragmentation of society into its economic and juridical forms of appearance is a result of definite social relations of production. The real individuals who inhabit these fragmented spheres are the same. It is the self-same individual who is at once a free subject and the victim of uncontrollable economic forces. The relations between the classes are at once juridic and economic.

In this historically constructed fragmentation, legal relations are one aspect of a dynamic system of capitalist production and reproduction, based on changing relations between capital and labour. This dialectical approach means avoiding the dangers of purely logical derivation of the legal form from an abstract characterisation of the capital-labour relation (Holloway & Picciotto, 1978; Holloway & Picciotto, 1979, criticising Balbus, 1977). Legal relations are not predetermined by the logic of the capital-form, nor by the needs or interests of the owners of capital alone. The concept of the legal form in the singular abstracts from the diversity of legal forms that are historically constructed as the relations between capital and labour change.

The starting point of the relations of production as a social relation between the classes is vital. Since the social relations between the classes are fragmented, the central antagonism takes the form of many specific conflicts, for example over housing, the environment, racial and gender oppression. It is important to stress that so-called social struggles are just as much aspects of class and are not merely incidental to struggles over wages and working conditions. All are rooted in the overall development of capitalist accumulation, even as they have their own dynamics; they cannot be reduced to simple class interest, since class unity is not pre-given but must be forged. Indeed the fragmentation of social relations continually creates and recreates divisions and conflicts of interest.

As forms of appearance of class relations, legal forms embody both domination (the will of the state) and reason (the rights of the people). As jurists put it, there is an inseparable connection in law between *voluntas* and *ratio* (authority and rights), positive command and subjective freedom. The realisation of class gains requires the transcendence of the specifically capitalist character of legal norms and procedures. At the most general level, bourgeois legal relations are oppressive in that they are based on individual legal subjects as property-owners and make no formal distinction between capitalist private property (which represents power over labour) and personal private property (which may be no more than labour power).

Thus in bourgeois law the right to work is recognised not as a right for the millions of unemployed, but as the right of the strike-breaker or non-union member. There is no right to decent housing, but only a right to be undisturbed in the possession of one's own home, whether it is a hovel or a palace. Other social rights, such as health, are not recognised as legal entitlements but depend on the vagaries of state provision.

Legal rights appear as natural but are in fact created and shaped by the state. Thus in Britain in the past dozen years, Thatcherism has rested some of its popularity on the creation of new rights, by various forms of privatisation, such as the right of residents to buy their council house, selling to the public or giving workers shares in nationalised industries, and putting public services such as hospital cleaning out to tender by private companies. Although Thatcherism has purported to be restoring market forces, in reality markets are highly structured and regulated by the state and finance-capital; so the creation of a property-owning democracy based on the right to own housing or company shares depends on financial manipulation, for example, tax-subsidisation of mortgages and employee share-ownership schemes, while municipal housing must pay high interest rates, and rents have been pushed up to market levels. The radical right has therefore been able to use state intervention to create individual rights and claim to be increasing the sphere of freedom, while the left has been forced to defend old and unpopular forms of public provision which have been slow to adapt and systematically disadvantaged.

In its practice, Marxism aims to socialise and democratise both the form and content of law. Liberal juridical forms are based on apparently free and equal legal subjects, generally applicable rules, neutral adjudication, the separation of prescription and enforcement, a representative legislature and a professional civil service. Behind these seemingly impartial legal forms, however, lie highly authoritarian and technicist forms of adjudication, enforcement and legislation. The democratisation of these forms is seen by critical Marxism as a high priority, the selection, composition, procedures and accountability of the judiciary being a case in point.

Critical Marxism addresses itself equally to the content of law, since it is structurally oriented towards protection of property rights of owners of capital, whether private or state, and against rights of workers. The problem of legal forms of regulation in general is that they refer only to the rights and not the needs of individuals. A society based on fulfilment of individual and social needs would no longer be regulated in ways which would be recognisable in terms of bourgeois legal forms. Bourgeois legal forms offer a minimum defence of freedom and equality, but are structured to protect private property. The point is not merely to denounce the legal form but to fight for the best possible form and content of law. When right and need begin to come together, this is what is meant by transcending the legal form itself. Even in advanced socialist societies law would rightly operate, only both its content and procedures would be changed to make it far more democratic in form and supportive of people's needs in substance.

Involvement with law should be seen as an integral part of broader social struggles, and legal tactics and strategies should be related to other forms of organisation and action. Taken alone, legal processes may be divisive and weaken social solidarities. Legal forms, however, cannot be avoided since the law provides both a medium of defence and a way of generalising the gains of particular struggles. There is often no other way of overcoming sectionalism than through the legalisation of rights which particular groups win in specific settings. To relate struggles to the form and content of law is not to juridify politics but to politicise jurisprudence. This is a lesson that has been well learned by many movements over the past two decades. An important example is the peace movement, whose activists have won important battles by integrating direct action and legal tactics within an overall strategy (Dewar et al, 1986). In Britain, suspicion of the law among socialists, especially in the trade unions, has led to attempts to ignore or avoid it instead of integrating strategies around law with broader political aims. To the degree that trade unions have argued only for legal non-intervention or immunity, that is, for the law to absent itself from industrial relations, they have been unable to develop an adequate counter-strategy to the labour laws of the Thatcher government. Now that the Labour–TUC policy has changed to advocating a 'positive framework of rights' for trade-unionism, there will have to be some hard thinking about the actual content of such rights and the form in which they are adjudicated and enforced.

One lesson of the 1984–5 miners' strike was that trade union solidarity by itself cannot always be an alternative to law. When the unions were strong, they did not use their power to generalise and institutionalise in law the gains they made as particular unions, a policy which would have gone some way to overcoming tendencies to sectionalism, but rather to keep the law at bay. When unions were economically weakened, their lack of legal foundation proved a major additional handicap. Although the government itself did not directly use its own new laws against the miners, it encouraged individual legal actions by dissident miners (based on common law) which magnified internal divisions about the procedures used in deciding on the strike. Grassroots solidarity and support from the socialist movement organised by local groups, women's groups and the 'far left' helped to prevent the destruction of the miners' union, but neither questions of intra-union democracy nor those of legality can be subsumed to the call for solidarity (Fine & Millar, 1985). Slowly unions are learning how to organise politically around the law, for instance, supporting and organising around workers' rights to ballot. The question facing them is not to oppose this right but to infuse it with a more democratic content and form: for example, when ballots are called, how ballots are conducted and how the right to a ballot is enforced.

Women struggling for equality have focused on rights such as that of equal pay for work of equal value and have also sought to overcome its limitations. Here, as in other areas of the social charter, European Community law has been invoked to reinforce the struggle, since the political pressures to ensure a social dimension for European integration have resulted in a programme, however limited and ineffective, for an equalisation of rights which provides legal space for workers and oppressed groups to exploit. In other areas the appalling record of the British government over rights of prisoners, immigrants, freedom of the press, etc., has been exposed by appeals to the European Human Rights Commission and Court in Strasbourg.

Organising in such a way as to relate legal forms to positive social and political content certainly lays open a potential for opportunism. It involves constant tactical choices, since the individual case can never be a pure class question. Sometimes a technical legal move or argument is best; sometimes it is possible to put a political point as part of a legal argument. It is desirable to aim for an open form of organisation which breaks down the separation of the legal professional and the lay client, and integrates the skill of the one with the direct involvement, experience and commitment of the other. Ironically, a useful model is the best sort of big business lawyering, which moulds and develops the law to fit its needs.

We hope that this outline has helped to show how critical Marxism does not counterpose a utopian ideal of communism, based on the abolition of all forms of law, to actual legal orders but rather exposes the real social antagonisms concealed beneath their apparently smooth surfaces (Rose, 1981). Far from constructing a phantasm of communal harmony, Marxism should be understood as striving – in a world in which freedom is a lonely child of subjection and injustice – for new social forms that will permit real personal and political liberty.

In its criticism of existing legal orders and projection of new forms of democracy, contemporary Marxism has returned to its enlightenment roots: integrating the civil rights of individuals with political rights of collective participation in the running of the state. In so doing, however, Marxism has found it necessary to push this project (see Fine, 1984) beyond the bounds of both liberal and so-called state-socialist legality, to the extent that both constrain rights within the narrow limits of actual property relations and then misrepresent these social boundaries as natural and unsurpassable.

Feminism: Paradoxes of the Double Bind
Anne Bottomley

Discovering Feminism...

At school (progressive, co-ed), when I decided I wanted to be a lawyer, the careers mistress said told me it was not a career for a woman. At 13 it was my first direct experience of discrimination. I decided to go ahead despite her advice and as a challenge. I had formulated an idea, I don't know on what it was based, that many women clients, particularly in family law cases, would prefer a woman lawyer. I tried this idea out on friends but they thought it improbable. No one in this progressive school credited my wish, as a woman, to be a lawyer.

I read law at university with a strong sense of having decided to become a lawyer despite being a woman and because of being a woman. I also knew that I wanted to be a radical lawyer. In the early 1970s the beginning of the law-centre movement had given a profile to the idea of 'lawyers for the people'. The combination of personal anger and political commitment which motivated me I later found was common among the feminist lawyers I met and worked with after I graduated. The struggle for the right to make our own choices, moving against the stereotypes imposed upon us, matched with a sense of wanting to improve conditions for others as well as ourselves, seem to me to be the foundation of feminism.

Feminism is rooted in the experience of our own lives. It is not a political programme or an academic study, but it can produce both. It is not one creed or philosophy. But some try to claim that they have the true feminism. It is not a movement or a party. But when one woman begins to name herself she will find others with whom she identifies in a common experience and commitment.

Feminism begins in our own biographies. I cannot begin to talk to you by constructing an abstract rendition of feminism, neither can I simply presume it and write of women in law. I have to begin with our own origins, experiences and expectations. What brings us together in this book is working with law. To make gender relations visible I have to address primarily, but, importantly, not exclusively, women and the position of women.

Women in Law ...

Superficially things have changed remarkably since I was an undergraduate. Women now represent not only *c* 50 per cent of law undergraduates but also *c* 50 per cent of those taking professional examinations and are far more visible in both branches of the profession. We have our first Court of Appeal judge and first Law Commissioner. In universities and polytechnics women form a good proportion of the staff. There are even some professors who are overt feminists. Law courses are taught with such titles as women and law, gender and law, and feminist perspectives on law. Feminism is a recognised presence in the more progressive law schools. It would seem that both as women and as feminists we have begun, in the words of the Irish President, lawyer and feminist Mary Robinson, to move on from rocking the cradle to rocking the system. However, the full picture is more complicated and attempting to unravel the many threads highlights the problems and paradoxes of rocking either cradle or system for contemporary feminists.

The increasing number of women entering law has to be placed against what the Equal Opportunities Commission has (infuriatingly) referred to as women's 'under-achievement'. Even taking into account the time-lag following the rise in women entrants, proportionally women are under-represented in the top ('high fee-earning') jobs. The Law Society has become concerned not only with this uneven profile but also with figures which show that the number of women leaving the profession is out of proportion to men. In the last decade the declining number of school-leavers entering the labour market led to a climate in which it was not only acceptable but seen as imperative to encourage women into key sectors of employment and keep them there. Feminist pressure for flexible employment patterns and provision for childcare became matched and strengthened by an incremental concern with employment figures.

For the immediate future women seemed to have a great deal to look forward to: we were gaining not only formal equality but a recognition of our needs and concerns as carers. However, the year 1990/1 has begun to throw this picture into confusion. After a period of boom, particularly in the south-east, the recession has hit a large number of firms and the Bar. Significant numbers of young lawyers have been made redundant. While the profession deals with retrenchment and restructuring, flexible work patterns and subsidised childcare are now seen by some as a luxury we cannot afford. The terms of the debate have been set by the market economy. The boom seemed to make possible so much we had fought for on the basis of principle but had won on the basis of good economic practice; the recession makes the frailty of this even more visible.

We have to be aware of structural limitations and not be easily persuaded by superficial improvements. How far can we achieve real change within the present socioeconomic, political structure? Our economic system is based on a market economy; the extent to which this places constraints on change must be realised but equally cannot be used to ignore or belittle the potential for improvements now. Even within a market system we are able to ask questions about what we are willing to pay for and subsidise. A commitment to allowing women (and men) to combine career and caring requires a financial contribution that must be borne by all earners. Even within our present economic and political structures there are fundamental choices to be made. Constructing those choices depends on our ability to create an agenda.

The climate of demands and expectations for us as lawyers is set as soon as we begin to study law (Rifkin,1985; Bottomley,1987). It is as undergraduates that we are initiated into the possibilities and limitations of law and lawyering. Unless and until gender issues are taken seriously in academic institutions, nothing will change. Look around you – to what extent do you see an active questioning of gender and legal relations in your law courses and among your colleagues?

Courses which use feminist material are too often simply subject areas deemed to be about women – most obviously family law. Even in these courses, when standard texts do refer to feminist material it is often introduced with a health warning against taking the arguments too far. Courses using feminist materials are usually taught by women, taken by women, and are presumed by our colleagues to be simply about women. A lecture on feminism may be given on other courses but is often seen as 'a lecture' and given by a woman lecturer invited in. The so-called core courses still ignore (with some notable exceptions) the rich seam of material available that would raise key issues usually rendered invisible in the subject area (eg, Pateman, 1988). Feminism has not really penetrated law schools; in some law schools it is now tolerated, in most it is ignored or, at best, marginalised. In as far as it is tolerated it is those aspects of feminism which most fit the prevailing orthodoxy that are encouraged and given credence by patronising male colleagues.

Recognising the fit between aspects of feminism and the prevailing orthodoxy is important. For many feminism is simply about women's rights. The emphasis on 'women' and on 'rights' are examples of a double bind – it is both right and terribly wrong. To concentrate on these is to presume that the problem for women is simply to achieve the benefits which men have; this presumes that all is basically right with the world if only we had equal access to it. This suits the prevailing political orthodoxy and the commonly held assumption that feminism is simply about giving women more chances rather than radically challenging men's lives as well. Feminism does insist on women's rights but equally calls for a fundamental questioning of the basis of our social order.

However, it is the struggle against discrimination which is the easiest concept for most people to identify with. This is not surprising – not only is it in the living memory of our mothers and grandmothers that overt discrimination was a regular feature of their lives, but the modern history of women's rights has to a great extent centred on the demand for equality. The nineteenth century resounds with battles against discrimination – exclusion from education and the professions, exclusion from the right to vote and to hold property. The culmination of this struggle was finally marked by the passing of the 1975 Sex Discrimination Act and Equal Pay Act.

The struggle for formal equality cannot be belittled – it was strongly fought over and each victory important. For many of our sisters in other countries the battle is still central to their agenda. We are privileged in the sense that we can afford to see the very constraints of the ideas of discrimination and equality. This is not to dismiss them as unimportant but rather to place them within a broader agenda and a more profound analysis of gender divisions. Equality means simply and only the right to be treated in the same way and given the same opportunities as those who already have them – in the case of gender equality the right to be treated as men, as if men are the norm and as if the present organisation of social relations is all we aspire to.

To recognise both the benefits and limitations of a formal equality programme, and that one aspect of feminism fits neatly into an extension of orthodoxy, allows us to understand why some sections of the left critique feminism as being simply a liberal programme. It is true that some feminists seem to go no further than a formal equality argument or to concentrate on this, but it is a fundamental misconception to equate feminism with no more than an extension of liberalism. It is too easy for those who already have the privileges of formal equality, and the benefits of structural inequality, to belittle the efforts of feminists to extend and use the tools and strategies that are available to improve women's position here and now. Further, for some contemporary feminists there is an attraction in taking the ideas of equality and discrimination and really pushing them to the limits – looking if you like for a radical programme of 'true' equality and truly tough anti-discrimination strategies that go far beyond the ideas and practices of orthodox liberal traditions.[1]

Mapping Feminism ...

It is difficult to try to define the different elements of feminism, and the differences between them, with brevity. I have already indicated one stream, of liberal-feminism, but this label is often used pejoratively and at best covers a wide range of differences.

In England, a major influence within feminism, unsurprisingly given our political heritage, has been Marxist theory and/or socialist commitment and practice. A great deal of literature in the 1970s and early 1980s was addressed to the question of the relationship between the politics and practices of the left and the women's movement. Unravelling the positions that were hammered out at this time is difficult, but simply we can identify one stream of feminism that is concerned with continuing to examine contemporary legal discourse as an aspect of state and class relations. For some this led on to an argument about the specificity of women's oppression; the model of a materialist analysis became one way to analyse the exploitative relations between men and women. Interestingly, in two examples (Delphy in France and MacKinnon in the United States), beginning with a Marxist model of class and state relations and moving then to an account of gender relations led them to posit theories in opposition to a Marxist explanation. Delphy remains a classic materialist in her concern to give special priority to economic relations between men and women (she has particularly looked at the marriage contract) but MacKinnon was more radical and moved on to argue that the fundamental relation between the genders is based on the exploitation of sexuality and that men bring to, and derive from, that exploitative relationship not simply power but the power of violence (she has written on rape, pornography and sexual harassment).

At this point we have moved away from forms of analysis identified with Marxism or socialism and towards work which tends to be associated with the term radical feminist: but again this needs to be handled with care. For some it does mean identifying men or maleness as the main enemy, for others such language is crude and there are major divisions in both theory and strategies. What holds radical feminism together is a concentration on relations of sexuality, power and violence. What divides is an argument about origins and consequently about the possibilities for change.

Within this framework both Marxist-feminist and radical-feminist positions attempt to understand causes. Put another way, it is about trying to find a model to explain the reasons as well as describe the effects; for most this model is found in patriarchy. The actual use of the term differs considerably between theorists but at its simplest it is used to explore relations of power and exploitation between men and women. Problematically, it seems to suggest that not only can a final explanation be found but further that it will be found in material conditions.

A concern that such a search might be too essentialist began to emerge among feminists in the 1980s. This fitted with trends in academic work as well as, to a great extent, mirroring the 'crisis on the left': people began to question whether one final reason could ever explain a complex web of social relations. Many feminists began to feel easier with the term patriarchal relations, used descriptively, rather than patriarchy.[2]

Paradoxically, at the same time as theory seemed to be loosening up in terms of building models, many (intellectual) feminists became influenced by ideas of gender differences in the use of language and modes of reasoning. This created a new equality/difference argument focused on the concept of a phallocentric society, concerned with the way in which language, symbols and modes of representation construct and utilise the masculine as the norm and the feminine as 'the other', the outside and the fatal allure of all things dangerous.[3] This was a rediscovery not simply of the vulnerability of women but of the fear men have of the female, drawing on psychoanalytical material as well as work on language. For some this became another form of structuralism, for others it is placed within a context of postmodernist thinking which is attractive because of the basic critique it offers of any form of essentialism. The paradox is that at each extreme the insistence on looking at the very deep divide in the way in which men and women think and understand their worlds seems to provoke the fear that it will either lead back into structuralism or, equally problematically, fall into a relativism that would make any form of decisive action impossible. I can share this concern, particularly when I look at some aspects of the intersection between feminism and postmodernism.[4] However, for feminists the grounding of any theory must come back to the combination of lived experience with a commitment to change. For that reason feminists are now strongly involved in debates about a revival of (for want of a better term) ethics: a language and mode of reasoning which allows us to make judgements and take stands (eg, Braidotti,1991) without being caught in the claim to final truths.

I have attempted this brief mapping exercise to expose the care needed when dealing with the term 'feminism'. We need to understand the different streams, and at the same time realise that it is often difficult to separate them. Some feminists do associate themselves with specific positions and the way in which they deal with legal issues is explained by this. Socialist-feminists often work within the area of labour relations, whereas radical-feminists often deal with issues of sexual violence in criminal law. Understanding differences in this sense is important but we should not overdraw them. Some feminists are quite eclectic and see it as valid to draw on different aspects and strategies, recognising that what holds feminists together is their radical questioning of gender relations. In terms of work on law, what is important is the constant reworking of 'strategies now' with a utopian vision, which keeps open and alive debates within feminism and between feminism and other radical critiques. Feminism can never be reduced to a series of external-to-feminism reference points; it cannot be gauged by simple judgement of one of its many aspects. It is the voice of women saying 'but ...'.

Reworking the Position of Women ...

To return to the Equal Opportunities Commission and specifically the question of women lawyers: if women are under-achieving, is this evidence of our failure to live up to the challenge or perhaps evidence of continued discrimination which eventually wears us down? Perhaps it is evidence of the quality of life we aspire to and, in the case of committed feminists, believe worth fighting for. In other words, we may be unwilling to be judged on how we lead our lives in terms that were designed by men.[5]

Are you willing to work all hours of the day? Are you willing to indulge in tactics and modes of argument that run contrary to your instincts as to what is right and fair? Are you willing to defend an accused rapist, and if so will you be willing to use the classic tactic of attacking the victim? Are you willing to help a husband hide his assets to protect them against the claims of a wife? Are you willing to play law as men play games – a game of strategy in which to win is all? Do you want to have children? Do you have someone to look after them when they are sick? Do you want to be more than simply a success at your job? Are you willing to be frightening to men? Are you prepared for the sexual allure that many men manage to read into a business suit or, even better, black robes ... (think of the images of women lawyers in film, LA Law and other media representations). Realise that men, many men, have real difficulty in dealing with you as an equal ... and do you want that anyway?

Yes, it is a cheap trick. I have posed a series of rhetorical questions and chosen extreme examples as well as commonplace ones. But all these issues have come up over and over again when I have talked with women friends. For feminists the dilemma is more acute because we are so much more aware of it – that is our double bind. We wanted to be lawyers despite and because of being women. We realise that the fundamental struggle is still very much with us and takes us both back into our role as lawyers as well as beyond it. My careers teacher was so wrong and so right. It is that paradox that feminism has to engage with. Can we, will we, when and how will we rock the system?

Acknowledgements

With thanks to those who read, commented, cajoled and helped me understand the mysteries of writing on a new magic screen – Belinda and Derek Meteyard, Christopher Stanley and Andy Dart. To Gian Giuliani for keeping a home fire burning.

Notes

1. It is important to distinguish between different political traditions. The radical-liberal position is popular among certain Americans (eg, Eisenstein, 1988) and often written from an academic background in political theory (eg, Pateman, 1988). It is also recognisable in some of the Scandinavian work; notably Dahl (1987). For an argument about the need to recognise the juridico-political base see Gibson (1990). I would add to this the need to recognise the academic discipline women bring to their work.
2. This movement is visible in Smart's work - from a concern with the missing dimension (1976), through an argument that patriarchy as a system only benefiting men doesn't exist but important aspects of male privilege do and therefore 'relations' is a better term (1984), to a preference for an analysis of power relations based on Foucault (1989, 1991). Interestingly she increasingly dismisses law as a dangerous power game which can offer nothing to women, whereas in 1984 she was open to the argument that law can offer a number of strategies for the improvement and defence of women's position. The use of closed models is very visible in her work - at present a closed model of law which, I would argue, is as problematic as a closed model of patriarchy.
3. The influence of such ideas is visible in eg Gibson (1990) and Young (1990). For an introduction to some of the basic themes see Jardine (1987).

4. The problems of men working with feminist ideas and with feminists are explored in Jardine & Smith (1987).
5. It is fundamental to me, as a feminist, to argue that the present advantages which accrue to men are nothing compared to the denial and warping that individual men undergo to conform to the image of the masculine. The future project must be about the radical transformation of the lives of both genders and of relations between them. This can only be to the advantage of all of us although the loss of male privilege will not be easy for most men to face. (What an understatement! Even the most radical men I know can still hardly glimpse the extent and depth to which they hold and use power; let alone begin to struggle with it.) For some clues see Olivier (1989).

The (Im)possible Pedagogical Politics of (the Law of) Postmodernism
Costas Douzinas and Ronnie Warrington

Outside or offside? Outside is the position of the judge, and the inquisitor. But academic debate has an effect. Being intra-textual does not make you extra-terrestrial.

But that is where the academic, at least in the social sciences, abandons the status of academic and becomes something more sinister, something that consciously tries to reach into thought processes, to shape them in a way that turns art, play, laughter and, yes, learning into truth with a capital T.

Hold it; let's go back. What were we saying? The responsibility? No utterances can be completely safe. Even your own thoughts, uttered only to yourself, affect your own actions and then others. So the most academic of discussions can affect the way people think and act and, in the end, what we are or may become.

But it would be quite wrong to see the postmodernism we are talking about in that way. That is because we can't draw up an agenda, a provisional programme that might help determine where all this gets us. That gets us into the reproduction of grand narratives.

What are you getting at?

That postmodernism distrusts the large-scale theories, the totalising theories that have been constructed to explain the social world. Real worlds or legal systems are not 'out there', perfectly formed or otherwise, waiting to be brought to light by theory. Postmodernism prefers provisional, small scale narratives that pay attention to different forms of speaking and writing; it listens for the repressed and oppressed dialectics that are apparently excluded but actually always within complex textual organisations. And it deliberately sets out to unsettle closed, comfortable, established systems of meaning. Marxism, for example, despite its utterly essential moral indignation and unswerving opposition to political domination and oppression, is a discourse which aspires to a total possession of an all-embracing, definitive truth. It reaches towards an understanding as complete and therefore perhaps as dangerous as any religion. But the point is, as Lyotard [1984] puts it, society itself does not form an integrated whole, but remains haunted by a principle of opposition. That principle of opposition is suppressed in most of the major theories that have influenced the build-up of the modern world, including Marxism; it needs to be brought out again. The end of grand narratives, as it is grandly called.

Oh, of course [testily]. But that is all a bit overdone isn't it? Totalitarian regimes of thought, Enlightened, pre-Enlightened, post-Enlightened are part of the thing we are all struggling against. But grand narratives are also maybe all we can hang on to. Do we not make grand narratives of the petty, stupid, dull, little things that make up our lives? Are not we all building the most ridiculous grand narratives all the time? A student wants to write an exam script that will pass; then one that will get a first; and what then? Why does she or he want a first? To get the better job, the better house, car and access to better restaurants, power, sex, drugs, drink and drachmas. Is not that a desperate clinging to a sort of petty grand narrative, one in which we all indulge and are all guilty of? And isn't the same true of the cosmic global narratives that constitute a politics of the postmodern age, wherever that is, or perhaps was? A series of little or local narratives. Ecologically, environmentally user-friendly, bloody green narratives. Is that not simply another way of grand narrativising? You build up a grand narrative of little narratives and think you have escaped grand narratives and developed new politics. Have you ever met a green friend of the earth who was open to anything but green narratives? And hang everything else.

OK. But what we are talking about is not the same as dogmas. If you recognise these dreams for what they are, inevitable but dangerous turns in the form of politics (ones that can sometimes even lead to readings of genocide as a genuine human good), then surely that is a start. After this you read people, situations, events, catastrophes, books as the always potentially other of what they are, or seem or desire to be. In doing this you open the tyranny of the oppressor to the discourse of the oppressed.

But do the oppressed have to construct their discourses by creating new privileged readings, in a world of increasing illiteracy forchristsake, via the master discourses, the arcane languages of some academic gurus in Paris or Yale? What do academic discourses do but produce, turn into another commodity to be appropriated and abused, the latest nothings of a new super-caste? And how new are these latest musings anyway?

That sounds like part of the general criticism that postmodernism merely repeats what it tries to criticise. Take a standard Marxist critique, like that of Callinicos [1989], for example. He makes a great fuss about the fact that many modernist themes are picked up in postmodernist discourses and that they often seem merely to echo some of the debates in art, literature, theatre, and to a lesser extent perhaps, philosophy that modernism introduced. For Callinicos this seems a fundamental critique. He makes a similar point when he argues along the lines that the posties use rational argument and are, therefore, somehow merely replaying a modernist (or perhaps Enlightenment) debate. But the point, as Derrida for one continually argues, is that the critique of reason always takes place from the standpoint of reason; a point Callinicos does grudgingly acknowledge. Just as the questioning or even the rejection of the Enlightenment takes place from within the Enlightenment; similarly the development to postmodernism takes place from out of the very modernism it is reworking, and inevitably uses modernist themes to do so. Callinicos's objection is not very significant here. Again, it is not simply that there is (or maybe that there is) nothing outside of the text. It is that the text, or Enlightenment reason, makes and unmakes the possibility of our thought, of our discursive potentials. We never step outside of Enlightenment reason not just because we lack the imagination or the will to truth, but because the outside is only set up in relation to the inside and can't exist without it. The outside is an expression of our relation with the inside. So reason cannot be critiqued without reason and it is the reason of the Enlightenment that shapes the reason that we use to critique reason. In that sense Habermas [1987] is mistaken in his battle to save reason, or communicative competencies. He is attacking the wrong targets. There is no difficulty with all the paraphernalia of reason and the wonderful possibilities that the Enlightenment opened up. It is true that some of Nietzsche's [1961] remarks do give the impression that he wanted to return to a sort of heroic time when men were men, before reason, before universal competition, as Marx might have put it, made Achilles the equivalent of the tortoise. But that is a poor reading of Nietzsche. A better one is to accept that reason is all we have, but that the scientific form of reasoning lauded by the Enlightenment, even if we could work out what that was, is not all there is to it. Not, then, that we want to abandon reason, but, as Heidegger [1968] might have put it, we have not yet learned to use reason. We have not, after all, reached the age of reason.

Yes, I suppose one thing that can be said for even the worst side of postmodernism, the celebration of global-warmed-multi-world-mass-production-identikit-lives is that it does challenge the dangerous idea that texts can get elevated to the status of the new *Capital* because they embody some ultimate or scientific reason. The publication of *Of Grammatology* [1976] exactly 100 years after the first publication of volume one of *Capital* also symbolically brings to an end the era of capitalism as the advanced society. The tumble into the infinite repetition and consumerism of the postmodern world, something that in effect Marx is forecasting in *Capital* itself, with its meticulous analysis of the possibility of the endless reproduction of commodities, heralds also the elevation of the banal, the trivial and the simulation of nothing into the greatest aim society or the individual can have. Postmodernism shocks because it can lead to an absolute commitment to the mirage; in its celebration of the image, any attempt to imagine something beyond the image becomes a madness.

But you were also saying that the reading of texts and people is all that there is to it. So a postmodern reading that helps do that in a way that is liberating, whatever that may mean, must be important.

Well, what is it that is so liberating, assuming you can read? To be able to read a text differently (of course not better) results only in a different reading.

I thought we agreed earlier that even thinking differently can be important. But thinking is not an abstract matter is it? To begin with, it has to be set in a context. Or rather, perhaps, an institution; in education, or politics or prison, or the factory – perhaps the differences between these examples are so slight that we should delete them – it is the setting that is vital, or maybe successful.

Why?

Because, generally speaking, we don't think beyond the institution. All that is now possible is more of the same. The experience that counts is the one that can be repeated everywhere, at all times and in all places, which is why Marx's example of reproduction within the factory was so effective. It is the institution that reproduces the same and guarantees more of it. Including thinking. But thinking at the same time is not predetermined by any context or institution. There are boundaries, orders, but the hope is that these can be, if not removed exactly, then at least rethought. It is the possibility of rethinking the accepted boundaries of thought that is always there, despite the context, that are important.

All right, so to what does this importance relate? It relates to seeing that people and texts do more and less than they claim, that meaning, what it is we communicate, though related to those degraded but not irrelevant ideas of authorial attention and reader position or grid is also something else, that is that in the differences between writer, text and reader there are spaces, supplements, traces, OK, which in any complex textual assembly are always capable of providing something more; that difference is both a danger and a potential liberator. In the differences, gaps, cliff edges, mazes and labyrinths, that is in the very uses of language, nothing and everything is at stake.

Spoken like a true text. But the politics of it can't just be this commitment to new, or different or open forms of reading, or discovery. What is there that the writer or speaker or body didn't realise? If post-modernism has any meaning at all for us, it relates to a different way of stating a political commitment that, in a sense, is always already predicated. Our own understanding of postmodernism is based on certain commitments, such as the denial of the authority of rules based on the exclusion of classes, races and of a specific gender – all done in the name of equality, and of disrespect masquerading as equal concern and respect; a rejection of the total triumphalism of western bourgeois values, smug and complacent at the best of times and doubly so during the collapse of so-called existing communisms. In short a commitment to causes, changes, aspirations and, perhaps, even grand narratives that go beyond the disagreements over particular texts.

So postmodernism is a way of committing oneself to a form of thought, without having to grind through the analysis?

No, not exactly. If we treat Marxism as one of the discredited grand narratives, though perhaps the most significant one, as you were saying earlier, how do we proceed? Perhaps postmodernism, with its celebration (and questioning) of the cash-trash-all-nexus is merely the final triumph of a pre-Enlightenment thought.

Meaning?

In some time before the many bourgeois revolutions one actually had a foundation for belief – God, community, state or human nature. Modernity questioned the foundation of all beliefs, except human understanding. Modernity's crisis was caused by its own reason for being. Its foundational faith in a new foundationalism – if nothing else, reason – was perceived as an unacceptable foundation; and that faith in reason came to be seen as merely a substitute for other foundational faiths which it had supposedly rejected. To that extent the new philosophers of truth, like Davidson [1984], do have a point. But without a faith in reason it is very difficult to speak at all.

You are making a pretty good attempt.

Look, can't you just say that poverty, deprivation, the slaughter of human beings is wrong, absolutely wrong, you could even say at all times? And what postmodernism might offer is a way of challenging the ultimate tragedy, the view that suffering, war, starvation, *the* grand narratives of our age, or even the results of earthquakes, let's face it, are not natural. The naturalism of our response to suffering is itself a construct of one of the cleverest, most devious, but most disastrous possible narratives. A narrative of all who say keep my place, my privilege, my power, my ability to control the space that I inhabit in the consciousness of others.

But that is precisely what we have been talking about: a cultural moment where it becomes possible to refuse the authority of this form of discourse, to deny its ability. The result can be the sort of sickening individualistic carelessness of the other that cultural postmodernism sometimes offers.

But not always.

No, though depressingly often ... But it is also a break point, a moment that may represent —

A new politics? A new narrative of domination?

A way of approaching the problem of politics as a problem. Which is exactly what the law student is about.

> Sweating over their books of law
> Desperately arguing with demented spades
> Post-haste comes fate knocking at the door
> Examinations, marks, classes, grades
> Give us certainty, truth, answers to a claim
> While justice is hanged on that tree of ill-fame

Deconstruction in particular actually sets itself in a very old and honourable tradition of criticism; one that says you start by reading the text carefully and that deconstructive readings of the text of law can be more faithful than those supplied by your average legal argument. What you find going on in judgements, articles and case notes is often a wilful misreading in order to put forward particular lines of development. Now what the law student learns is how to follow these creative misconstructions and misreadings that have been taken up. But they also learn not to see those others that are ignored, lost, negligently occluded. What deconstruction does is help read texts so that the lost parts, the suppressed and oppressed of the text are once again made available. They show the other possibilities, the ones the orthodox readings fail to notice. Not because they deliberately read them out – though in legal texts there is a fair amount of that too – but because they are read badly. Deconstruction as a philosophy of language is also an instruction in reading.

The point then is to assess the effect of the readings. And to do this you have to see not only how the ideas are being expressed but where they are put to work.

The context, as we were saying earlier.

Exactly. In law, for example, we can't just assume a general audience for 'law' or 'legal argument'. Judicial ideas or case law development take place in the specific environment of law courts, with the particular audiences of the judiciary and legal professions being the intended main recipients of the arguments. With doctrine, and even more so with strictly theoretical or jurisprudential discourses, the primary audience is the academy. This world, as real as any other, is the institutional setting determining the effectivity, or otherwise, of its discourse. And it is in challenging or changing orthodoxy within this world that alternative, or postmodern or Marxist academic critiques are to be assessed. Their importance lies in their effectivity, at least initially, in their chosen area of operation. The point I was trying to make before – textual analysis, especially in the academic setting, is in no sense irrelevant. On the contrary, it is the very thing that ensures effective or necessary work.

And the importance of postmodern readings is particularly interesting in a subject like law, where under the guise of an apparently oral tradition and practice –how does Goodrich put it? '... the legal tradition was based upon oratorical techniques of hearing, on aural memory ... skills of representational speech' – what is actually dominant is the written text. Law, at least common law, is based on writing though it actually appears to be an oral matter at heart. It is reading, though, that is at stake.

Yes, much legal discussion is a prime example of Derrida's argument, is it not?

What? You mean that *Of Grammatology* exposition?

You remember? That in so much of Western thought, traceable to Plato, the nearest we get to authenticity is speech, which itself is only an imitation of the pure essence of thought and intention. Writing is merely the attempt to communicate when speech is not available, and is therefore twice removed from reality, from the essence of things. It is only a poor copy of speech, itself a poor copy of the inner essence. And the Common Law replays that by insisting on oral presentations, oral evidence, oral judgements – within the Western tradition at least the closest approximation we have to authenticity, to truth. What Derrida does is question that whole debasement of writing by showing, in a certain counter-intuitive sense, that writing comes before speech, that not only is there no possible guaranteed access to authenticity via speech in a way that writing cannot deliver, but also that in a sense there is no speech without writing. The Common Law tradition therefore merely replays the fallen tricks of Western philosophy.

Don't decry it; its success is stupendous. In a sense it works. It actively convinces that the whole rigmarole of counsel, judges, witnesses, experts, all standing up asking and answering questions and speaking, actively produces the nearest possible thing we can have to a truth-finding process.

Mind you, it did get a bit of a battering in 1990 particularly. What with the Guildford Four, the Birmingham Six and the Maguire Seven.

But these are treated merely as exceptions that prove the rule. Mistakes are made but the general provision still holds: speech comes first.

And to return to the Common Law tradition, Derrida's argument works beautifully. Precedent is no longer oral memory or common inheritance; it is simply (and with the invention of data banks and the like only more so) the workings of the written tradition controlling what is supposed to be a pure oral process.

Exactly. A perfect example of the reversal of common sense and a nice manifestation of Derrida's arguments.

Of course, the standard objection is that speech actually existed or comes before writing or, at least at first blush, that seems most likely.

But that is quite irrelevant isn't it? Whichever came first in some absolute sense, whether neolithic people grunted before they drew on their caves or painted the kill before they learnt to discuss it – isn't it most likely that they developed alongside each other? – is not to the point. Crucial is that, in Derrida's reworking, what we see creating the communities we inhabit is the interpretation of written texts. Spoken text, as it were, only comes out of the written record, whilst being treated as the apparently more important, more authentic form.

Yes, just think about a law case for a moment. The summary facts, the pleadings, and the precedents all appear in written form. Counsel and judges then argue on those written statements, those cases etc. But the controlling discourses are the written ones. In the oral tradition of the common law, writing does indeed come first. Take something as basic as equity. In the technical common law sense, equity is meaningless without writing. Equity, the judgement of the court of conscience, followed a direct appeal to the representative of God's own representative, apparently an oral matter. But actually equity depends on writs, pleadings, judgements, orders, injunctions, in a word – documentation, all of which only make sense as written. Lawyers are therefore speakers about written matters which they themselves have already written and drafted (title deeds for example) before they are discussed and argued about in court. Law in court is an interplay between the spoken and the written, or rather an oral discourse about what was previously written, in statutes, law reports, pleadings and the like.

Which is why, almost more than any other applied theoretical discipline, law needs not just careful readers, it also requires readers who can pull texts out of their vacuums, make the silences speak, the apparent absences appear and these texts assume context, etc. If no interpretation is exhaustive then whether or not there is an infinity of interpretations is irrelevant. It is sufficient that more interpretations become possible.

But what has this got to do with a radical politics? The right can pull out their own leftovers quite as easily.

I suppose so.

But wait – just because deconstruction and postmodernism notoriously have been appropriated by some of the most unpleasant politics of the age doesn't mean anything. It is still possible to use it in a way the new age demands, or at least needs. Furthermore, as a critique, deconstruction has far more power than the 'misuses' [prove that] to which it has been put, especially in the US. But there is always the danger. If the history of Marxism teaches us anything it is that emancipatory discourses can be captured by the most oppressive of reactionary and brutal ideologies. But that is no reason for not struggling for those emancipatory discourses, merely a reason to avoid their misuse and to fight, textually speaking of course, for other ways of reading the world.

So politics is approached like a law text – what can be read out of this text or situation or moment – what is there that can be made to speak that challenges the deadening orthodoxy; how can the textual production of this particular artifact be rethought creatively in a manner that can be liberating? Is that it? Is that what this text/conversation that we/you have just spoken/written/read is meant to do? Or, pedagogically speaking, suggest is possible, or desirable?

Critical Legal Theory; The Power of Law
Sammy Adelman and Ken Foster

Law grinds the poor, and rich men rule the law
Goldsmith, *The Traveller*

Most ideas about law disguise its political nature and functions. The reason for this lies in the nature and form of law and how we think about it. The reality of power is obscured while the existing political order is rationalised in the rhetoric of equality, rights and the rule of law. There is little systematic work on law and power despite the fact that a defining feature of law is that it operates to facilitate exploitation and discrimination. It operates in this manner primarily in four spheres: class, gender, race and ideology. In most pre-modern societies power was exercised in ways unrestricted by notions of legitimacy and right. We therefore need to explain how this concept of 'law' is used to justify the political order of modern society and why it is neither perceived – nor, indeed, operates – as the naked domination of one group over another.

The pervasiveness of law in modern society means that law must be challenged from within by means of what we call legal insurgency. It is not enough to be critical of law and its underlying political structures; we need to move beyond mere criticism to critique and thereby expose the contradictions underpinning the principles, policies and doctrines of bourgeois law. The material effects of law and the ideological bases upon which it is manufactured must be analysed and deconstructed in order to comprehend the power of modern legal discourse as a dominant intellectual paradigm.

The ways of thinking about law which have dominated European social thought during the past 200 years constitute a paradigm which has variously been termed formalism, positivism, rational/scientific and modern. This paradigm disguises the structures of political power by making legal discourse appear to be neutral, value-free and scientific. It separates legal discourse from other discourses, political and moral discourses in particular. It abstracts human beings from their social existence by constructing them exclusively as the holders of legal rights and the subjects of legal duties. It fetishises the individual, and it reifies social and political relations between people.

Legal Formalism

Legal formalism, which we consider to be emblematic of this paradigm, has three principal dimensions. First, it represents the notion that law is made by the state and its agencies so that all legal rules appear imperative and willed by the political sovereign. Law is enacted by a legislature or announced by judges. It is derived from the state, which is seen as an external impersonal force which governs the people from above, which has unrestricted sovereignty and the absolute power to make rules. It is created by the legal institutions themselves and appears to be relatively autonomous of the natural 'social order'. The validity of law is determined not by its substantive content but by formal questions about its precedence, its pedigree and its procedural correctness.

The rise and legitimation of the bourgeois nation state is the key historical determinant of legal formalism. The modern state acts independently of real control by the governed despite the fact that its power, expressed in political and legal doctrines of sovereignty, is often rationalised as the democratic outcome of a social contract with the people. The law is perceived to be a state-approved set of rules commanding and controlling the people. This concept of the state causes two related difficulties. First, how does the state legitimate its place at the apex of political decision-making? This problem has historically been resolved in various ways: military victory or conquest, divine right, ownership of land, the natural or traditional order of the community, external power such as the papacy, a valid constitution, democratic election, or through revolution. Secondly, each political system has its own ideological methods of resolving the difficulty arising from the apparent conflict between the unrestricted power of the state and the protection of individual rights. The potential tyranny and arbitrariness inherent in uncontrolled power therefore come to be accepted as being limited by concepts of democratic accountability, legal controls over the political executive, formal universal rules equally applicable to all citizens, and the ostensible neutrality of those who make and administer the law.

The second characteristic of legal formalism is its indifference to substantive justice. Dominant groups and individuals exercise their power by subjecting every citizen to the same rules so that formal justice masks substantive social differences and inequalities. Legal discourse is isolated from the purview of political, social and ethical/moral discourses, and legal reasoning is severed from *any* external criterion which can be used to judge and evaluate social behaviour. Thus moral standards, ethical behaviour and, crucially, questions of justice are eliminated from legal reasoning. What the law is and what it ought to be are argued by legal practitioners to be independent questions. Indeed, modern judges are expected to be remote and disinterested.

Its third characteristic is its explicitly rational and scientific discourse, a product of the Enlightenment and hence an expression of a conscious desire to understand and control the material world. Legal formalism presents law as a gapless, logical and internally coherent system, in which correct legal decisions can be deduced by formal reasoning. These characteristics of formalism are frequently hailed as virtues yet merely serve to emphasise the false separation of judgement from political and social factors.

What is less often stressed is the extent to which this is part of a more general development of scientific thought. The emergence of scientific legal discourse from the late eighteenth century onwards paralleled the growth of medical and biological discourses and the development of political, social and economic sciences as distinct disciplines (Foucault, 1971 and 1979). Its expression in legal discourse is most clearly represented by John Austin's positivist jurisprudence and its mimicking of the methods of natural science. Legal science concentrates pre-eminently on the classification and division of concepts, on methods of induction and deduction, and on the analysis and synthesis of rules. Judicial decision-making becomes an experimental procedure in which hypotheses of abstract rules are proposed, evidence is found and tested, and conclusions are drawn by logical deduction. Even modern refinements of scientific procedure, such as the theory of falsification rather than verification, are paralleled in the legal method of writers such as Hart and Dworkin – for example in the finding of the hard case of extreme facts which will not fit the rule.

Law as Power

One of the few authors who has directly addressed the question of power in modern societies is Michel Foucault. He identifies power as being everywhere and flowing in different directions depending upon who is exercising it and in what context. He thus frees us from sterile conceptions of power being implemented in a top-down fashion by the dominant groups in society. On the other hand, this ultimately pluralist conception of power runs the risk of ignoring the significance of the group exercise of class, race and gender power through law. Foucault can also be faulted for identifying law as a declining discourse: as we head towards the twenty-first century it would appear that law has never been more central to the maintenance of capitalist, racist and sexist relations.

Our analysis of the centrality and ideological importance of legal formalism reveals that it is not coincidental that bourgeois law operates to the advantage of the powerful or that access to and treatment by the law is directly related to socioeconomic class. As Anatole France so succinctly put it, 'The law in its majestic impartiality forbids both rich and poor alike to sleep under bridges, to beg in the streets and steal bread.' (France, *Crainquebille*, quoted in Davidoff, 1952) Law has historically assumed forms which facilitate the accumulation of capital and which operate ideologically to secure the consent of those subject to it. The worker and the capitalist are equal only in the eyes of law, which operates semi-autonomously to mask, filter and mediate reality. Law generally benefits the dominant social classes because they construct the law even as they are constructed by it. The limited legal gains made by the dominated classes are generally the product of resistance or the co-optation so characteristic of the welfare state. These exceptions that prove the rule are crucial to the success of law's ideological hegemony.

The problem of class analysis, however, is that it does not adequately explain other forms of domination such as racial and sexual discrimination. The growing corpus of feminist writings on law has subjected bourgeois law to a thorough critique, demonstrating in the process how its categories – constructed by and for, and enforced predominantly by, men – are incapable of providing substantive justice for women because they in fact facilitate discrimination against women (MacKinnon, 1987, Smart 1989).

The concept of jurisprudence presumes an identifiable unity of law, hence basic principles of justice, rights or equity are presumed to underpin all aspects of law. Jurisprudence seeks to identify the source of these principles and therefore make generally applicable statements about the nature of law. Basic to this notion is the idea that these norms are relevant and binding to all areas of law (Smart, 1989, p. 69).

It is precisely this blanket approach by the law which makes possible the illusion that all citizens are completely autonomous, free-willed, fully aware of the law and fully in agreement with the major tenets of the dominant ideology – which is essentially that of the white Anglo-Saxon Protestant. It is not surprising, therefore, that the pregnant woman, the victim of racial discrimination, the Muslim in Britain or the political leftwinger should often find his or her *Weltanschauung* directly contradicted by law and legal ideology. Fitzpatrick has demonstrated how, in the liberal worldview underpinning bourgeois law (which celebrates individualism as it promotes conformity), 'racism is compatible with and even integral to law' (Fitzpatrick & Hunt, 1987, pp. 119–32).By focusing exclusively on the individual, and on intention to the exclusion of motive (see Norrie in this book), the legal system performs the sleight of hand of rescuing society from responsibility for racism while appearing to be an adequate means of dealing with it.

Class, gender and race are the primary material relations of exploitation, masked but yet built into the legal form. They are not, however, separate matrices of power relations. Rather they are interdependent, so that a single legal system facilitates different forms of exploitation and discrimination. Thus there is a relationship between the sexual division of labour (which predates class divisions, but which changes in relation to both the social and international divisions of labour) and different modes of production. Similarly, such a relationship exists between racial discrimination and colonialism and imperialism, and between law and the underdevelopment of the Third World. In South Africa, black women are thrice oppressed, as blacks, as women and as black women, and the legal structures of apartheid have directly or indirectly reinforced and facilitated all three forms of oppression.

Law is ordinarily generated, enacted and enforced by those with a vested interest in maintaining the *status quo*. It is therefore inherently conservative. If legal theory is to be progressive it must be critical and must address the role of law as a primary facilitator of exploitation and discrimination. In our teaching, research and practice we must seek to theorise, not in the abstract, but on the basis of the materiality of law: we must seek a materialist theory of law. Feminist legal theorists have demonstrated how traditional jurisprudence, insular and parochial as it is, can no longer ignore the claims and challenges of feminist legal theory, despite the latter's flaws and growing pains. The task now confronting us is to generalise such a critique to race, colonialism, imperialism and all other forms of domination and to seek to unify theory and practice. For it is only in the unity of praxis that legal theory can avoid the sterility of traditional jurisprudence and begin to make a meaningful contribution to social life.

Law as Resistance
Peter Fitzpatrick

Introduction

Whether law is to be resisted or whether it can be a form of resistance is an intensely debated issue in the politics of law. Feminist and minority activists in the United States strive to secure positions in law whereas most critical legal scholars there see law as indeterminate and intrinsically unreliable. In the United Kingdom some would see law as subordinate to a dominant power in society whereas others argue for its independent capacity to bring about progressive change. Here, I will outline these various stands, not to resolve them but to extract from them two distinct ideas of law. With one, law has that general, surpassing power necessary for the rule of law. With the other, law is limited and constituted in its involvement with various social relations. Resistance can have little assured place with the first idea of law but it does have a part in the second, not least in the undermining of law's pretensions to surpassing power.

Law and the Limits of Resistance

To set the scene, I will start with a story often celebrated for affirming law as resistance – Marx's account of the Ten-Hour Act, the Factory Act of 1848 which limited the hours of work to ten a day (Marx, 1954, pp. 264–81). The significance of this law lay not just in its limiting of the working day. It was the symbol, culmination and resolution of a long, general struggle between workers and employers. Given this, what is remarkable is not so much the achievement but its precariousness. As Marx so graphically shows, the act was sustained only by an intense politics involving workers, crown lawyers and factory inspectors opposing the manufacturers and judges sympathetic to them. Employers often evaded the act and even secured its modification in their own interests with the Factory Act of 1850. The Ten-Hour Act is hardly, then, an unequivocal instance of law as resistance.

Nor has the general issue since been settled. Versions of the dependence of law would see it, to take examples from Marxism, as a component of a superstructure determined by an economic base, or as relatively autonomous within a somewhat more complex structure where the economic remains ultimately determining. But others advocate the taking seriously of law and of many other social forms that the left is said to have treated negatively or dismissively to the detriment of its political effectiveness. So, one is supposed to be realistic about, for example, police and profitability, and this not only because people see good in them and people have votes, but also because these social forms will in some ways need to be maintained in a future socialist society. So law, as one such social form, is granted an independent political existence and the capacity for progressive social change.

A marked variation on this theme comes from recent sharp debates within critical legal studies in the United States. The prevalent view sees 'the legal process at large and its discrete doctrinal components' as 'fundamentally indeterminate and manipulable' (Hutchinson and Monahan, 1984, pp. 211–12). That indeterminacy and manipulation will typically favour dominant interests. Rules, rights and processes in law insidiously attract people with a promise of enduring standards and objective determination, but provide neither. There can be no significant basis or focus here for resistance. But from the perspectives of minorities this line of

> critique ... is familiar, imperialistic and wrong. Minorities know from bitter experience that occasional court victories do not mean the Promised Land is at hand. The critique is imperialistic in that it tells minorities and other oppressed peoples how they should interpret events affecting them. A court order directing a housing authority to disburse funds for heating in subsidized housing may postpone the revolution, or it may not. In the meantime the order keeps a number of poor families warm. This may mean more to them than it does to a comfortable academic working in a warm office. (Delgado, 1987, pp. 307–8)

I would like to suggest that these disagreements reflect two distinct dimensions of law. The first we could call a relational dimension. For the proponents of taking law seriously, and for the advocates of minorities, the idea of law tends to be an operative one. Out of the infinity of what law could be and could do, it is doing and being something specific. In this way law is formed in the diversity of its links with other social relations. This law creates a diversity of fields each with characteristic meanings and limits which come to be usual but not invariant, resolved but not set. These fields often give effect to resistances, as with the Ten-Hour Act. Or, to take a current example, we find improbable legal pockets of humanity and tolerance in the immigration law of the United Kingdom created by the sustained activity of legal practitioners particularly through the appeals process. In this diversity of situations, a modest general claim could be made for law as resistance along the lines that the stability involved can limit the ruler as well as the ruled. This claim is often inflated into a virtue unique to the rule of law but it is no more than what is involved in any formalisation of power.

Which point serves to return us to the thesis of indeterminacy in critical legal studies, since any formalisation can be rendered indeterminate. But the dimension of law in which this can be done is different to that relational dimension we have just considered where law would cease to exist if it were rendered comprehensively indeterminate. Law in this other dimension resides definitively in some unifying, 'sovereign' location such as the state. It is set apart from social relations even if it will often be thought of as connected in a general way to society or as ultimately dominated by some element of society such as the economic. Whatever this connection or whatever law's ultimate basis may be, the intrinsic claim of the rule of law is that law is a transcendent, all-encompassing power. It cannot in its own terms be limited in the interests of a power outside of itself. Thus resistances established in law remain contingent on change or abolition through a rule of law which does not grant them any existence outside of its own domain. We could call this the surpassing dimension of law. The gains of the Ten-Hour Act, as we saw, were not assured within law. The overtly partisan resort by recent governments in the United Kingdom to law's surpassing dimension has dramatised its significance for resistance. To take but one example, rights of trade unions and of workers once seemingly secured in law have been taken away or drastically modified. The general point is that resistance cannot be assured through law in its surpassing dispensation. This conclusion is complicated where there are constitutional provisions securing positions against normal legal change. But constitutions can be amended and, more ominously, they are interpreted. To take another recent example, in the landmark decision of *Roe v. Wade* ([1973] 410 US 113), the US Supreme Court used the constitutional right to privacy seemingly to secure a right to abortion but it has now subjected this right to the prospect of contrary regulation by state legislatures (*Webster v. Reproductive Health Services* [1989] 109 S Ct 3040). This surpassing dimension of law, in its incompatibility with any settled condition, has operated to resist ascribed status whether sexual, racial or feudal. But, overall, its record on this score has been at best ambivalent (Fitzpatrick, 1987).

Resistance and the Limits of the Law

So far I have argued that although resistance can be effective in law's relational dimension, it can ultimately be countered in law's surpassing dimension. Without abandoning that conclusion, I now want to show that it can also be reversed, that law as relational can, paradoxically, surpass law as surpassing. That is, we can use law as relational to locate limits and restraints on the ability of surpassing law to negative resistance. One obvious way is to strengthen those elements which go to constitute law relationally. The Ten-Hour Act was secured and finally sustained because an effective politics remained integral to law in that situation. The dilution of the Act in the Factory Act of 1850 could be traced to a weakness in that politics (Marx, 1954, pp. 269–77). To take another example, the increasing resort to informal and popular justice as alternatives to law has remained largely subordinated to state law because an alternative basis for it has not been secured. The outcome is dramatically otherwise where there is an alternative basis drawing on the involvement of the community, as with the Newham Conflict and Change Project (Miller, 1986).

But, as the persistence of popular and informal justice, even in their compromised forms, indicates, there is a distinctiveness to them in their ability to regulate areas which state law cannot. Informal and popular justice supplement state law. The supplement provides what is lacking. It serves to complement and to complete that which is supplemented. The very presentation of informal and popular justice as essentially different to law confirms law as apart from and independent of the informal and the popular – confirms it as the preserve of a formal, official authority. But, as Derrida has it, the supplement is also 'dangerous' (1976, pp. 144–5). It remains outside, challenging the completeness and the adequacy of that which is within. This challenge has been greatly exploited by organisers of popular justice in the Third World to create legal processes that resist state law and operate beyond its bounds (see, for example, Baxi, 1985).

Henry's illuminating case studies of the use of law in workplace discipline in Britain provide another instance (Henry, 1982). Here was an area state law could not regulate directly in capitalist society without undermining the authority of employers. An alternative source of discipline was derived from the popular legal skills of workers to erect forms of private justice in the workplace. Henry found that this did lead to 'tension' between this involvement of workers and the potential the involvement had to 'undermine management's ability to control' (Henry, 1982, p. 374). The challenge thus posed by this form of popular justice was countered by the manipulation of the informal nature of the proceedings so as to confine them to procedural matters, thus avoiding any substantive engagement with the terms of management's authority (Henry, 1982, pp. 375–7). To make those terms subject to dispute and appraisal before a legal forum within the workplace, to introduce into the workplace in this way elements of the freedom and equality of legal subjects, would confront the arbitrary authority of 'management' with these characteristic legal modes and values. Such a confrontation would evoke limits of law which the initial resort to popular justice was meant to circumvent. It would also locate points of fundamental resistance to the authority of employers. This line of analysis could, broadly, be replicated for various sets of social relations to which law is linked, such as the family and state administration (see Donzelot, 1980). The sum of the limits that result would reveal law in its surpassing dimension as restricted to a particular configuration of interests and as vulnerable in its claim to a transcendent rule.

Conclusion

I have argued that we can better understand law as resistance if we see it in two dimensions. With one, law assumes a unified identity surpassing social relations. With the other, law is created in its integration with the diversity of social relations. This relational dimension of law supports resistances but they can be undermined by law in terms of its surpassing dimension. However, the relational dimension of law returned the favour, as it were. It served to demarcate limits on law in its surpassing dimension. Law proved to be a potent mode of resisting law.

2
Critical Legal Education

On the liberal view it seems to me almost the entire legal system of a country outside a small central core of criminal and civil law becomes indefensible.

(Roger Scruton, *The Meaning of Conservatism*, 1984 p. 71)

The [market] is in fact a very Eden of the innate rights of man. It is the exclusive realm of Freedom, Equality, Property and Bentham. When we leave this noisy sphere where everything takes place on the surface and enter the hidden abode of production on whose threshold there hangs the notice 'No Admittance Except on Business' a certain change takes place in the physiognomy of our *dramatis personae*. He who was previously the money owner now strides out in front as a capitalist; the possessor of labour-power follows as his worker. The One smirks self-importantly and is intent on business. The Other is timid and holds back, like someone who has brought his own hide to market and has nothing to expect but – a tanning.

(Karl Marx, *Capital*, Volume I, 1976, p. 280)

The ambition of the Critical scholars is revolution, not reform. For them, intellectual critique is merely a prelude to, and platform for, political action.

(Allan C. Hutchinson and Patrick J. Monahan, 'Law, Politics, and the Critical Legal Scholars: The Unfolding Drama in American Legal Thought', *Stanford Law Review*, 1984, vol. 36, p. 199)

Preface

One of the central concerns of this handbook is to promote major changes in legal education. This chapter, therefore, has a double purpose. First, (as indicated in the Introduction) to explore the ways in which traditional legal education can be said to be both a training in subordination and a training for subordination. To examine, in other words, how 'black-letter' doctrinal teaching trains students to accept the notion of law not only as a complex of neutral impartial rules but also as a set of legitimate hierarchies of authority – the teacher substituting for the judge as the high priest of truth. This is a training in and for subordination to law, judges, courts and the professional hierarchy and involves an attempt to destroy all critical thought in order to produce an alienated and subordinated person 'fit to practice'. Secondly, to interrogate the hidden and suppressed premises upon which all legal subject areas are based. The task here is to make visible those unacknowledged assumptions which lay behind the constitution of particular subjects, and in so doing to subvert their claims to political, economic and social neutrality. In other words, to force the dominant tradition and its supporters and exponents to engage in an intellectual and political debate about the present definition and substance of their particular subject area.

Our overriding objective is to empower teachers and students with the necessary critical weapons with which to mount an attack upon the 'citadel'. To this end, the following contributions provide a critique of the dominant methods of teaching and texts in a range of subject areas, and an alternative bibliography.

We see the handbook, in this respect, as providing an introduction to Pluto's Critical Supplements, part of the series Law and Social Theory. These supplements will offer an extensive critique of orthodoxy and will enable readers to pursue in greater depth the issues raised in the handbook. Books currently in preparation cover Torts, Land Law, Family Law, Contract, Trusts and Jurisprudence.

We would encourage our readers to invite our authors to address seminars in their own law departments where the issues raised can be discussed and pressure developed for change (see author addresses, pp. 224–5). Our authors are also willing to provide copies of their teaching syllabuses to those who would like to develop new courses in their own institutions or to critique present courses.

Legal Education as Training for Hierarchy
Duncan Kennedy

Law schools are intensely political places. The trade-school mentality, the endless attention to trees at the expense of forests, the alternating grimness and chumminess of focus on the limited task at hand – all these are only a part of what is going on. The other part is the ideological training for willing service in the hierarchies of the corporate, welfare state.

To say that law school is political is to say that what teachers teach along with basic skills about what law is and how it works is wrong, is nonsense; that the message about the nature of legal competence, and its distribution among students, is wrong, is nonsense; that the ideas about the possibilities of life as a lawyer that students pick up from legal education are wrong, are nonsense. But it is all nonsense with a tilt; it is biased and motivated nonsense, rather than random error. It is nonsense which says that it is natural, efficient and fair for law firms, the legal profession as a whole, and the society that the legal profession services to be organised in their actual patterns of hierarchy and domination.

Because most law students believe what they are told, explicitly and implicitly, about the world they are entering, they behave in ways that fulfil the prophecies the system makes about them and about that world. This is the link that completes the system: students do more than accept the way things are, and ideology does more than damp opposition. Students act affirmatively within the channels cut for them, cutting them deeper, giving the whole a patina of consent and weaving complicity into everyone's life story.

The First-year Experience

Law students are usually ambivalent on entering law school. They enter thinking that being a lawyer means doing a highly respectable and highly paid job, but also that it is something more than that, something somehow connected to social justice. They also think of law school as extremely competitive, as a place where one needs a tough, hard-working, smart style. They enter law school with a sense that they will develop that side of themselves. Even if they disapprove, on principle, of that side of themselves, they have had other experiences in which it turned out that they wanted and liked aspects of themselves that on principle they disapproved of. The initial classroom experience sustains rather than dissipates this ambivalence.

The teachers are overwhelmingly white, male and deadeningly straight and middle class in manner. The classroom is hierarchical with a vengeance, with the teacher receiving a degree of deference and arousing a degree of fear reminiscent of the sixth form. But the sense of autonomy you had there is gone. In its place is a demand that you master a new language, and a new way of thinking at which the teachers supposedly excel, and which they use, occasionally or frequently, directly or indirectly, with intention or haphazardly, in both lectures and seminars, to engender a feeling of subordination and of hierarchy. It is humiliating to be frightened and unsure of yourself especially when what renders you unsure is a lecture or seminar arrangement that suggests at once the patriarchal family and a Kafka-like riddle state.

The law school classroom *is* culturally reactionary.

But it is also engaging. You *are* learning a new language and it *is* possible to learn it. Pseudo-participation makes one intensely aware of how everyone else is doing, providing endless bases for comparison. The teachers offer subtle encouragement as well as not-so-subtle reasons for alarm. Performance is on one's mind, adrenalin flows, success has nightly and daily meaning.

It quickly emerges that neither the students nor the faculty are as homogeneous as they first appeared. Some teachers are more authoritarian than others; some students accept while others react with horror to the infantilisation of the first days or weeks. There even seems to be a connection between classroom manner and substantive views, with the 'softer' teachers seeming to be more 'liberal'; more sympathetic perhaps to plaintiffs in tort cases, more willing to hear what are called policy arguments, as well as less intimidating in class discussion. But there is a disturbing aspect to this process of differentiation: in most law schools it turns out that the tougher, less policy-orientated teachers are the more popular. The 'softies' seem to get less across. They let things wander and one begins to worry that their niceness is at the expense of a metaphysical quality called 'rigour', thought to be essential to success in exams and in practice. Ambivalence reasserts itself.

There is an intellectual experience that somewhat corresponds to the emotional one: the gradual revelation that there is no purchase for left or even committed liberal thinking on any part of the smooth surface of legal education. The issue in the classroom is not left against right, but pedagogical conservatism against moderate, disintegrated liberalism. No teacher is likely to present a model of either left pedagogy or vital left theoretical enterprise, though some are likely to be vaguely sympathetic to progressive causes, and some may even be moonlighting as left lawyers. Students are struggling for cognitive mastery and against the sneaking depression of the pre-professional. The intellectual content of the law seems to consist of learning rules – what they are, why they have to be the way they are – while cheering the occasional judge who seems willing to make them marginally more humane. The basic experience is of double surrender: to a passivising classroom experience and to a passive attitude toward the content of the legal system.

The first step toward this sense of the irrelevance of liberal or left thinking is the opposition in the first-year curriculum between the technical, boring, difficult, obscure legal case and the occasional case with outrageous facts and a piggish judicial opinion endorsing or tolerating the outrage. The first kind of case – call it a cold case – is a challenge to interest, understanding, even to wakefulness. It can be on any subject, so long as it is of no political or moral or emotional significance. Just to understand what happened and what's being said about it, you have to learn a lot of new terms, a little potted legal history, and lots of rules, none of which is carefully explained by the casebook or the teacher. It is difficult to figure out whether you have grasped it, and difficult to anticipate what the teacher will ask and how you should respond.

The other kind of case – call it a hot case – usually involves a sympathetic plaintiff and an unsympathetic defendant. On first reading it appears that the defendant, a multinational company, has screwed the plaintiffs, a poor farming family, by renting land for strip-mining with a promise to restore it to its original condition and then reneging on the promise. The case has a judicial opinion that awards a meaningless couple of hundred pounds to the family rather than making the company perform the restoration work.

The point of the class discussion will be that your initial reaction of outrage is naive, nonlegal, irrelevant to what you're supposed to be learning, and maybe substantively wrong into the bargain. There are good reasons for the awful result, when you take a legal and logical large view as opposed to the knee-jerk passionate view, and if you can't muster those reasons maybe you aren't cut out to be a lawyer.

Most students can't fight this combination of cold cases and hot cases. The cold case is boring, but you have to do it if you want to become a lawyer. The hot case cries out for response, seems to say that if you can't respond you've already sold out; but the system tells you to put away childish things, and your reaction to the hot case is one of them. Without any intellectual resources in the way of knowledge of the legal system and of the character of legal reasoning, it will appear that emoting will only isolate and incapacitate you. The choice is to develop some calluses and hit the books, or admit failure almost before you've begun.

The Ideological Content of Legal Education

One can distinguish in a rough way between two aspects of legal education as a reproducer of hierarchy. A lot of what happens is the inculcation through the formal curriculum and the classroom experience of a set of political attitudes towards the economy and society in general, towards law, and towards the possibilities of life in the profession. These have a general ideological significance, and they have an impact on the lives even of law students who never practice law. Then there is a complicated set of institutional practices that orient students to willing participation in the specialised hierarchical roles of lawyers. Students begin to absorb the more general ideological message before they have much in the way of a conception of life after law school, so I will describe the formal aspect of the educational process before describing the ways in which the institutional practice of law schools bear on those realities.

Law students sometimes speak as though they learned nothing in law school. In fact, they learn the skills to do a number of simple but important things. They learn to retain large numbers of rules organised into categorical systems (requisites for a contract, rules about breach, etc.). They learn 'issue spotting', which means identifying the ways in which the rules are ambiguous, in conflict, or have a gap when applied to a particular fact situation. They learn elementary case analysis, meaning the art of generating broad holdings for cases so they will apply beyond their intuitive scope, and narrow holdings for cases so they won't apply where it at first seemed they would. And they learn a list of balanced, formulaic, pro/con policy arguments that lawyers use in arguing that a given rule should apply to a situation despite a gap, conflict or ambiguity, or that a given case should be extended or narrowed. These are arguments like the need for certainty and the need for flexibility, and the need to promote competition.

Law schools teach these rather rudimentary, essentially instrumental skills in a way that almost completely mystifies them for most law students. The mystification has three parts. First, the schools teach skills through class discussions of cases in which it is asserted that law emerges from a rigorous analytical procedure called legal reasoning, which is unintelligible to the layperson but somehow both explains and validates the great majority of the rules in force in our system. At the same time, the class context and the materials present every legal issue as distinct from every other – as a tub on its own bottom, so to speak – with no hope or even any reason to hope that from law study one might derive an integrating vision of what law is, how it works, or how it might be changed (other than in an incremental, case-by-case, reformist way).

Secondly, the teaching of skills in the mystified context of legal reasoning about utterly unconnected legal problems means that skills are taught badly, unselfconsciously, to be absorbed by osmosis as one picks up the knack of 'thinking like a lawyer'. Bad or only randomly good teaching generates and then accentuates real and imagined differences in student capabilities. But it does so in such a way that students don't know when they are learning and when they aren't, and have no way of improving or even understanding their own learning process. They experience skills training as the gradual emergence of differences among themselves, as a process of ranking that reflects something that is just 'there' inside them.

Thirdly, skills are taught in isolation from actual lawyering experience. Legal reasoning is sharply distinguished from legal practice, and one learns nothing about practice. This procedure disables students from any future role but that of an apprentice in a law firm organised in the same manner as a law school, with older lawyers controlling the content and pace of depoliticised craft-training in a setting of intense competition and no feedback.

The Formal Curriculum: Legal Rules and Legal Reasoning

The intellectual core of the ideology is the distinction between law and policy. Teachers convince students that legal reasoning exists, and is different from policy analysis, by bullying them into accepting as valid arguments about legal correctness that are circular, question-begging, incoherent, or so vague as to be meaningless. Sometimes they are policy arguments (for example, security of transaction, business certainty) which are treated in a particular situation as though they were rules that everyone accepts, but that will be ignored in the next case, when they would suggest that the decision was wrong. Sometimes they are exercises in formal logic that wouldn't stand up for a minute in a discussion between equals (for example, the small print in a form contract represents the 'will of the parties').

Within a given subfield, the teacher is likely to treat cases in three different ways. There are the cases which present and justify the basic rules and basic ideas of the field. These are treated as cursory exercises in legal logic. Then there are cases which are anomalous – 'outdated' or 'wrongly decided' – because they don't follow the supposed inner logic of the area. There won't be many of these, but they are important because their treatment persuades students that the technique of legal reasoning is at least minimally independent of the results reached by particular judges and is therefore capable of criticising as well as legitimating. Finally, there will be an equally small number of peripheral or 'cutting-edge' cases which the teacher sees as raising policy issues about growth or change in the law. Whereas in discussing the first two kinds of case the teacher behaves in an authoritarian way supposedly based on his or her objective knowledge of the technique of legal reasoning, here everything is different. Because we are dealing with 'value judgements', that have 'political' overtones, the discussion will be much more freewheeling. Rather than every student comment being right or wrong, all student comments get pluralistic acceptance, and the teacher will reveal himself or herself to be either a liberal or a conservative rather than merely a legal technician.

The curriculum as a whole is rather similarly structured throughout. It appears once again to be, but is not really a random assortment of tubs on their own bottoms, a forest of tubs. There are certain underlying premises. First, there are the ground rules of late-nineteenth-century laissez-faire capitalism. Teachers teach them as though they had an inner logic, as an exercise in legal reasoning, with policy (for example, commercial certainty in the contracts course) playing a relatively minor role. Then there are the second- and third-year courses which expound the moderate reformist programme of welfare capitalism and the administrative structure of the modern regulatory state. These courses are more policy-oriented than first-year courses, and also much more ad hoc. Teachers teach students that limited interference with the market makes sense and is as authoritatively grounded in statutes as the rules of laissez-faire are grounded in natural law. But each problem is discrete, enormously complicated, and understood in a way that guarantees the practical impotence of the reform programme. Finally, there are peripheral subjects, such as legal philosophy or legal history and clinical legal education. These are presented as not truly relevant to the hard, objective, serious, rigorous analytic core of law.

This whole body of implicit messages is nonsense. Teachers teach nonsense when they persuade students that legal reasoning is distinct, *as a method for reaching correct results*, from ethical and political discourse in general (that is from policy analysis). It is true that there is a distinctive lawyers' body of knowledge of the rules in force. It is true that there are distinctive lawyers' argumentative techniques for spotting gaps, conflicts, and ambiguities in the rules, for arguing broad and narrow holdings of cases, and for generating pro and con policy arguments. But these are *only* argumentative techniques. There is never a correct legal solution that is other than the correct ethical and political solution to that legal problem. Put another way, everything taught, except the formal rules themselves and the argumentative techniques for manipulating them, is policy and nothing more. It follows that the classroom distinction between the unproblematic, legal case and the policy-oriented case is a mere artifact: each could as well be taught in the opposite way. And the curricular distinction between the nature of contract law as highly legal and technical, by contrast, say with environmental law, is equally a mystification.

These errors have a bias in favour of the centre political program (in any of its Major, Kinnock or Ashdown variations) of limited reform of the market economy and pro-forma gestures toward racial and sexual equality. The bias arises because law-school teaching makes the choice of hierarchy and domination, which is implicit in the adoption of our particular rules of property, contract and tort, look as though it flows from and is required by legal reasoning rather than being a matter of politics and economics. The bias is reinforced when the centre reformist programme of regulation is presented as equally authoritative but somehow more policy-oriented, and therefore less fundamental. The message is that the system is basically OK, since we have patched up the few areas open to abuse, and that there is a limited but important place for value-oriented debate about further change and improvement. If there is to be more fundamental questioning, it is relegated to the periphery of history or philosophy. The real world is kept at bay by treating clinical legal education, which might bring in a lot of information threatening to the cosy liberal consensus, as free legal drudge work for the local community or as mere skills-training.

It would be an extraordinary first-year student who could, on her or his own, develop a theoretically critical attitude towards this system. Students just don't know enough to figure out where the teacher is fudging, misrepresenting, or otherwise distorting legal thinking and legal reality. To make matters worse, the two most common kinds of left thinking the student brings are likely to hinder rather than assist in the struggle to maintain some intellectual autonomy from the experience. Most liberal students believe that the left programme can be reduced to guaranteeing people their rights and to bringing about the triumph of human rights over mere property rights. In this picture, the trouble with the legal system is that it fails to enforce the rights formally recognised. If one thinks about law this way, one is inescapably dependent on the very techniques of legal reasoning that are being marshalled in defence of the status quo.

This wouldn't be so bad if the problem with legal education were that the teachers *misused* rights reasoning to restrict the range of the rights of the oppressed. But the problem is much deeper than that. Rights discourse is internally inconsistent, vacuous or circular. Legal thought can generate equally plausible rights justifications for almost any result. Moreover, the discourse of rights imposes constraints on those who use it that make almost impossible its functioning effectively as a tool of radical transformation. Rights are by their nature 'formal', meaning that they secure to individuals legal protection for, as well as from, arbitrariness – to speak of rights is precisely *not* to speak of justice between social classes, races or sexes. Rights discourse, moreover, simply presupposes or takes for granted that the world is and should be divided between a state sector that enforces rights and a private world of 'civil society' in which atomised individuals pursue their diverse goals. This framework is, *in itself*, a part of the problem rather than of the solution. It makes it difficult even to conceptualise radical proposals such as, for example, decentralised democratic worker control of factories.

Because it is logically incoherent and manipulable, traditionally individualist, and wilfully blind to the realities of *substantive* inequality, rights discourse is a trap. As long as one stays within it, one can produce good pieces of argument about the occasional case on the periphery where everyone recognises value judgements have to be made. But one is without guidance in deciding what to do about fundamental questions and fated to the gradual loss of confidence in the 'convincingness' of what one has to say.

The alternative left stance is to undertake the Procrustean task of reinterpreting every judicial action as the expression of class interest. One may adopt a conspiracy theory in which judges deliberately subordinate 'justice' (usually just a left liberal rights theory) to the short-run financial interests of the ruling class, or a much more subtle thesis about the logic or needs or structural prerequisites of a particular 'stage of monopoly capitalism'. But however one sets out to do it, there are two difficulties. The first is that there is just too much detail, too much raw matter of the legal system, and too little time to give everything you have to study a sinister significance. It would be a full-time job just to give instrumental Marxist accounts of the cases on consideration doctrine in first-year contracts courses.

The second difficulty is that there is no logic to monopoly capitalism, and law cannot be usefully understood, by someone who has to deal with it in all its complexity, as superstructural. The legal rules and concepts that permeate all aspects of social thought *constitute* capitalism as well as responding to the interests that operate within it. Law is an aspect of the social totality, not just the tail of the dog. The rules in force are a factor in the power or impotence of all social actors (though they certainly do not determine outcomes in the way liberal legalists sometimes suggest they do). Because it is part of the equation of power rather than simply a function of it, people struggle for power through law, constrained by their limited understanding and limited ability to predict the consequences of their manoeuvres. To understand law is to understand this struggle as an aspect of class struggle *and* as an aspect of the human struggle to grasp the conditions of social justice. The outcomes of struggle are not preordained by any aspect of the social totality, and the outcomes within law have no inherent logic that would allow one to predict outcomes scientifically or to reject in advance specific attempts by judges and lawyers to work limited transformations of the system.

Left liberal rights analysis submerges the student in legal rhetoric but, because of its inherent vacuousness, can provide no more than an emotional stance against the legal order. The instrumental Marxist approach is highly critical of law but also dismissive. It is no help in coming to grips with the particularity of rules and rhetoric because it treats them, a priori, as mere window dressing. These theories fail left students because they offer no base for the mastery of ambivalence. What is needed is to think about law in a way that will allow one to enter into it, to criticise it without utterly rejecting it, and to manipulate it without abandoning oneself to *their* system of thinking and doing.

The Modelling of Hierarchical Relationships

Law teachers model for students how they are supposed to think, feel and act in their future professional roles. Some of this is a matter of teaching by example, some of it a matter of more active learning from interactions that are a kind of clinical education for lawyerlike behaviour. This training is a major factor in the hierarchical life of the legal profession. It encodes the message of the legitimacy of the whole system into the smallest details of personal style, daily routine, gesture, tone of voice, facial expression – a plethora of little p's and q's for everyone to mind. Partly, these will serve as a language – a way for the young lawyer to convey that he or she knows what the rules of the game are and intends to play them. What's going on is partly a matter of ritual oaths and affirmations – by adopting the mannerisms, one pledges one's troth to inequality. And partly it is a substantive matter of value. Hierarchical behaviour will come to express and realise the hierarchical selves of people who were initially only wearers of masks.

Law teachers enlist on the side of hierarchy all the vulnerabilities students feel as they begin to understand what lies ahead of them. In law school, students have to come to grips with implications of their social class and sex and race in a way that is different from (but not necessarily less important than) the experience of school. People discover that preserving their class status is extremely important to them, so important that no alternative to the best law job they can get seems possible to them. Or they discover that they want to rise, or that they are trapped in a way they hadn't anticipated. People change the way they dress and talk; they change their opinions and even their emotions. None of this is easy for anyone, but progressive and left students have a special set of humiliations involved in discovering the *limits* of their commitment and often the instability of attitudes they thought were basic to themselves.

Another kind of vulnerability has to do with one's own competence. Law school wields frightening instruments of judgement, including not only the classified degree system but also the more subtle systems of teacher approval in class, reputation among fellow students, and out-of-class faculty contact and respect. Left students sometimes begin law school with an apparently unshakable confidence in their own competence and with a related confidence in their own left analysis. But even these apparently self-assured students quickly find that adverse judgements – even judgements that are only imagined or projected on to others – count and hurt. They have to decide whether this responsiveness in themselves is something to accept, whether the judgements in question have validity and refer to things they care about, or whether they should reject them. They have to wonder whether they have embarked on a subtle course of accommodating themselves intellectually in order to win teacher and peer approval.

In their relations with students, and in the student culture they foster, teachers get the message across more directly and more powerfully. The teacher/student relationship is the model for relations between junior solicitors and barristers and between senior partners and barristers, and also for the relationship between lawyers and judges. The student/student relationship is the model for relations among lawyers as peers and for the age cohort within a law firm or set of chambers.

In the classroom and out of it, students learn a particular style of deference. They learn to suffer with positive cheerfulness interruption in mid-sentence, mockery, *ad hominem* assault, inconsequent asides, questions that are so vague as to be unanswerable but can somehow be answered wrong all the same, abrupt dismissal, and stinginess of praise (even if these things are not always and everywhere the norm). They learn, if they have talent, that submission is most effective flavoured with a pinch of rebellion, to bridle a little before they bend. They learn to savour crumbs, while picking from the air the indications of the master's mood so they can learn the difference between a good day and misery. They learn to take it all in good sort. So it will be with many a robed curmudgeon in years to come!

The final touch that completes the picture of law school as training for professional hierarchy is the recruitment process. As each firm, with the tacit or enthusiastically overt participation of the law schools, puts on a conspicuous display of its relative status within the profession, the profession as a whole affirms and celebrates its hierarchical values and the rewards they bring. This process is most powerful for students who go through the elaborate procedures of firms in the top half of the profession. These include, nowadays, first-year summer jobs, dozens of interviews, second-year summer jobs, more interviews etc., etc.

This system allows law firms to get a *social* sense of applicants, a sense of how they will contribute to the nonlegal image of the firm and to the internal system of deference and affiliation. It allows firms to convey to students the extraordinary opulence of the life they offer, adding the allure of free travel, expense-account meals, fancy hotel suites and parties at country clubs to the simple message of money.

When students award prizes for the most rejection letters and for the most unpleasant single letter, they show their sense of the meaning of the ritual. There are many ways in which the boss can persuade you to brush his teeth and comb his hair. One of them is to arrange things so that almost all students get good jobs, but most students get their good jobs through twenty interviews yielding only two offers.

By dangling the bait, making clear the rules of the game, and then subjecting almost everyone to intense anxiety about their acceptability, firms structure entry into the profession so as to maximise acceptance of hierarchy (see John Fitzpatrick's second article and Watkinson in Chapter 3). If you feel you've succeeded, you're forever grateful, and you have a vested interest. If you feel you've failed, you blame yourself. When you get to be the hiring partner, you'll have a visceral understanding of what's at stake, but by then it will be hard even to imagine why someone might want to change it.

Inasmuch as these hierarchies are generational, they are easier to take than those baldly reflective of race, sex or class. You, too, will one day be a senior partner and, who knows, maybe even a judge; you will have mentees and be the object of the rage and longing of those coming up behind you. Training for subservience is learning for domination as well. Nothing could be more natural and, if you've served your time, nothing more fair than to do as you have been done to.

I have been arguing that legal education is one of the causes of legal hierarchy. Legal education supports it by analogy, provides it with a general legitimating ideology by justifying the rules that underlie it, and provides it with a particular ideology by mystifying legal reasoning. Legal education structures the pool of prospective lawyers so that their hierarchical organisation seems inevitable, and trains them in detail to look and think and act just like all the other lawyers in the system. Up to this point I have presented this causal analysis as though legal education were a machine feeding particular inputs into another machine. But machines have no consciousness of one another; inasmuch as they are coordinated, it is by some external intelligence. *Law teachers, on the other hand, have a vivid sense of what the profession looks like and what it expects them to do.* Since actors in the two systems consciously adjust to one another and also consciously attempt to influence one another, legal education is as much a product of legal hierarchy as a cause of it. To my mind, this means that law teachers must take personal responsibility for legal hierarchy in general, including hierarchy within general education. *It is there because they put it there and reproduce it generation after generation, just as lawyers do.*

Maybe my preoccupation with the horrors of hierarchy is just a way to wring the last ironic drop of pleasure from my own hierarchical superiority. But I don't interpret it that way. The denial of hierarchy is false consciousness. The problem is not whether hierarchy is there, but how to understand it, and what its implications are for political action.

Critique and Law:
Legal Education and Practice
Alan Hunt

Introduction

Legal education in Britain is on the verge of profound changes. This essay sets out to explore the intellectual and political context of the reform of legal education and of the issues which a project of radical reform needs to confront and resolve.[1]

All is not well in legal education. In the past pressure for reform has come mainly from legal academics, but today it is the legal profession which is currently initiating the process. This development poses an interesting challenge to the critical legal community. For, while much of the stimulation of critical legal thought came from dissatisfaction with legal education, the critical camp has never had a very well-formed strategy for legal education and has principally concentrated on grounding legal education in a sound theoretical framework. This theoretical focus has tended to ignore the more practical implications of the inescapable vocational aspirations of the great majority of law students. The challenge facing critical legal studies is to confront the difficult problems that need to be tackled in striving for some integration of theory and practice within legal education.

I will explore a number of current alternatives to expository legal education. Important though these have been in stimulating discussion and experimentation, I shall argue that, in their different ways, they are only partial solutions. My central argument is that it is both possible and desirable to go beyond these pragmatic or partial critiques and that a model of critical legal education offers such an alternative.

The Dissatisfaction with Expository Legal Education

There is a widespread dissatisfaction with the expository tradition and the inordinate amount of time that we require our students to spend 'learning the law' in a context in which there is an apparently unending expansion of rules of substantive law. The volume of learning is such as to inhibit the possibility of students being able to stand back and consider even the general course of development of legal doctrine, let alone to grapple with questions about the relations between doctrine and policy, between principles and rules, and the relationship between law and the political, economic and social development of contemporary society.

The dissatisfaction also stems from the tension in the relationship between the academic and vocational/professional dimensions of legal education. The goal of teaching students to think like lawyers becomes less than satisfactory when we admit that neither academics nor prac- titioners have any very satisfactory view of just what these skills amount to. 'Thinking like lawyers' was a conceivable educational objective when the ideal model was that of mooting as a preparation for a career as an advocate. But this model embodies only a small part of what only a few graduates will end up doing. Once we recognise that lawyering is probably more about interviewing skills, negotiating strategies, financial and office management, etc., then the orthodox model is less and less satisfactory.

Partial Critiques of Expository Orthodoxy

The post-war development of legal education has witnessed a number of 'partial critiques' of the expository tradition. I describe them as partial because, while their inspiration is dissatisfaction with the existing state of legal education, they all, to a greater or lesser extent, accept or work within the parameters laid down by the expository tradition. The topography of contemporary legal education consists of a substratum of the expository tradition overlaid with a variety of more recent features that are incorporated in a wide variety of forms, hence the increasingly pluralistic course structures and curriculums. The main partial critiques are as follows.

(a) Legal Methods
The focus on legal methods is to provide a general framework which can underpin substantive law teaching. It has been strongly oriented to the acquisition of student skills in the handling of legal materials. Its most immediate impact has been to seek to replace the traditional English Legal System course with its strongly institutional focus and very formalistic treatment of precedent and statutory interpretation. The most important exemplification of this alternative 'methods' model has been provided by Twining & Miers (1982).

The emphasis on legal method is compatible with a range of intel- lectual perspectives on legal education. The strong version of the expository approach, doctrinalism, is very sympathetic to founda- tional studies in legal reasoning, but possibly less at ease with a more radical strand within the method approach which permits the identi- fication of a variety of styles of legal reasoning. There is wide support for a focus on manipulative skills in handling legal materials, but the focus remains fairly traditional in its view of what legal materials are – the appellate judgement and the statute still retain pride of place.

(b) Expansion of the Syllabus

The typical undergraduate curriculum has expanded significantly over the past decades. In part this was a response to a real increase in the volume of law (for example, growth of administrative law, consumer law, etc.). In part it is a reflex of changing patterns of legal practice (for example, the rise of family law as matrimonial issues grew in importance for practice). This expansion of subjects in the law curriculum has been a counter-balance to the dominance of rich man's law in the traditional curriculum, and is manifest in the rise of labour, welfare and housing law.

Yet these new subjects have replicated the concerns and preoccupations of the expository tradition with the emphasis upon syllabus coverage and contemporaneity of treatment of case and statute law. The paradox is that in such subject areas, because of their regulatory character, the volume of substantive material leads to the treatment being even drier than that accorded to more traditional subjects.

(c) Sociolegal Trend

From the mid-1960s onwards, there was a noticeable growth of sociolegal material into most but by no means all law degrees. The general form of these developments was to add, usually as options, subjects variously labelled as Sociology of Law, Law and Society etc. The aim was to focus on law in action and to criticise the expository approach for ignoring both the constituting influences on the form and content of law, and the impact or consequences of law. Such courses usually espoused an input–output model. The input of social, political and economic causation was manifested in the popularity of emergence studies of statute law. The output focused upon an action model of law conceived as a process with a number of key decision stages. The other feature of the trend was its introduction of theories normally excluded from the official corpus of jurisprudence. Max Weber and Karl Marx began appearing in reading lists for the first time.[2]

The significance of the sociolegal trend has been its explicit challenge to the appropriate boundaries of legal studies. Its limitations have stemmed from its self-marginalisation within the comfortable environment of the specialist option. This location has provided an outlet for some law teachers and students. But the result has been that the main structure and content of legal education remained unchanged. This was significantly the consequence of sociolegal studies largely ignoring the domain of legal doctrine; the legal sociologists concerned themselves with the wider social origins and consequences of law, while the field of doctrine itself was left unexamined and safely within the expository tradition.

(d) Law in Context

The most distinctive impact upon the approach to the teaching of substantive law has come from a trend epitomised by the Law in Context series published by Weidenfeld and Nicolson. Its significance is that, unlike the sociolegal trend, it did not abandon the arena of legal doctrine. Indeed, its primary expression has been in the production of alternative texts in many, but still not all, substantive law fields.

The law-in-context trend, with its focus on the production of texts, has never had any very clearly formulated intellectual agenda about what constituted the context nor how that context was to be related to the treatment of substantive law. In its weakest version the context consists of nothing more than a descriptive account of the background, sketched in broad economic, social and political terms, within which the substantive law exists; the main bulk of such a text then proceeds within an expository approach. A second variant uses a policy-oriented perspective: legal doctrine is seen as the bearer or embodiment of social policy. This position generates an evaluatory view in which substantive law is checked against these policy goals.

A preliminary assessment of contextualism needs to recognise its significance in challenging the expository tradition in its own arena of substantive law. It is this feature which attests to its real but generally unspoken critique of orthodox legal education. However, its lack of apparent attention to its own methodology has resulted in its impact being uneven and largely dependent upon the strength or weakness of particular texts.

(e) Clinical Legal Studies

The expository tradition, while purporting to provide an academic foundation for lawyering, remains inside the realm of the law library, immunised from real clients. The clinical legal studies movement seeks to take seriously the vocational aspirations of law students by providing 'real' experience. It seeks to highlight the issues and skills in the advice-litigation complex that do not feature in expository legal education. At its best the clinical approach facilitates the consideration of alternatives to litigation rather than assuming litigation to be the natural result of legal problems.

The clinical approach bears many of the same features that have influenced the expansion of the syllabus, namely, the concern for those areas of law which impact upon sections of the population with unmet legal needs. It is strongly influenced by the model of the law-centres movement and tries, more or less explicitly, to open up radical alternatives to conventional legal practice. This alternative practice is grounded in a political commitment to new clients who are not served, but on the contrary are adversely affected, by rich man's law; these clients are potentially all those who are disadvantaged economically, politically or socially.

The clinical legal studies approach has encountered serious practical problems, not least a lack of cooperation from certain sections of the profession. But beyond these wider issues it has not resolved its relationship with expository lecture-room teaching. Without a more radical restructuring of the curriculum it is likely that clinical experience will remain at best an addition to, rather than an alternative to, the expository mainstream.

Critical Legal Education

In order to respond to the critique of the expository tradition and the limitations of the currently available partial critiques it is necessary to argue the case for a fundamental restructuring of legal education. I would term this project critical legal education. My proposals are self-consciously maximalistic; they seek to present a coherent alternative to the existing model. I do not suggest that the old model can be scrapped and the alternative introduced fully formed. In practice the process of change will be one of reform rather than revolution, but if the reform process is to have any direction it is necessary to specify what its goals are. To this end I focus on these goals, considering the means of realising them only illustratively and in so far as is necessary to amplify and justify them.

My claim is that the goal of resolving the tension between academic and vocational objectives can best be realised by enhancing student understanding of legal phenomena. The intellectual goals can be summarised as follows.

(a) Critique
It should be based on the method of critique which takes seriously the founding assumptions of legalism (which are presumed in legal studies) but does not treat them as eternal verities. Although there is considerable room for discussion about the constituent assumptions of legalism, I would suggest (for the purpose of illustration) the following: a unitary 'legal system'; the formal separation of state and law; and the 'centrality of law'. The focus should be on the problematic nature of these notions and their relationship to the wider society.

(b) Theoretically Grounded Legal Education
Current legal education is atheoretical but is pervaded by a powerful implicit theory; for present purposes I suggest that it lies somewhere between Austinian imperative and the Hartian model of rules. An alternative framework would start from the position that law, as a

complex social phenomenon, should be approached from a number of different perspectives, each with its own strengths and weaknesses. Critical legal education should not seek to prioritise any single theoretical perspective.

The obvious question arises: how to give adequate attention to theory in an already crowded curriculum? Some brief comments can be made about possible solutions. The separation of theory from substantive law, which is epitomised in the normal separation of jurisprudence from substantive law subjects, should be avoided. Each substantive law field should incorporate its own required theoretical framework. For example, one would envisage property law drawing significantly upon political philosophy (Locke, Macpherson, etc.) while family law would probably draw more heavily on the sociology of the family, demography, etc.

There will be controversy concerning the process of drawing on theoretical traditions with their own internal intellectual histories. But, handled sensitively, it should be possible to draw upon sociology, philosophy or economic theory without first offering general courses in these disciplines.

To give adequate space to locating substantive law within a theoretically articulated framework requires a much more selective approach. This means abandoning the goal of coverage which is exemplified in the scrutiny of core syllabuses by the professional bodies. The most important implication will, therefore, be the need to enter into dialogue with the professional bodies in order to move away from the coverage criterion to one which focuses upon the way in which courses provide an appropriate mix of intellectual foundation and legal skills.

(c) Historically Grounded Legal Education
The great disservice done by medievalist legal history is to have brought about the eradication of history in any form from the typical law curriculum. History must be seen as having a central place in the law curriculum, not as a self-contained strand, but integrated within the teaching of substantive law. This requires a major shift in what is understood by legal history; most immediately, a shift from medievalism to modern legal history. But it also requires a shift from the preoccupation with the internal development of legal doctrine towards a socioeconomic orientation.

(d) Legal Doctrine and Legal Skills
Critical legal education must be centrally concerned with legal doctrine. It should not commit the errors of most sociolegal studies (indicated above), and the selective approach to syllabus planning should facilitate a much stronger skills orientation to original legal materials (which the current expansion of syllabuses does not). Such an orientation will not

be without its problems. The tendency should not be to assume a model of a single set of lawyering skills (associated with the assumption of a single form of legal reasoning) but to expand the range of materials handled by students, beyond statutes and law reports, and to introduce them to the variety of forms of legal reasoning (for example, the interaction between reasoning from analogy, by deduction, from policy, principle or moralism etc.).

(e) Beyond the Little Boxes

The expansion of the typical law curriculum produces a highly fragmented student experience of encounters with compartmentalised bodies of rules, unified by some, usually unspecified, process and presented as constituents of an integrated totality, the Law.

The critical legal approach must question this legal monism, the Law, and develop the curriculum so as not to imply a neat and taken-for-granted natural classification of sub-disciplines. This can be tackled at one level by an emphasis upon the cross-cutting and conflicting classificatory schemes (public/private, civil/criminal, etc.). But beyond this the aim should be to design syllabuses that consciously disrupt orthodox boundaries. Thus, for example, the public regulatory character of much private law can be accentuated. Additionally, foundation courses can be designed which emphasise the regulatory character of private/facilitative law.

Conclusion

In my view such a critical legal education would better serve the vocational aspirations of law students by providing them with more relevant skills within an intellectual framework which emphasises the contingent character of legal practices and processes, and highlights their changing relations with other mechanisms of social ordering and regulation. By carefully restricting the sheer weight of the contemporary curriculum it would offer, not only the scope for more selfconscious intellectual development, but also an emphasis on methods which will produce students better able to handle in a self-assured and critical fashion the widening range of occupational openings available to them.

The critical perspective should not seek to impose an alternative model curriculum with the same high degree of uniformity of the current model. Any attempt to embody the aims outlined above would inevitably lead to a much more varied array of law degrees. Such diversity would be a considerable strength, favouring different degrees of specialisation in both teaching and research, and offering a more attractive choice to intending students. A more pluralistic array of law degrees would require a new and more mature relationship between the professional bodies and the academic institutions.

The current dissatisfaction with the condition of legal education can be turned into a period of creative development. Already some of the self-imposed bonds of the orthodox curriculum have been removed and a greater range of experimentation can be observed across a range of institutions. This essay has argued that these possibilities can be further extended and developed, not to produce a new orthodoxy, but to promote legal studies in a richer diversity that will enhance not only undergraduate courses but also scholarship and research.

Notes

1. This paper builds on and in important respects departs from an earlier paper (Hunt, 1986).
2. For evidence of the radical shifts that have taken place in the content of legal theory and jurisprudence syllabuses see Barnett & Yach (1985).

The Law of Contract
Alan Thomson

How many contract courses begin with the teacher asking a bemused class how many contracts they have already made that day before skilfully revealing, through talk about bus rides and buying bars of chocolate, the centrality and pervasiveness of contracts. By implication a course is promised that will go to the very heart of the social order as well as being of obvious practical relevance. Yet what follows in courses based on the standard textbooks dramatically fails to fulfil either of these expectations. Although in the student imagination the law of contract tends to become the lasting model and measure of 'real' law, its practical relevance is extremely limited, and as for going to the heart of the social order, this is denied from the moment in those first examples when it is assumed that contract is the 'natural' form of social relations, and the only issue becomes how they are to be regulated.

Yet in spite of, or rather because of, these shortcomings, the law of contract continues to occupy a peculiar and central place in legal education whose influence extends across the entire curriculum. Purified by a careful process of exclusion, it conveys to students a particular idea of law as a whole – an idea of what law essentially is. Through carbolic smokeballs, old oats and the intricacies of offer and acceptance, students not only begin to learn the lore which will identify them as guardians of the mysteries of the law, but also come to learn what 'real' law is. Like the reality constructed in our primary socialisation as children, the reality of law which the law of contract first constructs tends to retain for ever its massive power over us.

To see through this, and thereby to understand that what lies beyond the technical rules are the deeper and more lasting lessons that the law of contract teaches, one must first dispose of the widespread assumption that the importance of the law of contract in the law school is a reflection of its importance in practice.

While it is undoubtedly true that in a world increasingly dominated by market exchange the institution of contract is of central importance, it does not follow that so too is the law of contract as constituted by the standard texts. First, as any legal practitioner knows, since the law of contract consists only of general rules and principles it rarely provides more than a very partial picture of the relevant legal rules in any real situation. Today there are few types of contract which are not governed by special legal rules, and/or are subject to particular public law provisions. Generally these do not supplement the supposed general principles (such as freedom of contract), but run counter to them. Only by more or less rigorously excluding these 'special' rules can the idea of the law of contract be sustained.

Secondly, if the importance of the law of contract of the textbooks were a reflection of its importance in practice, it is inexplicable why so much space is given to topics such as consideration, offer and acceptance, privity, and mistake, which rarely arise in practice. Conversely, it is equally puzzling why so little attention is given to such practically important issues as contract drafting, interpretation and nego-tiation. Is it because these latter issues are necessarily concerned with the terms of contracts, and it is in their terms that contracts most clearly reveal themselves as the expression of relations of power rather than the embodiment of principles?

Thirdly, many empirical studies show that the law of contract has a limited effect on the way people in business operate in practice, rarely determining the outcome even when a dispute arises.

While it looks initially like a great waterfall running into every corner of life, it turns out that by the time the law of contract has flowed down to the real world it is reduced to a mere trickle which only holds in a few crevices. Indeed it is difficult to avoid the conclusion that so little relation does it have to the real world of the practising lawyer, let alone that of the businessman, tenant or the consumer, that it is little more than a creation of the academy, constituted by the very texts which purport to describe it. This suggests that it is a form of knowledge which has dominion only in the classroom and the exam-ination hall where the student encounters the carefully crafted problem situation in which anything that would challenge the view that general principles can provide answers has been legislated out of existence.

Indeed I would argue that the modern law of contract is not merely constituted by the student texts (for which there is ample historical evidence from its origins in the nineteenth century), but that it is constituted by exclusion.

Thus the precarious claim to importance of the law of contract depends not only on excluding special statutory provisions and references to the realities of legal and business practice, but, most importantly, on a continuous attempt to exclude the uncertainties and indeterminacies in contract doctrine which challenge some of its central constitutive claims, namely the possibility of deducing answers to particular situations from purely legal general rules and principles, and without recourse to political and moral argument and assumptions. This is achieved in various ways: by carefully constructing and purifying the facts of problem situations, thereby concealing the political and other value preferences implicit in choosing what is to be considered legally relevant; by deploying the ubiquitous trick of precedent, namely suggesting that just because the decision in the instant case is logically consistent with certain chosen precedents it, and no other decision, logically follows; and, on no better grounds than that it is a contract course, by continually excluding as irrelevant ways of conceiving the relationship between the parties as other than contractual, thereby continuously concealing from the student the fact that law merely solves the problems it itself creates. Furthermore, by focusing exclusively on the interparty relation, the law of contract simply conjures ideas of justice other than interparty fairness out of existence. Questions of social and distributive justice, which relate to consequences and which threaten the orderly world of rules and principles, are simply outlawed from the toytown world of the contract class.

In this way the liberal individualist conception of justice (which restricts justice to general rules of just conduct and ignores the fact that different people and groups have different access to the resources of wealth, education and power), remains unchallenged as the silent underpinning of the law of contract. Just rules are conveniently conflated with a just world. Indeed one of the features of The Law of Contract which appeals to students is that since it is comprehensible without any knowledge of the real world, a simple idea of justice as the-same-rules-for-all suffices. It is important to recognise that this apparent comprehensibility is only possible if one excludes from sight the unequal world to which the law of contract applies.

Particularly revealing of how the law of contract is constituted by exclusion is the way it skirts around the real substance of contracts, and rarely reaches the parts that matter to the parties: their terms and contents. Thus most of its doctrines are about peripheral issues such as formation, privity, assignment and breach. Furthermore, by drawing its material purely from instances of dispute, it focuses on the exceptional as opposed to the unexceptional realities daily sustained by the terms of contracts. Of course in recent years the idea of freedom of contract – the official excuse for standing back from the contractual terms – has been encroached upon by ideas of unconscionability, duress and inequality of bargaining (as in UCTA, the Unfair Contract Terms Act of 1977). Because of the generality of such encroachments, the standard texts have not been able to retain their distance and ignore them. But in teaching them as mere supplements to the body of contract law, to be considered only when the edifice is firmly in place, traditional expositions have sought to minimise the danger they pose by their open-ended standards and their capacity to disclose real people and consequences beneath the classroom abstractions of As and Bs. In truth, however, such doctrines are indeed dangerous supplements, for they threaten to expose what, to preserve its identity, the law of contract must necessarily suppress, namely that contract is an instrument of power, not only in a few exceptional cases, but in its very nature. To understand this is to open the way to revealing how contract merely serves to provide a cloak of legitimacy to the underlying structural inequalities of power in society, such as those of class, gender and race. If we think there are good reasons why the little old lady should not be held strictly to all the terms of a hire-purchase contract just because she has 'agreed' to them, why (for example) should the employee, often with less real choice than the old lady, be held to his or her contract of employment? Do not all contracts merely give legal expression to the relative power of the parties?

So far, then, I have suggested that the law of contract conceals more than it reveals about the social order in a world based on market exchange; that it is constituted by excluding and suppressing; and that it is little more than an academic creation whose validity scarcely extends beyond the artificial world of the classroom. If this were all we could perhaps dismiss it simply as an irrelevant academic exercise, a mere waste of time, which, through inertia, has somehow survived from a time long gone when it was genuinely believed that there were discoverable universal rules and principles. However, in my view, the law of contract as it is traditionally taught is more than a mere waste of time. It is positively pernicious, for it performs important ideological functions for the existing social order. It is this that enables us to understand why it retains its central place in the law school curriculum.

As I have suggested, it is the law of contract which conveys *par excellence* to students an image of what law as a whole is, and of what 'real' law is like. This image has various related aspects. First, it is an image of law as founded on a mixture of commonsense and an everyday sense of justice, albeit one refined over the centuries by the relentless application of pure reason. In short, through the law of contract, law appears as a form of wisdom, the product of reasoned reflection on experience, which, like all forms of wisdom, is only to be challenged by the foolish. Secondly, through the law of contract, law appears a logically coherent set of rules, principles and concepts, which in all but exceptional cases generates clear and determinate solutions. In short, law appears, at least potentially, as a self-sufficient form of reasoning. Thirdly, the law of contract projects an image of law as a set of rules which logically follow from a restricted number of self-evident principles which can be abstracted from particulars and consequences. Fourthly, it presents law as both eternal and universal, like the laws of physics; something whose rules, though discovered at particular times and places, once discovered have a timeless and universal validity. Fifthly, by purging virtually all reference to statute, so that the law of contract appears to be an almost pure creation of the common law, it projects an image of real law not as manmade but as the product of judicial discovery.

The law of contract, then, projects an image of law as a whole as the universal and eternal wisdom which reason has discovered, and communicates an idea of law as beyond policy and politics – the neutral language of commonsense and justice. Furthermore, denied any other viewpoint, students are likely to treat an exposition of the rules as a description of how the world really works. The law of contract creates a master-image of the well-ordered society; a society in which law appears as the 'haven of justice', divorced from the dirtiness of business, politics, power and the conflict of interests and of values; a society which rises above the uncertainties and incoherences of political and moral argument. This is the first and most general lesson which the law of contract teaches. However, it also teaches two more particular ideological lessons.

First, it serves to make the contingent fact of capitalism, the appearance of social relations as market-exchange relations, look like the necessary facts of life, by concealing that the conceptualisation of social relations as contractual is not outside history but *has* a history. Secondly, by creating the appearance that, through the law of contract, such relations are, or can be made, subject to universal principles of commonsense and justice, it serves to put the justice of the market-based social order beyond question. By projecting the (liberal) image of social order as purely the product of individual choices, and by assuming that one can equate a person's interests with what he consents to, the law of contract renders power largely invisible, thereby making the relations of power that constitute capitalism look like relations of justice. Put differently, the law of contract takes at face value, and gives legal expression to, the self-image of capitalism as an order of opportunity, choice and voluntary exchange in which all individuals can participate on equal terms. What that conceals is not only that opportunities and choices are not equally available, and that exchanges are often far from voluntary, but also that the only choices on offer are those consistent with maintaining the existing system of capitalist production relations. This precisely requires that those relations be seen as no more than the product of voluntary individual exchanges.

In short, in contract classes the student may learn little of practical utility but he or she learns two of the vital lessons on which the legitimacy of capitalism depends, namely what 'real' law is, and that market capitalism is, or at least can be made, an order of justice. What, then, can a critical contract course do, and what might it look like?

The first and most obvious thing it can do is to avoid participating in constructing the image of contract law, and thereby law as a whole, which has been sketched above. This means de-centring the textbooks, using them selectively and suspiciously rather than allowing them to define and dominate the course. By viewing cases as the central legal text and the orthodox textbooks merely as a gloss or commentary upon the cases, which offer one possible reading rather than a statement of the law, one creates an idea of law which is at once more open and uncertain. Moreover, by contrasting the official reading of the textbook with the various other possible readings of the cases one is able to draw out the unspoken assumptions and political and moral preferences which give the appearance of coherence and certainty to the official reading.

Secondly, a critical course must move beyond the artificial world of the Court of Appeal to explore the realities of contracting practice, the consequences of such practice, and the legal interpretation of it. By viewing contract not as a statement of rules in some ideal world but as a practical tool which may be deployed with greater or lesser skill, and which reflects the power of those using it, inequality of bargaining and unfair contract terms are revealed not as a gloss or awkward addition on a logical body of rules based on freedom of contract, but as inherent in the nature of contractual relations. For example, studies on the use and non-use of the law of contract in practice do not simply reveal the context in which the text of the law (conceived as self-sufficient) operates, but rather the context reveals the character of the text: one of power.

Thirdly, by focusing not on the so-called 'general' law of contract, but on the particular categories of contract, such as marriage, employment and consumer contracts (which are excluded from the standard texts precisely so that the claim that there is a general law of contract can be maintained), one challenges the image that these contract texts purvey, namely that social relations are regulated by reason, justice and commonsense. Nothing demonstrates more simply the ideological role of the orthodox contract texts than showing how rarely in practice the rules they proclaim operate without qualification, and how the law of contract is little more than a mirage constructed by academics which maintains a connection with justice only by abstracting from all particular circumstances and effects.

Fourthly, rather than seeing each case as little more than an example of the application of preexisting rules and principles (introduced primarily for clarification), each case should be seen for what it was: the occasion or opportunity for judicial decision. Consequently it should be interrogated in terms of what led to the particular decision; what political and moral attitudes informed judicial opinion; and what assumptions make that opinion plausible. By drawing out the dominant liberal individualism and the very occasional glimpse of other views informing contract cases, one cannot avoid confronting the fact that contract law is not outside politics but part of it.

Fifthly, by opening up, through the cases, the incoherences, uncertainties and indeterminacies which the textbooks so skilfully conspire to conceal, one necessarily reveals that the law of contract, to the extent that one can talk of it at all as a whole, is not a set of universal rules outside particular times and places, but has a history, not only in the sense that the rules have changed, but in the more important sense that conceiving of social relations as contractual relations is historically relative. Only when legal decisions appear to be the product of pure 'legal logic' does it seem possible to dispense with history, just as the truth claims of science, if accepted, appear to render the history of science superfluous.

While the history of contract can be and has been written from many viewpoints, it is difficult to deny the central importance of viewing it as an aspect of the history of capitalism, and of viewing contract as both the practical instrument and the legal ideological expression of the relations of market exchange (see Grigg-Spall and Ireland in this chapter). Together with property law it has become one of the principal means of giving legitimacy to the class relations of capitalism. Furthermore, since the law of contract tends to become the model or measure of law in general, to leave unchallenged the relationship between contract and capitalism is to leave unquestioned the relationship between law in general and capitalism. This is not to deny that to view the history of contract in terms of the history of capitalism alone may be insufficient.

Finally, and most importantly, by opening up contract law in these ways, exploring it in terms of its consequences, drawing out the political ideologies it silently expresses, revealing the historical circumstances of its development, and demonstrating the potential openness of the cases, one brings into sight exactly what the textbooks suppress, namely ideas about the expression of social relations in terms which give voice to quite different ways of conceiving living together. Thus while contract gives legal expression to society as a collection of isolated distrustful strangers, submitting only to general rules out of enlightened self-interest, to challenge contract is to struggle to conceive of and express other ways of living together, based for example on altruism, ideas of solidarity or on constructing norms through engaging in genuine conversation and discussion. Today the dilemma is to respond to this challenge without simply suggesting the largely discredited option of extending the role of the state, for that is to replace the tyranny of the law of contract with the tyranny of state administration of people. Both deny people control over the conditions of their own existence.

Criminal Law
Alan Norrie

Introduction

The predominant approach to the teaching of criminal law in the United Kingdom stems from the theoretical assumptions of legal positivism. Legal rules can be examined as a discrete body of knowledge, isolated from the analysis of politics, sociology and other disciplines which might otherwise be thought to be relevant. These rules are grouped around central principles (for example, of individual liberty and responsibility) which are orthodoxically presented as lying at the heart of the law and which govern to a large extent the organisation of the standard texts. Criminal law consists of a set of rules based upon principles of individual justice and is to be understood as part of an enterprise that is essentially, though imperfectly, rational. My argument will be that the philosophical individualism that lies at the heart of criminal law is flawed and limited in important ways, and that the result of this is that legal doctrine, far from being a potentially rational and principled whole, as lawyers in the legal positivist tradition argue, is in its essence as much characterised by unreason and lack of principle. The key to understanding is to expect continuous tensions and illogic, not to look for rationality and coherence.[1]

Law and the Juridical Individual

My starting point is the ideological form of the abstract juridical individual, which lies at the core of criminal law doctrine. This ideology, which has both psychological and political elements, places the individual at the centre of legal and moral discourse, and is reflected in criminal law doctrine through principles of individual responsibility, and rules which respect the freedom of the individual. But this legal individualism is a particular form of individualism, developed out of a particular historical period[2] and having very definite limits imposed upon it.

Psychological Individualism
The law's starting point is the idea of a rational, intentional, voluntary actor, but this actor is viewed in isolation from the social context within which his or her actions occur. This idea, which informs the general principles of individual responsibility, is fundamentally myopic in that it ignores the nature of criminality as a social phenomenon, and consequently has to find ways of excluding that nature from its gaze.

Political Individualism
The individualism of the law is political as well as psychological. The individual is presented as an actor who is free from political interference except in so far as this is permitted by an already established system of laws. This guarantees his or her freedom because the law is a rational, deductive system which controls what the state, including the judges, can do. Further, the basic principles of state intervention in criminal law are principles of individual right, stipulating the requirement of a responsible ('guilty') individual before punishment can be awarded. This liberal view of the judicial role is again incomplete, for while the judges do work within a doctrinal tradition of individualism and rationalism, these elements operate as conditional, rather than absolute, constraints upon their thought. The judges are not simply the neutral occupants of a value-free role, they form part of a sociopolitical elite, which operates through a discourse of rationalism, individualism and neutrality. They are, as one judge put it, 'at least as much concerned as the executive with law and order' (Lord Devlin quoted in Griffiths, 1985) and this concern runs counter to the values of political individualism within doctrine. This ambiguous role of the judges accounts for two kinds of contradiction which riddle criminal law. One concerns the existence of conflicting substantive standards within doctrine, as the judges move unreflectively from rules which more strongly assert the requirement of individual responsibility to rules which are weaker in this respect, making it easier to convict the individual. A second contradiction relates to the judges' ambivalent attitude to the requirements of logic. Sometimes a judge will extol the virtue of reason as the most binding requirement on his decision, while at other times he will discount it as a matter of secondary importance.[3] Frequently, he will pay lip-service to it, while surreptitiously denying it in his arguments.

Exemplifying the Critical Approach
Psychological Individualism in Criminal Law

Actus Reus
The law's assumption that the individual is a self-activating social atom comes up against the inherent social reality of individual life. There is first of all the question of the voluntariness of acts. This is interpreted

very narrowly (*R. v. Bratty* [1963] AC 386), so that an act is only involuntary if the individual psyche is actually unconscious. Yet there are other kinds of involuntariness, which possess much more of a social dimension, that the law chooses to ignore. For example, there is the involuntariness which accompanies drug addiction, where the psyche is operative but ensnared in the social and physiological context of the addiction. Similarly, there is the question of whether an individual who breaks a law for religious beliefs that he or she regards as binding has acted voluntarily. The criminal law would deny this vehemently, since it would allow many people to get off on crimes of conscience. Yet, where a strongly held religious belief was that of the victim of a crime, who refused a blood transfusion as a consequence and died, this was understood as a case where the victim had acted involuntarily (*R. v. Blaue* [1975] 3 AER 446), with the consequence that the accused was still potentially guilty of murder.

Similarly, causation operates to locate an individual as the cause of a crime, while denying all the surrounding causal circumstances within which the defendant's action occurred. In a famous American case (*Commonwealth v. Welansky* in Clarkson & Keating, 1984, pp. 326–28), involving a fire in a nightclub, a prankster removed a light bulb, which led to a waiter lighting a match while replacing it, which led to a fire, which left 500 people dead. The owner of the club had installed defective wiring and flammable materials, and had failed to ensure that the fire exits were operative, while the local authority fire department had the week before passed the club as safe. In this set of multiple causes, at which level should responsibility lie? Only the owner was convicted, but what of the fire department, the prankster and the waiter? What of the broader social factors that lead nightclub owners to use cheap, flammable materials in order to cut financial costs and increase profits? If the profit motive were a cause, one could nonetheless be sure that it would not be found in the dock (Lacey, Wells & Meure, 1990, pp. 243–52). Because of the need to attribute causation to an individual, whose causal acts always occur within a wide social context, the law is inherently unstable. It splits off the individual from the social by using a distinction between factual and legal causation, but the nature of the latter has never been properly explained, so that the law looks like a series of ad hoc, criteria-less decisions. In a world of multiple causation, it cannot be otherwise.

Finally, in omissions, the same problem emerges from the law's roots in nineteenth-century individualism, where the existence of a duty to act was always more easily linked to the idea of a contract, and the capacity of individuals to pay their way, rather than to the idea that individuals as social beings were largely interdependent, even in the 'obvious' context of the family (Glazebrook, 1960). Because the law has these roots, it finds it extremely difficult to create duties of care where the judges think that social interdependence ought to be upheld. Thus in *R. v. Stone and Dobinson* ([1977] 1 QB 354), where the brother of a deceased woman and his common-law wife had omitted to care for her while she was living in their house, the judges could find no solid legal basis for the liability of the defendants and so imposed, without existing legal authority, a duty of care on blood relatives and those who 'undertake' (the judges exploited the ambiguities of this term)[4] to look after ailing third parties.

Mens Rea

A similar issue emerges in the refusal of the law to take the motive of the accused into account. Intentions are not conjured out of thin air, they are the product of practical human decisions combining desires (motives) and beliefs (Moore, 1984, Chs.1 and 2). The traditional individualist analysis recognises this, but regards the motives leading to the formation of intentions as psychological (anger, jealousy, greed) rather than as socially formed. Were it to recognise the social context within which individuals come to act, and to see motives as stemming from the location of individual acts, it would not be so easy to blame the individual. The way around this has been so to structure legal doctrine that intention becomes crucial to liability and motive becomes irrelevant. Then, at the end of the trial, when justice has been done and a criminal has been properly convicted, the doctrine can be put on one side and motive allowed back into the courtroom, in the non-threatening guise of a factor in mitigation of sentence.

Historically, there was a clear political aim behind the separation of intention from motive. The poor or dispossessed might claim that their theft or rebellion was not wrong at all but was rightful in a context of starvation or oppression (Hay, 1977). This amounted to saying that they had acted from a good or justifiable motive. Lawyers are able to marginalise such overt challenges to the order of things by denying the relevance of motive to crime (Hale, 1971; Hay, 1977). A good example is in the law of theft, where motive is relevant on the question of whether an accused acted dishonestly (Theft Act 1968, s2). This gives rise to an important tension: should the judges accept that the question of dishonest motive is at large for defendants to argue about in front of juries and magistrates, or should they try to find a definition of dishonesty that excludes such possibilities? The issue is political, since lurking behind their deliberations are the figures of the animal-rights activist and the latterday Robin Hood (*R. v. Ghosh* [1982] QB 1053). In practice, they have gone for an unsatisfactory compromise which seeks, unsuccessfully, to exclude politics from the courtroom (Williams, 1982, pp. 728–30). The issue arises also in the defences of duress and necessity, for these amount to claims that the accused was not responsible for his or her motive, which resulted from natural or social circumstances beyond the accused's control. The problem stems from a *reductio* argument (Lord Simon in *R. v. Lynch* [1975] 653 at 686–7). Do people form motives to commit crimes because of threats of violence (duress) or the necessity of their situation? In our society, many people are homeless and hungry, so that if necessity were admitted as a defence, this 'would open a door which no man could shut' (Lord Denning in *London Borough of Southwark v. Williams* [1971] 2 AER 175). The result of this contradiction between individual responsibility and the social context of wrongdoing is the highly anomalous one that some kinds of coercion (those that fall under the head of duress) are recognised as leading to acquittal, but others (those under the head of necessity) are not.

Political Individualism in Criminal Law

The abstract individual is at the core of legal doctrine as a political atom, which the law must respect. But the question remains of just how much content the law will give to this concept, and this is a matter for negotiation as the content rubs up against the judges' conception of what is necessary in the interests of *raison d'etat* or 'law and order'. In this situation, law's respect for individuals is not stable, but shifting, according to the political climate, the views of particular judges, and even the particular facts of the case on appeal.

In intention, this can be seen in the shifts that have taken place in the mens rea of murder from the objective 'natural and probable consequences' test of *Smith* ([1961] AC 290) to the subjective probable consequences test of *Hyam* ([1974] 2 AER 54) to the virtual certainty test of *Moloney* ([1985] AC 905), *Nedrick* ([1986] 3 AER 1) and *Hancock & Shankland* ([1986] 1 AER 644). These three quite different and contradictory accounts of what is meant when we say that an individual intends an act have all been central to the mens rea of murder in recent years. Nor is the matter resolved by the recent cases, for there remain important conflicts within them (Norrie, 1989). At the back of all three rules, there lurk important political objectives. Thus in *Smith*, the objective test arose in the context of the killing of a police officer shortly after the abolition of the 'constructive malice' rule, while in the latter cases, an important consideration emerging out of the judgements is the possibility of convicting a political bomber for murder rather than manslaughter when he or she plants a bomb intending only to frighten.

In recklessness, the law is in a terrible mess because of the judicial desire to remove subjective questions of awareness of risk from the remit of the jury, which, as a popular body, is regarded by many judges as unreliable (Smith & Hogan, 1988, p. 236). This has led to the existence of two standards of recklessness according to the crime charged, with often paradoxical results (Smith & Hogan, 1988, p. 67). The question of whether an accused must have been aware of a risk, or whether it is sufficient that a 'reasonable man' would have recognised it, is part of a broader tension within the law between subjective and objective tendencies, which arises in the law of mistake (*DPP. v Morgan* [1976] AC 1982, *R. v. Gladstone Williams* [1983] 78 Cr App R 276, *Beckford v. R.* [1987] 3 All ER 425, *R. v. Graham* [1982] 1 WLR 294), of provocation (*R. v. Camplin* [1978] AC 705), and of duress (*R. v. Graham, R. v. Howe* [1987] AC 417) as well as in relation to recklessness. Cases usually have the appearance of falling on one side or the other of this divide according to happenstance rather than design. Thus where a mistake relates to the actus reus, or to the defence of self-defence, an honest mistake will suffice, but where it is a mistake as to the existence of duress, it must be a reasonable one. Generally speaking, an objective test makes it easier for the prosecution to gain a conviction because it is unnecessary to inquire into the particular subjective state of mind of the accused, while a subjective approach attracts the approval of the academic writers within the positivist tradition, since such an approach affirms a 'thick' notion of liberal political individualism. It is noteworthy that a considerable amount of passion rides on this issue, but the academics claim too much when they argue that a subjective approach is the proper orientation of the law. That would only be so if the law were, as they claim, a rational, principled whole. It is not, it is a conflicting gruel of contradictory ingredients because of the contradictory location of judicial ideology at the intersection of liberal principle and politics.

These conflicting pressures become most apparent where an appeal forces the judges into a corner because the logic of the existing rules points in one direction, but their political instincts point in another. The liberal theory proposes that it is their heads which should rule their hearts, but this by no means always happens (Norrie, 1990, Ch. 8). Thus in *Caldwell* ([1982] AC 343), the subjective test for recklessness was well known and had been recommended to Parliament by the Law Commission as the test to be applied in the Criminal Damage Act 1971. While Lord Diplock conceded the need to establish the intention of Parliament, he made no reference at all to the Law Commission's view, and condemned a rule that had been in operation for most of the century as 'fine and impracticable' ([1982] AC 341). Similarly, in *Majewski* ([1977] AC 443), the problem of intoxication was dealt with by establishing an untenable distinction between crimes of basic and specific intent. The problem for the judges is that intoxication is both the source of much crime and a potential route to the denial that a person formed the necessary intent. They got around this by saying that for the more serious crimes, labelled crimes of specific intent, evidence of intoxication could be relevant to mens rea; on the less serious ones, labelled crimes of basic intent, it could not. They have never explained satisfactorily the basis for the basic/specific distinction or how the intent in crimes of basic intent was in some way not a 'real' intent to be established according to the evidence. Equally, in duress, the judges played around with the distinction between principals in the first and second degree to murder in the cases of *Lynch* and *Abbott* ([1977] AC 755), without ever explaining satisfactorily why the defence was available in the former but not the latter instance. Eventually, they admitted this themselves, but resolved it by overruling their own decision in *Lynch* (in *R. v. Howe* [1987] AC 417).

In all these cases, it transpires that the law's logic is by no means an immovable object, protecting individuals against state policy. Where needs must, rationality will be discarded, and frankly so.

Conclusion

The legal positivist is right to see the 'law' as an important phenomenon, but wrong to imagine that it can be understood as a politically neutral system of rules governing any polity. Criminal law is a mechanism of social control which evolved out of the struggle for power and control between conflicting social classes, but one which is mediated by an ideology of political and psychological individualism. That ideology gives rise to a set of categories at the heart of the law which operates both to condemn and to protect individuals. It is the contradictory nature of that position that is at the nub of criminal law doctrine through the systematically conflicting inclusions and exclusions of acts and contexts, of individual and sociopolitical interests. These conflicts give to criminal law its stubbornly irrational appearance. From this standpoint, we not only understand the criminal law in a critical way, we also understand it better.

Notes

1. In what follows I concentrate solely on the structure of criminal law doctrine, not because I think it alone is important, but because it is that structure which lies at the heart of the traditional criminal law course, and which has tended to be ignored in critical accounts. I will not discuss the broad variety of contextual materials which portray the ways in which the criminal law works in practice. These are extremely important to a full understanding of criminal law, but they tend to have a limited connection with the core legal principles which are at its heart.
2. There is no space to elaborate the historical material here, but it is important to understand that modern criminal law systems were a product of the period of the bourgeois Enlightenment, and are thoroughly marked in their basic assumptions by this origin. Foucault's book (1979) was the first modern work to recognise the

significance of the individualist form of penal theory in this period, a form that remains critical to criminal law today.

3. Compare the views expressed by Lord Hailsham in DPP v. Morgan [1976] AC 182 and R. v. Howe [1987] 1 All ER 771, and by Lord Edmund Davies in Abbott v. R. [1977] AC 755, R. v. Caldwell [1982] AC 341, and DPP v. Majewski [1977] AC 443.

4. Dobinson had helped the deceased and so had in one sense 'undertaken' acts of kindness. She had not, however, given an 'undertaking' so to act. Dobinson would paradoxically have escaped liability had she more callously done nothing at all to assist the deceased.

Tort Law
Joanne Conaghan and Wade Mansell

The subject of tort is one of the most beguiling to students whose conception of legal study is that it is about discrete subjects apparently clearly defined and governed by a satisfying intermingling of statute and case law. If the textbooks are to be believed, tort appears to consist of a number of general principles (in most cases strongly corresponding with common sense) exemplified by case applications which seem, if the premises of tort are accepted, logical, coherent and essentially just. Additionally, the cases themselves are often memorable because of the bizarre and commonly tragic facts with which they often deal. They support the view that humour is intimately connected with misfortune. Individuals being struck on the head by cricket balls, suffering dermatitis through impure underpants, trapped in a toilet with a defective door, vomiting because of decomposed snails in opaque ginger-beer bottles are the very stuff of tort.

It seems, then, that tort is a morbidly attractive subject to study and an at times exhilarating subject to teach – rigorous, principled and even entertaining. Yet, despite these manifest attractions, the lure of tort is somewhat diminished by a closer critical examination: logic, coherence and justice too often give way to chaos and aimlessness; rationality, far from being a characteristic of the torts system, becomes a major weapon in its assault; politics assumes a dominant and contentious position. The popular image of tort remains both coercive and appealing because it is not obvious that as a system of loss distribution tort is very haphazard. Nor are its politics explicitly revealed and rehearsed in a traditional study of the subject. Conventional texts, such as Winfield & Jolowicz, proceed on the basis that tort law consists of a basically uncontentious and apolitical body of principles (Rogers, 1989). This encourages a view of tort law as largely commonsense and corresponds fairly closely with many students' perception of what is just and fair. These things impede the development of a reflective and critical approach to the subject. Tort law appears apolitical because it is experienced as largely uncontentious and we do not, therefore, tend to question its politics. But the politics are there and it is vital to understand that tort, its texts and its syllabuses are inherently political. The whole foundation of tort law reflects a particular philosophical and ideological perspective (based on individual rather than societal responsibility for misfortune) which is, in our view, highly contentious. Indeed, if the basic subject matter of tort is concerned with how the law responds, or fails to respond, to the misfortunes which afflict individuals in our society, it can be strongly argued that the tort system represents a political solution which is undesirable both because of the arbitrariness of its results and because of the underlying callousness of its ideology. It can also be contended that the legal form which tort doctrine assumes, as a body of knowledge which is coherent, principled and neutral as to outcomes, operates as a major impediment to any significant political change.

Of course, this criticism itself is also political and its underlying premises should be made explicit: it is that society should assume considerable responsibility for the misfortunes of its members, and that political and legal energy should be redirected, away from tinkering with torts law and towards the construction of alternative loss-distribution mechanisms based upon the acceptance of social responsibility for individual misfortune.

At the heart of the law of tort lie a myriad of complex political and moral issues which rarely surface. To critique is partly to excavate, but the critical lawyer cannot approach the subject like the disinterested scientist examining the finds of an archaeological dig. To acquire a critical understanding of law involves an acceptance of the impossibility of a neutral, disinterested point of view. This produces a strange and paradoxical result. The rejection of neutrality undermines the legitimacy of those positions which posit themselves as neutral by showing that they are, in fact, partial rather than universal points of view, and so confers greater legitimacy on those points of view generally regarded as partial and political. In other words, it shifts the terms of the debate. The issue is no longer what is the correct (that is, objective, verifiable) legal position but rather what is the *preferred* legal and political solution. Articulating the politics of law is thus a crucial step in the process of securing a 'good society' through open discourse and participatory decision-making. It is in this sense that the critical project is a radical one. But there is another dimension here. By focussing on tort law as something other than the affirmation of a neutral, common sense position and by seeing it instead as a partial and contingent point of view, one is free to imagine and to pursue alternative arrangements.

With these goals in mind we will consider more closely the nature of the tort system. Our primary focus will be the tort of negligence which assumes a position of supreme importance in the conventional texts and in most tort syllabuses, and whose reasoning and ethos has permeated other areas of tort particularly through the ubiquitous concept of 'reasonableness'.

Critiquing Negligence

A critical exploration of negligence might take a number of different forms. First, one might exhume and examine the political and moral underpinnings of its doctrines. Secondly, one could focus on the *form* of negligence as an allegedly coherent and rational body of rules and consider to what extent this form corresponds with its content. Finally, one might look at a number of interpretive perspectives on negligence as a way of unravelling the complex political and moral norms which compete for recognition and realisation in the courtroom and the classroom.

Law and Values

It is clear that negligence is imbued with political and moral values which, although never far from the surface, are rarely articulated and even more rarely questioned or challenged. Why, for example, should omissions often be treated as incurring less liability than 'acts'? Why should the intervention of a third party act as a brake on liability when damage is done and the defendant is a negligent cause of it? Why should mental distress and economic loss be treated differently from physical damage? These questions conjure up generally accepted rules and principles which permeate the tort of negligence (though neither their boundaries nor their doctrinal status is very clear) and which are often defended in moral terms. Thus, it is contended that moral responsibility for omissions is somehow less than that for acts and therefore should not attract the same liability even where the damage is identical. This assumption is in turn based on ideas about limiting individual responsibility, particularly in relation to obligations imposed by the state. It is argued that the imposition of positive obligations on people diminishes freedom and discourages action, inventiveness and, consequently, economic growth. In other words, the legal tendency to treat omissions differently from acts reflects the economic and political perspective of market capitalism. Again, careless actors are somehow viewed as less responsible if, in the arbitrary scheme of things, some third party comes between them and subsequent harm. The old and venerated concept of *novus actus interveniens* operates here to shift our attention away from the negligent behaviour of the defendant towards the more immediate wrong inflicted by the intervening actor and posits the absurd conclusion that the original negligent actor is no longer at fault for the apparently non-ideological reason that he or she is not a 'legal cause' of injury. This authoritative pronunciation of causation is a smokescreen which clouds the presence of a policy operating to limit the responsibility of individuals for their acts. This is further illustrated in the tendency to eschew mental-distress and economic-loss liability on the grounds that they place too heavy a burden of liability on the defendant. It is likewise assumed in such cases that somehow economic loss and mental distress open up floodgates which are better left closed.

Of course, alternative rationales based on economic efficiency, deterrence, insurance, risk distribution and compensation can also be offered in defence of, or in opposition to, any of these doctrines. But the presence of such competing alternatives simply serves to reinforce the strongly political content of these doctrines. The point remains that tort law does not operate in a value-free zone but takes its content, shape and direction from norms which should rightly be a primary focus of its study.

Consideration of the assumptions underlying torts doctrines (and their controversial nature) opens up for discussion a host of issues which are rarely addressed and certainly never adequately explored in the traditional texts. Critical are the problems arising from the centrality of the concept of fault in the tort of negligence. Essentially, negligence embodies the principle that where harm to someone is caused through the fault of another party, that party will be liable to compensate for the injury and loss caused. This statement is of course unacceptably broad as the qualifications relating to duty, breach and damage exhaustively discussed in every text on tort indicate. But the basic idea is that it is just that those who injure through carelessness should compensate and that those who suffer through carelessness should be compensated by the perpetrators of the careless act. This focus upon the *cause* of the injury or loss in determining whether compensation is due results in the differential payment of compensation to those who have suffered identical harm by different means. Fault dictates full compensation, but, in the absence of fault, losses must lie where they fall subject to the meagre and uncertain benefits of the current welfare system.

The merits of the fault principle are not in our view so self-evident as to require such inattention to its demerits. While the maxim 'no liability without fault' may make a certain sense, its corollary – no compensation without fault – is much more questionable because identical needs are met with different responses on the basis of a difference which is irrelevant to the need itself. Why *should* fault determine who gets what? Equally importantly *does* fault, in fact, determine who gets what, and when it does not, why not? Furthermore, what is fault? How is it recognised? The traditional answer, namely that fault involves unreasonable behaviour, is merely to restate the question in a different form. These sorts of questions about the moral content of negligence doctrine – marginalised by the 'black-letter' focus of the conventional text – are at the centre of a critical approach to legal education.

The Form of Law

A common impression of the *form* of negligence is as an essentially 'black-letter' discipline with perhaps more woolly edges than most and a more explicit if nevertheless limited role for policy considerations in the determination of results. This is certainly the impression created by classical tort texts such as Winfield & Jolowicz, and Street (Rogers, 1989; Brazier, 1988). Students are encouraged to see negligence law as rule-based. The task for the student is to discover the rules and also to discover which 'rules' are uncertain or unresolved. They are provided with a framework within which the rules fit and the implication is that rules which do not readily fit the framework are the 'hard cases' of particular interest at least to examiners. Underlying such a presentation of negligence is a belief that it is, to some extent at least, coherent, logical, rational and deducible from previous cases and fundamental principles. In reality, however, negligence doctrine abounds with demonstrable incoherence.

The internal incoherence of negligence is evidenced in almost all aspects of doctrine including definitional questions surrounding duty and breach; the attempt to present as objective concepts such as foreseeability and the 'reasonable person', which are subjective and intuitive; the morass of complications concerning the law on negligent misstatements; problems caused by cases where injury or loss is caused by more than one factor or when the direct causal link is difficult to establish; rules of remoteness and foreseeability, particularly when the defendant may be held liable for consequences of his or her negligence which, while a direct result of foreseeable consequences, are not in themselves foreseeable (the 'thin-skull' rule of *Smith v. Leech Brain & Co. Ltd* [1962] 2 QB 405). Students flounder helplessly in these areas as they attempt to grasp the lifelines offered to them by the textbooks – the rule which will illuminate the puzzle of intervening acts or harness the disorder of the duty question. Likewise, they do not probe too deeply into the tricky questions raised by a serious consideration of tort law's best distinctions – such as omissions and acts, economic loss and physical damage, direct and indirect consequences – in case they should be confronted with the awful realisation that these concepts are fairly meaningless. Consider in this respect the recent case of *Murphy v. Brentwood DC* ([1990] 3 WLR 414) and ask whether it can be honestly said that their lordships in this case have had any more success in maintaining the spurious distinction between economic loss and physical damage in the context of defective premises than they had in their previous *tour de force – D & F Estates Ltd v. The Church Commissioners for England* ([1989] AC 177).

Despite such manifest uncertainty within particular doctrines, the traditional textbook writers, together with commentators in scholarly journals, continue to perpetrate the myth of doctrinal coherence subject to room-for-argument or areas-of-uncertainty qualifications (Brazier, 1988, pp. 226–7). Furthermore, judges and commentators alike continue to cling to the organising concept of fault as the universal principle underlying the edifice of negligence. It does not seem to matter that negligence law is riddled with situations in which the fault principle is mysteriously and inexorably suspended, as in the cases concerning nervous shock or economic-loss recovery.

Nor does it seem to matter that in practice fault has little to do with tort recovery but is in fact hostage to the availability of insurance. It is extraordinary how little attention is paid to the major disparities between negligence as an academic and legal category and negligence as an operational reality. For law students negligence consists of appellate cases which reach the pages of Winfield & Jolowicz, while negligence, the system, is presented as something quite different and less important. While *Atiyah's Accidents, Compensation and the Law* (Cane, 1987) remains the authoritative text addressing the disparity between negligence in books and negligence in practice, its trenchant criticism of the system seems to have had only a marginal effect upon academic courses in negligence (Cane, 1987). Yet the problems addressed by Atiyah concerning the operation of negligence actions – such as delay, cost, quantification, settlement and uncertainty of result – are by no means marginal. To realise that the administration expenses of the negligence system amount to some 85 per cent of the value of the sums paid out as compensation (or 45 per cent of the total of compensation and operating costs), emphasises that the system is as unsatisfactory practically as it is theoretically (Pearson, 1978, vol. 2). To enter the arcane realms of calculating injury and loss, both present and future, in money terms is also revelatiory. The form of negligence as a 'black-letter' discipline quickly loses much of its alleged coherence when viewed through the lens of 'what really happens'.

Interpretative Perspectives on Law

This essay clearly adopts a particular interpretive perspective. It is one which challenges the central conception of fault and individual responsibility in the allocation of compensation. It also maintains that in operation negligence is an irrational system for redistributing loss arising from particular circumstances. It *is* a system only in that it does some things consistently, but as a system of compensation it is remarkable for its overall inconsistency. As such, it has few defenders beyond those who profit from its operation. The criticism of negligence, then, is both from within and from without. We maintain that it fails first on its own terms as a rational, self-perpetuating, self-evaluating system of neutral rules and secondly as a social response to particular goals – those of compensation and loss redistribution. Of course, such an assertion opens up for debate the whole question of what goals or objectives torts law is or should be pursuing. This is a question about which there is divergent opinion. In our view, such divergence must be an important focus of critique because clearly different approaches to evaluating the system (for example, in terms of economic efficiency, or deterrence, or compensation, or fault and individual responsibility) generate different assessments of the system's worth and different prescriptions as to its cure. Even tensions within cases, between judgements and different judicial styles, can often be understood in terms of conflicts about goals (or even about whether the law of torts is goal-oriented at all rather than simply a mechanism to facilitate the pursuit of a variety of individual goals). It is essential to examine the law of negligence in the wider context of arguments about its political and social role. Such a focus serves a dual purpose in providing a forum within which the political content of torts can be properly aired and explored and in giving students a framework which aids their understanding of the evolutionary and dynamic aspects of torts doctrine. At the same time this makes it impossible to present the subject as a static 'black-letter' discipline, an approach more likely to blur than to illuminate the student's grasp of the subject. Such an approach encourages the student to regard negligence not as a set of rules but rather as a series of arguments which compete for persuasivenesss, drawing upon institutional resources (such as precedent), the ascendancy of a particular moral tradition (usually fault-related) and political acceptability. Through such an approach students not only experience law as political and controversial (which it is) but also acquire the sort of skills and insights which inform and direct legal practice.

Conclusion

Of course, this essay has an agenda. We are exploring the law of negligence in light of the need for a humane and adequate compensation system. But if we have an agenda, so do all writers and commentators on tort; so do the judges who develop the doctrine; so do the litigators who formulate arguments in terms of their particular clients' demands. To view the law of tort as anything other than an armoury of conflicting agendas is to be both naive and myopic. To teach the law of tort without addressing this insight is to fail to teach at all. It is, rather, to mislead.

Inevitably such exploration raises for discussion a wide range of issues which space does not allow us to examine here – questions about how and why the tort system continues, given its demonstrable inefficiencies; upon what epistemological premises it rests; whether its credibility depends to any great extent on its alleged rationality; what principles and policies should determine the question of compensation in our society; and finally whether any of these questions can usefully be asked in a world where capitalism is dominant.

The critical student should arm herself (or himself) with a scepticism of what passes as 'received' knowledge in the texts, in lectures and in classes. She should refuse to take for granted as wisdom that which is written by the learned of the law. She should proceed on the basis that law, including negligence, is intimately connected with politics, particularly the politics of resource distribution, and finally she should not allow the authority of the text, the teacher or the institution to invalidate her understanding and assessment of the issues which she confronts.

Property Law
Andy Clark, Kate Green and Nick Jackson

Introduction

The institution of private property plays a significant part in preserving material inequalities and legitimating the uneven distribution and use of power in contemporary societies. It is therefore an important object of critical inquiry. The aim of this article is to develop some ideas about what critical property courses might be like. Although the elements of any particular course – its content, analytical approach, standpoint and teaching and assessment methods – may vary, the overall aim of a critical course is to liberate the critical capacities of students and teachers. We begin by reviewing the elements of 'traditional' property courses and then proceed to suggest ways in which these elements may be approached in the context of critical property courses. In doing so our purpose is to formulate an agenda for discussion rather than to provide rigid principles.

Standard Property Courses: Critical Perspectives

A critical commentary on the standard course is necessarily a parody which takes little account of real variations between existing courses.[1] Critical property-law teaching already takes place, but it is often located at the margins of apparently non-critical courses where it remains largely invisible. At the same time, the orthodoxy of the

'Cheshire worldview' of land law and legal education continues to retain a firm grip on mainstream property-law teaching (Anderson, 1984; Cheshire, 1926). It is the articulation of this orthodoxy through the standard course that provides a focus for our criticisms.

Content

Bearing the title 'property law', the standard course claims to be all about property. Despite its apparent breadth, the course tends to have a highly specific focus, concentrating exclusively on a particular selection of rules about land. 'Public' aspects of land such as planning or the finance of leasehold housing are generally excluded, as are objects of property which fall outside the legal category of 'land'. Thus, for example, the standard course is unlikely to include any serious consideration of the various proprietorial concepts through which corporate finance is structured or through which images are constituted as objects of property (Edelman, 1979; Grigg-Spall, Ireland & Kelly in this chapter). This is not to indict the standard course for its lack of comprehensiveness, rather it is to draw attention to the unquestioned acceptance of selection criteria based upon a narrow set of past priorities, and to challenge an educational practice which requires students to focus on the minutiae of a limited number of rules without expressly formulating a coherent strategy for selecting particular topics while discarding others.

Analytical Approach

In terms of its aims and its practice, the analytical approach of the standard course is limited to the use of 'black letter' techniques. Learning how to use these techniques effectively is an important part of legal education. But the hidden assumption is that these techniques are the *only* method of analysing law. The overall effect is debilitating for it precludes comparison of different modes of reasoning and reflection upon the variety of ways in which lawyers approach property. For example, whereas the high-street lawyer may see property law in terms of the routine steps required to process conveyancing transactions, the city lawyer is more likely to view it as a conceptual structure to be moulded in the interests of corporate capital. Equally, the standard course provides few opportunities for developing other legal skills. In most cases, the course is structured around its chosen textbook. Yet the search for coherence has traditionally led textbook writers to present property law as a logical structure of abstract concepts. The textbook approach exerts a considerable influence on the way judges and other lawyers confront their work, but it is by no means the only influence. In its emphasis on the absorption of 'pure' legal technique, the standard course prevents rather than encourages understanding of the range of factors which may underlie any given decision in law.

Standpoint

The standard course is usually presented in terms that are neutral, technical and apparently devoid of political content. Problems of balance are absent because there appears to be nothing to balance. Yet this standpoint can also be seen as one of reverence with a number of different nuances: land law is held to incorporate the wisdom of the ages yet is attuned to modern requirements; it is seen to rest on an atemporal logical structure but, in the hands of 'practical men' (judges, legislators and conveyancers), it progresses inexorably towards a state of near-perfect functionality.[2] This self-image lacks plausibility and the underlying orthodoxy is all the more heavily imposed on students because of the implicit claim to neutrality.

Teaching and Assessment

The teaching method tends to be based on the empty-vessel principle – teaching consists of transmitting the contents to the waiting minds of students. This inevitably engenders a relationship of dependency in which students come to rely on their 'master's voice'. Independent thinking or reading around the subject is effectively discouraged (see Kennedy in this chapter). This pattern is reinforced by the narrowness of assessment methods which effectively require students to reproduce 'right answers' in examinations designed apparently to induce a sense of hierarchy and powerlessness. The hidden message is that it does not pay to be critical of anything.

Designing Critical Property Courses

Our aim here is not to put forward a model critical property course and to replace the orthodoxy of the standard course with some alternative dogma for critical interventions which must themselves be open to question. What follows is an attempt to explore some of the issues which enter into the design of critical property courses. It is central to the idea of a critical course that it be oriented towards the possibility of social change. Existing rules and practices cannot simply be examined on their own terms, but must be opened up to the possibilities of different and better worlds. Within this broad framework, there is room for a wide range of critical standpoints which may involve differing conceptions of the relationship between the course and the possibilities of social change.

Content

If the axiom of criticality cannot determine the specific content of a critical course, the requirement that a critical property course should be about property is also problematic. Nevertheless, it is possible to suggest some guidelines. A course which concerns itself overtly with property must at some point address the question of what property is. The purpose of asking this question is not to instigate a (necessarily sterile) search for the 'correct definition'. Rather it is to provide a platform for questioning assumptions about different conceptions of property. Analysis of these assumptions can give important insights into the institution of property in contemporary society.

A preliminary analysis might begin by differentiating between thing-ownership and bundle-of-rights conceptions of property. In everyday discourse property is frequently used to refer to thing-ownership and is equated with things (objects of property). Ownership is assumed to be full or absolute. Hence, property is seen in terms of the individual relationship between a person and his or her 'thing'.[3] In contrast, legal discourse represents property in terms of clusters of individual legal relationships between people (subjects of property) and assets. Ownership is seen as a bundle-of-rights through which enti-tlements and obligations in respect of assets are determined. Moreover, rights may be limited and divided between legal persons, thereby enabling the fragmentation of ownership and control. This produces an abstract notion of property which can be applied flexibly to the protection of different forms of wealth (Cotterrell, 1986). However, from a critical perspective, an important feature of both these conceptions of property is the absence of any reference to power. Whereas the former fails to recognise the inter-subjective aspects of property relations, the latter, despite its relational emphasis, focuses exclusively on individual legal relations between subjects and refuses to acknowledge the social, economic and political dimensions of these relations. As a result both conceptions conceal the operation of power through the regime of property. At the same time it is evident that property relations *are* implicated in the day-to-day exercise of power by some people over others and that law is used to legitimate and to limit its operation. Critical property courses could build on these insights to pursue an idea of property as a shifting network of contingent power relations.

In developing *such* an analysis of property in terms of power relations, emphasis needs to be placed on tracing the various ways in which specific legal forms and techniques are deployed in structuring the distribution and use of power in specific situations. Thus, the powers exercised by various categories of property owners require specific analysis so that the operations of power may be traced into specific legal forms as well as into specific relationships. For example, in according corporations legal personality and applying the Lockean justification of ownership as the just deserts of honest labour, the law provides a mechanism for the corporate ownership of earnings. Yet this use of the corporate form also has the effect of dispossessing the honest labourers – the workers – of their just deserts. Similarly, in terms of the relationship between authors and publishers of copyright works, legislative techniques have been deployed, alongside the ideology of 'author's right', to further the interests of publishers at the expense of authors (Porter, 1989) and, in the context of pension funds, the 'propriety' of the personal trustee-beneficiary relationship is used to legitimate the relationship between pension-fund managers and workers (Cotterrell, 1986). By employing the same legal form in different circumstances, the acceptable legitimation of one kind of property/power relation serves to conceal another kind of property/power relation.

The relationship between public and private dimensions of property/power relations provides another area of investigation. While property relations are usually taken to fall within the private sphere, the state plays an active role in creating and protecting property rights. In advanced capitalist societies the political task of reconciling the maintenance of private property rights with the development of personal political and economic rights has become increasingly problematic (Bowles & Gintis, 1986). Examples can be found in the tensions between private land-ownership and freedom of movement, copyright ownership and access to information, and demands for the recognition of employment and social security rights as property rights. Taking the first of these examples, private land ownership coupled with the action for trespass represents a significant restriction on people's freedom to go where they please. For the most part this is not conceived in terms of the exercise of power by landowners over others, but is seen as natural or inevitable. On the occasions when the issue does surface (for example, the miners' strike or the hippy convoy) (Vincent Jones, 1986), the power of the landowner to restrict the movement of others is rarely questioned. Any attempt to do so is likely to invoke an appeal to privacy (for example, 'Would you be prepared to let strangers wander through your home?') which ignores the distinction between home-ownership and other types of land-ownership in seeking to justify exercises of power which have little to do with privacy.[4]

An examination of the distribution of wealth in terms of 'who owns what and how' is another way of studying property. This would include analysis not only by class, but also by gender and race. These investigations could be integrated with studies of, for example, the rules concerning the 'referability' of contributions in the context of beneficial interests in land. Here the principles of 'honest labour' and 'giving effect to the intentions of the parties' combine to conceal the discriminatory rules governing property relations between men and women with regard to their homes and to structure power relations within the private or domestic sphere of the household. Further studies in this area might focus on the dichotomy between public and private property. In our language property is virtually synonymous with private or exclusive property. Common property which is, by definition, ownerless, would appear to represent a contradiction in terms. Property lawyers lack the grammar and vocabulary required to investigate 'non-private' ownership, whether in the form of state ownership of resources and enterprises, or shared ownership of matrimonial property, or common land rights (Edgeworth, 1988; Murray, 1987). In this context, anthropological and sociological studies of Australian and American Indian attitudes to land-ownership and African customary land rights offer scope for enlarging ideas about what property is or could be (Bohannan, 1964; Maddock, 1983; Hirschon, 1984). At the same time, colonial histories tell other tales of English land law.

There are many other ways in which property might be investigated. In advocating an approach based on ideas of property as power our aim is to develop a theoretical coherence to the content of critical property courses which can be used to inform the selection of specific topics.

Analytical Approach
Our earlier criticism of the 'black-letter' approach of the standard course should not be taken to imply that a critical course would discard doctrinal analysis and research. Rather, critical property courses would aim to introduce a range of approaches, thereby providing a comparative basis for assessing different analytical techniques and modes of reasoning. In this context, critical courses have the potential to offer more sophisticated environments for the development of legal skills. In seeking to integrate doctrinal analysis with various kinds of contextual study and policy analysis, critical courses would necessarily move outside the narrow domain of cases and statutes. Relevant sociological, political and economic literature might be introduced, together with reports and policy documents issued by government agencies and interest groups, with the aim of generating a more sensitive understanding of how law is made and how it operates in practice. Students may also be encouraged to undertake empirical research projects using survey and documentary research methods.

For example, although it may be possible to learn the law relating to mortgages as an abstract body of rules, a coherent understanding of the contemporary significance of these rules requires study of the contexts, policies and practices which influence their operation. The production and consumption of housing, and particularly the commodification of housing, provide important contexts for the study of mortgage law. Thus, an analysis of the property/power relations between mortgagees and mortgagors might draw upon studies in the sociology and political economy of owner-occupation which focus on a comparison of different types of housing tenure, the relationship between housing markets and capital finance markets (including the role of building societies and other lending institutions), the development of housing policies and the ideology of home-ownership (Ball, 1983; Craig, 1986; Daunton, 1987; Gough, 1982). This context could also be used to compare specific law reform proposals with broader policy proposals. (Ball, 1986; Law Commission, 1986). More intensive study might focus on a specific area, such as the powers of mortgagees in relation to possession and sale. In addition to analysing relevant statutory provisions and case reports, students may be encouraged to investigate the incidence of non-repayment, the policies and practices of institutional lenders in dealing with non-repayment, and the consequent problems of homelessness (Doling et al., 1985; Ford, 1988; National Consumer Council, 1990). Such a study might include analysis of published reports and statistics, observation of possession proceedings in court, and survey research involving building-society managers, lawyers, money advice workers and dispossessed mortgagors.

Standpoint

While the standard course implicitly claims to convey objective truth, critical property courses could be developed from a number of different standpoints, none of which provides a unique or privileged position from which to uncover the 'truth'. The standpoints adopted in critical courses would be overtly stated and, therefore, open to criticism. It would be possible and perhaps desirable to combine a number of standpoints within a single course. However, critical courses would not necessarily seek to provide balance.

Teaching and Assessment

One of the main aims of any critical course must be to encourage students to develop their own critical skills and perspectives. In many cases, this will require the development of new forms of classroom relationship in which students and teachers become 'co-travellers' on the critical path (see Kennedy in this chapter). New relationships will entail new forms of responsibility. For students, the role of fellow traveller demands a willingness to cooperate in a collective educational enterprise and participate in setting and achieving educational objectives. It will also place heavier responsibilities upon teachers. In particular, teachers can expect to face hard questions about methods of assessment. It should be understood from the outset that the implications of critical legal education extend not only to what is taught, but also to how it is taught and to how the course as a whole (both teaching and learning) is assessed.

Concluding Remarks

The standard property course is deficient in its content, analytical approach, standpoint and methods of teaching and assessment. It is the product of historical evolution rather than contemporary choice. Critical property courses can improve on the standard course, even in terms of standard (for example, vocational) criteria. Without wishing to preempt the choices of individual teachers and students, we have suggested that critical property courses can usefully build on a general framework of 'property as power', and have sought to demonstrate that this can facilitate a range of critical inquiries into the ways in which property relations constitute and reflect power relations and the variety of forms which these may take in different societies.

Notes

1. For example, a course based upon Megarry & Wade's *The Law of Real Property* (1984, 5th edn, London: Stevens) is likely to differ significantly from one based on Gray's *Elements of Land Law* (1987, London: Butterworths), but note Harwood's (1989) critical review of the latter in *Modern Law Review*, vol. 50 pp. 272–9.
2. These nuances of reverence are illustrated by the following examples from Megarry & Wade: 'The first thing that the student must understand is that the basis of the subject remains the "old" law, and that the elements of this must be understood before the new statutes can be understood' (p. 1). (Note that the 'new statutes' referred to here are those introduced in 1925.) 'Judges have been able to mould [licences] freely to meet new situations, particularly in the area of family interests where they wish to give efficacy to vague and informal transactions which would otherwise be legally futile' (p. 799). 'In the main, the English law of property rests on the logical development of clear principles' (p. ix). The 1925 reforms 'are without doubt the greatest single monument of legal wisdom, industry and ingenuity which the statute-book can display' (p. 1144). (Compare this with Offer's [1977] detailed analysis of these reforms as the outcome of 'long-term conflict between the lawyers and the state for the control of land transfer' in 'The Origins of the Law of Property Acts 1910–1925', *Modern Law Review*, vol. 40, pp. 505–22.)
3. This conception is also prevalent in economic analyses of property. For example, Barzel (1989) argues that 'property rights of individuals over assets consist of the rights, or the powers, to consume, obtain income from, and alienate these assets', in *Economic Analysis of Property Rights* (Cambridge: Cambridge University Press) p. 2.
4. Compare Parkin's (1979) remark that 'the possession of a toothbrush or an oilfield confers similar rights and obligations on their owners, so property laws cannot be interpreted as class laws', *Marxism and Class Theory: A Bourgeois Critique* (London: Tavistock) p. 50.

Company Law
Ian Grigg-Spall, Paddy Ireland and Dave Kelly
(Readers following the Marxist perspective in this book should read Edie et al. and Grigg-Spall and Ireland prior to this article)

The conceptual structure of modern company law reveals much about the social relations of capitalist society and their reified and fetishised forms of appearance. Indeed, its historical emergence and development can only be properly understood in the context of an analysis of the various forms taken by capital. In standard company law texts, however, the conceptual structure of company law and the forms of consciousness of which it is part are treated as ahistorical givens and left unexamined. A critical approach to company law must begin with what these texts take for granted.

The Doctrine of Separate Personality

The doctrine of separate corporate personality is the cornerstone of modern company law. It is founded on a conception of the incorporated company not simply as an entity with an independent legal existence from its shareholders but as an object which is cleansed and emptied of them. It is this depersonalised and reified conception of the company that enables it to be 'completely separated' (Gower, 1979, p. 100) from its members. Traditionally, this 'complete separation' is seen as flowing from the legal act of incorporation, a point usually illustrated by reference to *Salomon v. Salomon and Co. Ltd* ([1897] AC 22). Correspondingly, a sharp line is drawn between incorporated companies, which are objects in themselves whose members stand in a completely external relationship to them, and *unincorporated* organisations which are merely collection(s) or aggregation(s) of individuals, in which the members *are* the company.

This view as to the origins of the complete separation of companies and their members – and, therefore, of the conceptual foundations of modern company law – is untenable. An examination of eighteenth- and early nineteenth-century cases and texts makes it clear that at that time incorporation did *not* entail such a separation. Incorporation did create an entity, the incorporated company, which was legally distinguishable from the people composing it, but there was no suggestion that this entity was completely separate from its members. On the contrary, up to the middle of the nineteenth century incorporated joint stock companies were consistently identified with their component members and conceptualised not as depersonalised objects, but as entities composed of those members merged into one, legally distinguishable, body. An incorporated company was its members 'united so as to be but one person in law ...'.

The prevalence in the early nineteenth century of this view is revealed, with particular clarity, linguistically. Nowadays, an incorporated company is usually referred to in the singular, as 'it', confirming its depersonalised, reified status. In the early nineteenth century, however, when they were perceived as associations of people merged into one body, joint stock companies – incorporated and *un*incorporated – were frequently referred to in the plural, as 'they'. (For one example see *Ex parte the Lancaster Canal Co.* (Mont & Bligh 94 [1828]).)

Those who adhere to the conventional view that complete separation is a function of the legal act of incorporation sometimes recognise that up to the mid-nineteenth century incorporation did not have this effect. However, they attribute this either to the confusing influence on the law of *un*incorporated joint stock companies, or to contemporary misapprehensions about the nature and effects of incorporation. It was not until *Salomon* in 1897, they argue, that the 'implications' of incorporation 'were fully grasped even by the courts', since which time 'the complete separation of the company and its members has never been doubted' (Gower, 1979, pp. 97–100). Neither of these explanations stands close scrutiny. The 'complete separation' of companies and their members emerged for the first time in the mid-nineteenth century. It was reflected in the changed consequences attributed to incorporation, but incorporation was *not* its source. Its origins are to be found in the changing economic and legal nature of the joint stock company share.

The Changing Legal Nature of the Share

Throughout the eighteenth and early nineteenth centuries, the term 'share' was 'used in its natural sense to denote ownership of an appreciable part of [a] whole undertaking' (Scott, 1912, vol. I, p. 45). Legally, shares in joint stock companies, *in*corporated and *un*incorporated, were viewed as equitable interests in the assets of the company. Their legal nature, therefore, depended on the nature of those assets: they could be either real or personal estate depending on whether or not the company owned land. Up to the early 1830s it was consistently being held that company shares were realty if the company owned land. Crucially, while the share was legally perceived in this way, shareholders – the equitable co-owners of those assets – were necessarily closely identified with their companies. They could not be 'completely separate'.

From the 1830s, however, the legal nature of shares began to be reconceptualised, and by the mid-nineteenth century the close link between shares and the assets of companies had been severed. In the crucial case, *Bligh v. Brent* (2 Y & C Ex. 268), decided in 1837, the issue before the court was whether a company's shares were realty and within the Statute of Mortmain. In accordance with the prevailing view, counsel argued that the company's shares were realty because the company owned land. In every joint stock company, he asserted, 'the shareholder has an estate of the same nature as the company'. Despite the overwhelming weight of the authorities, the Court rejected this view. The case, they argued, turned on 'the nature of the interest which each shareholder is to have', and in their view shareholders in incorporated joint stock companies had interests only in the profits of companies and no interest whatsoever in their assets. The shares were personalty, irrespective of the nature of the company's ownership of land.

Bligh v. Brent was the turning point, although uncertainties remained for some years after, particularly in relation to the nature of shares in *un*incorporated companies and in companies whose business activities were closely connected to land. By the mid 1850s, however, these had largely disappeared. In *Watson v. Spratley* (10 Ex. 222), decided in 1854, the court had to determine the nature of the shares of an *un*incorporated mining company. It held that the matter turned on 'the essential nature and quality of a share in a joint stock company', and declared its shares to be interests only in profits. Henceforth, shareholders, even in *un*incorporated joint stock companies, had no direct interest in the assets of their companies. Shares were personalty irrespective not only of the nature of a company's assets, but of its legal status. In short, they were an entirely separate form of property; legal objects in their own right. Critically, with this development, a legal space emerged between joint stock companies and their shareholders. The company owned the assets, both in law and in equity; the shareholders owned the shares, a new, quite separate and intangible type of property in the form of a right to revenue.

To understand the emergence of the modern doctrine of separate personality, with its reified conception of the company and complete separation of company and members, we need to trace the historical processes whereby the share and other similar titles to revenue emerge as legally recognised, autonomous forms of property.

Rights to Revenue as Forms of Money Capital

The most appropriate starting point is Marx's analysis of these titles to revenue as forms of what he calls interest-bearing or money capital. The ideal typical money capital transaction is a loan in which, in return for an increment in the form of interest, money is temporarily transferred from its legal owner to another person who uses it in the production process. Analytically, the transaction involves the transformation of money into money capital: a move from money as a means of facilitating exchange to money as a commodity in itself which commands a price. As Marx explains, this transformation can only take place under certain historical conditions – conditions in which labour power has become a commodity. It is the class relation between capitalist and wage-labourer which permits the transformation of mere money into capital. Interest, the return that accrues to money capital, is part of the surplus value produced by wage-labour (Harvey 1982; Marx 1974a).

This transformation of money into money capital is not, however, apparent in the basic motion underlying the capitalist mode of production:

$$M \rightarrow C \xrightarrow[\searrow MP]{\nearrow LP} P \rightarrow C_1 \rightarrow M_1$$

The capitalist spends money (M) to purchase certain commodities (C), labour power (LP) and means of production (MP). These are utilised in the production process (P) to produce other commodities (C_1) whose value is greater than those used in their production. The latter commodities are then sold for a sum of money (M_1) which is greater than the original money expended. The difference in magnitude between M and M_1 constitutes surplus value or profit and accrues to the capitalist. Money here is merely a means of facilitating exchange although it operates as 'capital *in* the production process' (Marx, 1974b).

For this movement to occur, however, capitalists must have sufficient money to start production. Historically, from the early days of industrial capitalism, the development of a credit system, in which money was transformed into money capital, was essential to enable the centralisation of sufficient capital for production to begin. This was especially true in areas where fixed capital costs were high such as canals and railways (Landes, 1960). In this process the 'normal' circuit of capital became:

$$M \rightarrow C \xrightarrow[\searrow MP]{\nearrow LP} P \rightarrow C_1 \rightarrow M_1 \xrightarrow[\searrow PE \text{ (Profit of enterprise)}]{\nearrow I \text{ (Interest)}}$$

The functions of contributing funds and of utilising those funds in the production process came to be performed by different people: money capitalists contributed funds, industrial capitalists utilised them. The industrial capitalists ensure that surplus value is produced, but as they borrow the capital they use they have to surrender part of the surplus value created to the money capitalists. The surplus value generated in production thereby comes to be divided into two qualitatively distinct parts: profit of enterprise which accrues to the industrial capitalist and interest which accrues to the money capitalist. Interest represents a relationship between two capitalists, and as such, necessarily entails antagonism between them as they contest the division of surplus value. With the development of an ever more sophisticated credit system, new financial instruments emerge, pushing money and interest bearing capital into a prominent role in relation to accumulation (Marx, 1974b). In this process, usury, which had for centuries been outlawed as against nature, came to be seen as natural and commonsense (Koffler, 1979).

Rights to Revenue as Property: the Nature of Fictitious Capital

Part of the process whereby this happens is the legal constitution and recognition of these new financial instruments – these new forms of money capital – as autonomous forms of property. At common law these titles to revenue were initially classified as 'choses in action'. This category – which by the eighteenth century covered instruments such as bills, notes, cheques, government stock and joint stock company shares – was used to describe all personal rights enforceable only by action and not by taking physical possession. Titles to revenue were, therefore, conceptualised as rights personal to the parties bound by the obligation. As such they were non-assignable and incapable of being independent forms of alienable property. At common law they could not even be stolen and legislation was needed to deal with them. Similarly, in early incorporated companies, the instrument of incorporation had to specifically provide for the transferability of shares, which were otherwise considered to be non-assignable. Gradually, however, 'some of the choses in action ... changed their original character and [became] very much less like merely personal rights of action and very much more like rights of property' (Holdsworth, 1937, pp. 531–2).

Marx argued that the key to understanding this development lies in the barriers that inhibit the circulation of money capital and the need to overcome them. When capital exists as money it is exchangeable, liquid and mobile. Once 'loaned' against future surplus-value production, however, it becomes tied to specific assets, and problems arise if lenders are not willing to give up control of their money for sufficient time for borrowers to finance their operations. Historically, the principal solution to these problems was the establishment of developed markets for titles to revenue, permitting money capital to preserve its flexibility and liquidity. Crucially, under these conditions these titles develop a capital value of their own, and become a form of capital in themselves, emerging as 'fictitious capital'. As such they come to be legally recognised as new autonomous forms of property.

The separate capital value of these titles is established in the market through the process whereby revenues are capitalised. A periodic income or revenue is capitalised by calculating it, on the basis of the prevailing rate of interest, as an income which would be realised by a capital loaned at this rate of interest. So, for example, if one had an annual income of £50 and the prevailing rate of interest was 10 per cent, that income would represent the annual interest on £500. That £500 would be the fictitious capital value of the legal title to the annual £50 (Hilferding, 1981, pp. 107–16).

It is as markets develop in these titles, enabling them to develop capital values of their own, that they emerge as autonomous forms of property. As Marx noted, as this happens, 'capital more and more acquires a material form, is [increasingly] transformed from a relationship into a thing'. This thing, 'which embodies ... the social relationship, ... acquire[s] a fictitious life and independent existence'. It is in this form that the social relationship comes to exist in our consciousness. Moreover, as this occurs, 'the conception of [such] capital as a self-reproducing and self-expanding value, lasting and growing eternally by virtue of its innate properties, is thereby established'. In short, the circuit of money capital appears as $M \rightarrow M_1$, money capital seeming to possess the inherent ability to command interest. Interest seems to accrue merely as a result of legal agreement between two individuals, and the circuit of money capital assumes a phenomenal form that appears quite separate from, and external to, the circuit of productive capital (Marx, 1972, p. 483; Marx, 1974b, p. 394).

One of the major purposes of Marx's analysis of fictitious capital was to expose the fetishisation of money that underlies the legal recognition of these titles to revenue as new forms of property, as self-expanding 'things'. In the eighteenth and early nineteenth centuries, when titles to revenue were still usually regarded as choses in action rather than property in themselves, revenues were generally seen as connected to specific social relations, as reflected in classical political economy. The reification and fetishisation of these titles broke the direct link between revenues and productive activity, and were the basis for the development of new forms of economic, political and social consciousness (see Ireland and Kelly in this chapter). These new forms of consciousness abandoned the notion of labour as the source of value and declared capital – a thing – to be equally productive. The fetishisation of money capital, through the legal constitution of its phenomenal forms as property in themselves, led inexorably, therefore, to the dominance of exchange or market ideologies from the mid-nineteenth century and to a view of capitalism as a non-exploitative and classless system (Clarke, 1982).

The Share as Fictitious Capital

As with other forms of money capital, the basic condition for joint stock company shares to emerge as separate forms of property with capital value in themselves is the development of a generalised market in them. This generalised market in shares did not emerge until after 1825 (Reed, 1969). Prior to this period there was no public market in shares and therefore shares could not develop as fictitious capital with a value in themselves. As a consequence, they inevitably retained a direct link to a company's productive assets and were legally conceptualised not as property in their own right, but as equitable interests in those assets. In these circumstances, shareholders could not be 'completely separated' from their companies. This was reflected in the contemporary view of joint stock companies, incorporated and *un*incorporated, as entities composed of shareholders merged into one body; as aggregates of people; as 'they's. People still 'formed themselves' into companies as in the 1856 Companies Act (19 & 20 Vict. c 40).

In the period after 1825 the nature of the share was transformed. The principal cause was the rapid development of the railway system. Railways involved massive outlays on fixed capital, requiring the aggregation of large amounts of money capital. The smaller denomination, freely transferable share was the chosen form of centralisation. The railways brought, therefore, a dramatic increase both in the number of shareholders and in the number of shares available for trading.

The effects of these developments on shares, however, were qualitative as well as quantitative. Shares were not only more numerous, they were now marketable commodities, liquid assets, easily converted by their holders into money. They were titles to revenue capable of being capitalised; a form of fictitious capital, separate from the productive capital of the company. Legally, they were judicially redefined as objects of property in themselves. Most important of all for the future development of company law, with the legal constitution of this new form of property, a gulf emerged between companies and their shareholders and between shareholders and their shares. Companies owned the productive capital, the actual assets; shareholders owned the fictitious share capital, the shares, which they could now sell at will. Shareholders were not completely separate from their companies. They no longer formed themselves into companies, but formed companies, objects external to them as in the 1862 Companies Act (25 & 26 Vict. c. 89). A company was no longer a plural entity, a 'they', people merged into one body; it was now a singular entity, an 'it', an object emptied of people. Both the company and the share had been reified.

Reconsidering Company Law

Contrary to the orthodox view, therefore, the source of the modern principle of separate personality is not incorporation but the historical processes whereby the joint stock company share emerges as a form of fictitious money capital. Analysis of these processes offers a methodology for the study of company law which involves an excavation of the specifically historical conditions and social relations which led to the emergence of joint stock companies as a phenomenal form of industrial capital and the share as one of the phenomenal forms of money capital. This method 'reasons from the forms in which economic phenomena present themselves on the surface of society to the material network of essential relations peculiar to the mode of production in question which explain why the phenomena should take such forms' (Sayer, 1979, p. 17). Such an analysis not only enables us to understand the conceptual foundations of modern company law, it also enables us to grasp that exploitation and class struggle between wage-labour and capital and between fractions of capital (industrial and money) are the essential relations underlying the joint stock company and the share. We can also begin to see how the company and share forms serve to obscure those relations.

We believe that this analysis, in demonstrating the centrality of law to the development of the circuits of money capital, has some important implications for critical legal studies in general. Recently, a number of critical legal theorists have correctly emphasised the ways in which law, as well as being constituted by capitalist social relations, is actually constitutive of them. For example, in forwarding such a constitutive theory of law, Karl Klare suggests that the legal process is 'one of the primary forms of social practice through which actual relationships embodying class power [are] created and articulated' (Klare, 1979). Having made this important point, however, Klare tends to focus specifically on people: on the legal dimensions of their personal relationships and on their legal constitution as individual legal subjects. In so doing, he fails to recognise that capitalist social relations come to be reified and depersonalised; that is, that class relations under developed capitalism cease to be personal but come, to a significant extent, to be embodied in things, some of which – like the joint stock company share – are constituted *in law* as autonomous forms of property. To oversimplify, a precondition of the full development of the notion of the individual legal subject existing in apparent isolation (the premise of fully developed bourgeois theory) is the disconnection of revenues from social relations. Crucial to this process is the legal reification and mystification of titles to revenue; that is, their constitution as things in themselves, as self-expanding, autonomous forms of property.

Labour Law
Alastair Edie, Ian Grigg-Spall and Paddy Ireland

Contextualist Labour Law

Only since the early 1970s has labour law emerged as a fully separate legal category. Before that, its field of operation was subsumed within the general laws of contract and tort and it was typically depicted as contract and tort with a boilersuit on. Since its emergence it has become one of the best examples of 'contextualist' legal study (see Hunt in this chapter).

In even the most impenetrable of 'black-letter' law degrees, labour law courses promise consideration of the law alongside the 'realities' of industrial relations and collective bargaining, with much cross-referencing between the law and the work of specialists in industrial relations, industrial sociology, labour history and so on. This is, in a sense, unsurprising, for so much of labour law is the direct product of state policy and state legislation that it simply cannot display the same level of apparent autonomy that characterises traditional common law subjects.

Measured against the mind-numbing backwardness of many law courses, this engagement with law's social context is progressive. However, the depth of analysis that it offers is limited by its essentially social democratic perspective on the world; it's a partial, rather than a total, critique (see Hunt in this chapter). This is to be expected, for the whole terrain of the subject has been mapped out by social democrats. There can be no other area which since its inception has been so colonised by Labour Party sympathisers. Academic labour lawyers have played an important role in the formulation of Labour Party policy and have written extensively for its think-tank, the Fabian Society. The doyen of labour lawyers, Sir Otto Kahn-Freund QC, had a social democratic pedigree stretching back to his editing of the English translation of Karl Renner's *The Institutions of Private Law and their Social Functions* (Renner, 1949). Inevitably, the political worldview of these originators and leading figures features in the organisation of the subject. It is not a matter of chance that books and courses on labour law are divided into individual and collective labour law; that central importance is attributed to collective bargaining and agreements; that the contract of employment is almost universally derided as a legal fiction; or that the law of strikes is judged by reference to its ability to arbitrate the interests of capital and labour (Kahn-Freund, 1972). These organisational principles represent a view which sees a qualitative difference between the individual and the collective; which sees trade union organisation as a countervailing power to organised capital; which preaches that a key to the regulation of the command power of the employer lies in casting off the mask of apparent reciprocity.

In essence, contextualist labour law focuses on the relevance of law and legal practices to the needs of those involved, especially workers. Where there is a perceived lack of correspondence between legal rules and practice and identified needs, normative and institutional changes are proposed. Certain fundamental assumptions, however, are always left unquestioned. This is the case even though conflict theories of industrial relations have come to be preferred to unitary theories. Wage-labour (that is, selling yourself for a wage) and the law and the state as modes of regulation are assumed to be natural and inevitable features of human existence. The capital–labour relationship is treated as natural and the task is defined simply as its institutional regulation.

Even the Thatcher decade, which, with its heightened attacks on workers and workers' organisations, should have raised questions about these assumptions, has had little or no impact. The response of traditional labour lawyers has essentially been to continue as before. Some have gone on producing proposals for a new system of labour law and the replacement of the contract of employment by some new status agreement, all of course, on the assumption of the eventual return of a Labour government (Hepple, 1986; Wedderburn, 1987). Others have sought to outflank the Thatcher government by enthusiastically supporting the Europeanisation of labour law and/or seeking to involve the courts in the judicial review of the formerly closed space of the private workplace (Bercusson, 1990; Ewing & Grubb, 1987). A number have simply fallen silent: 'Is labour law dead?' asks one academic (Ewing, 1988).

Critical Labour Law

A purely contextualist labour law cannot, therefore, be sufficient for the critical lawyer. Using the perspectives of historical materialism (see Fine & Picciotto in this book; Grigg-Spall, Ireland & Kelly in this chapter), a genuinely critical approach can be developed, enabling the basic concepts of labour law to be examined. This method, as Derek Sayer says, 'reasons from the forms in which economic phenomena present themselves on the surface of society to the material network of essential relations peculiar to the mode of production in question which explain why the phenomena should take such forms' (Sayer, 1979, p. 17). Such a 'transcendental analytic' enables us not only to grasp that exploitation and class struggle between wage-labour and capital are the essential relations underlying the contract of employment, but also to explain how its present legal form serves to obscure those relations.

Historically, the legal form taken by wage-labour has undergone considerable change. Up to the mid-nineteenth century it was legally conceptualised in terms of master and servant. As such, it directly reflected and expressed class division, subordination and exploitation. Only from the later nineteenth century did wage-labour come to be legally conceptualised in contractual terms; as a contract between formal equals. This legal form is still dominant and the employment legislation of recent years, has re-emphasised the contractual conceptions. The contract of employment remains, therefore, the central category of labour law.

It is characterised by three principal elements: exchange, free will and equivalence. Wages exchange for labour; agreement determines the mutual relations; the relation of formal equality is established by the equivalence of the commodities to be exchanged – wages for labour. Its content belies this contractual form. First, close examination of wage-labour reveals that there is no exchange at all (and certainly no equivalent exchange). From an individual standpoint (that of social democracy) the worker is paid for 'necessary labour' – that is, for the time taken to produce sufficient commodities to cover the wage. But from a class point of view all labour is rendered free since all workers are paid from the wealth accumulated from past generations of workers (Marx, 1970). The form of exchange is a 'mere semblance'. The capitalist, it is true, pays the worker the value of his or her labour power in money, but this money is merely the transmuted form of the product of his or her labour. The capitalist class is constantly giving back to the working class part of what they themselves have produced (Marx, 1970 p. 712).

Secondly, wage-labour has nothing to do with free will; not just because we have no real choice but to sell ourselves for a wage (or starve) but also because the availability, structure and payment for these jobs is dictated by the capitalist system, as recessions demonstrate time and again.

The question, therefore, becomes: how have class relations of exploitation, coercion and subordination – accurately reflected in the old legal form of master and servant – come to take their current contractual legal form where they appear as relations of exchange, free will and equivalence?

For some, it is the simple result of an ideological trick: the 'contract' of employment is a fiction. For materialists, however, the illusory legal representation (with its enormous political consequences) arises from social experience, not from ideological trickery. The move from the old status-based master–servant laws to the contractual, employer–employee conception must be historically traced to changes in social relations and their forms of appearance.

From Master and Servant to the Contract of Employment

Prior to 1875, workers were not treated as equal before the law. They were subject to the master-and-servant legislation which reflected the common-law conception of the master's absolute authority over the servant. At common law the position of the master to the servant was analogous to that of parent to child or, at that time, husband to wife. Onerous duties were imposed on servants and it was a criminal offence (punishable by imprisonment) to disobey the master, leave work without his permission, fail to attend work, or 'commit any other misconduct or misdemeanour'. The relationship was an open and visible legal relationship of subordination and domination; a non-negotiable-status, rather than a contractual, relationship.

Workers only came to be treated as formally free and equal to their employers after 1875, with the repeal of the master-and-servant legislation. Ideologically, this was of great importance, for the class-based, exploitative nature of wage-labour so clearly expressed in master–servant concepts was now concealed beneath a contractual form. Thereafter, 'the position of the ruling class [was] not supported by a privileged legal status' (Simon, 1954, p. 160). Formally, capitalists no longer had any rights which workers did not have. Their relation was no longer determined by status, but by contract, and the law regulating their relation was now a part of the ordinary law of contract. More generally, this process laid the foundations for law's claim to full autonomy from socioeconomic relations, because it could now be plausibly argued that law no longer expressed and reflected class domination and exploitation. All men (if not women) were formally equal before the law; law, therefore, could lay claim to being classless.

The explanation for this development is to be found in changes that took place in production processes during this period and, in particular, in the methods whereby profits were made (in Marxist terms, whereby surplus value was extracted). That is, in the transition during the nineteenth century from 'manufacture' to 'machinofacture' and from what Marx called absolute to relative surplus value.

Despite the so-called industrial revolution, eighteenth- and early nineteenth-century production methods were predominantly labour intensive and characterised by the employment of skilled wage-labourers, by 'manufacture'. The division of labour within workshops took the form of the simple cooperation of skilled workmen who, although they were increasingly tied to a particular task, were nonetheless of 'singular importance within the total labour process' (Kinsey, 1979, p. 54). In Marx's words: '... the whole body is paralysed if one of its members is missing' (Marx, 1970, pp. 346–7). Throughout this period, therefore, workforce discipline was a problem for capitalists, who needed to subjugate skilled labour in order to orchestrate production. The power of private property – that is, the absolute right of the capitalist 'to use and abuse, and exclude others, at his will, from the means of production' – had to be 'complemented by coercive legislation and common law which tied the worker in time and place to capital' (Kinsey, 1979, p. 54); hence the use of the Statute of Labourers 1399, the Statute of Artificers 1563, the Poor Law, and the master-and-servant legislation. In this period, wage-labour was only 'formally subordinated' to capital.

Crucially, at this time it was apparent that the source of profit (surplus value) was labour power. The connection between profit and labour time was more visible, for the largest input into the production process was living labour. This was reflected in the struggle over the length of the working day. As Marx wrote: 'In the period of manufacture, if one considers capital in the actual process of production as a means of extracting surplus value then the relationship is still very simple and the actual connection between labour power and profit imposes itself upon both workers and capitalists in their consciousness. The violent struggles over the limits of the working day demonstrate this strikingly.' (Marx, 1970; Peter Fitzpatrick in this book) In the words of one master to a factory inspector: 'If you allow me to work them an extra ten minutes a day, you put £1,000 a year in my pocket' (Marx, 1970). In political economy, these insights were reflected in the labour theories of value of Smith and Ricardo, and in the open recognition of the importance of status and class (hence, political economy, not economics).

Indeed, many historians argue that because of the visibility of exploitation at this time, large sections of the working class had revolutionary, anti-capitalist views (Abercrombie, Hill & Turner, 1980; Lazonick, 1978). They sought the 'abolition of wage-labour' rather than 'a fair day's work for a fair day's pay'. In consequence, many trade union rule-books, dating from this period, state as their declared aim the taking into social ownership of the means of production, distribution and exchange.

The gradual transition to 'machinofacture', involving the use of machines and factory production, brought profound changes. Under manufacture the workers made use of tools and simple instruments; under machinofacture the machines made use of them. The coming of machine and factory production, therefore, created mass labour, brutally displacing the skilled labour of the craftsman with the unskilled labour of the machine-minder. The pace and nature of work came to be dictated by the machine, with workers increasingly rendered mere appendages. Greater profitability was now principally achieved (as it is today, at least in the First World) by making labour more productive, rather than by lengthening the working day. In Marxist terms, the emphasis was on relative rather than absolute surplus value. In this deskilling process, the workers were partially disempowered, for they were now much more easily replaced. It became possible for capitalists to employ larger numbers of women and children who were weaker organisationally, as well as cheaper. The emergence of machinofacture, therefore, greatly broadened the labour force available to capital. Moreover, the machine not only increased productivity, it also enabled capitalists to control the intensity of the work process *in*directly, through the regulation of the speed of the machine. Domination seemed to emanate from the nature of the machines rather than from persons; the personal rule of the capitalist was replaced by the apparently impersonal rule of the machine.

Indeed, in this process, the class nature of production relations became even less clear. Owners progressively withdrew to become mere shareholders and loan/stockholders (drawing dividends and interest) and managers and technicians took over the actual running of production. The formerly obvious and visible nature of class authority in the workplace was eroded; management could claim to be a purely scientific and technical matter (see Kinsey, 1979, p. 58). Even more significantly, the move to machinofacture and factory production contained within it the seeds of a complete fetishisation of relations between wage-labour and capital, and a complete concealment of exploitation.

As we have argued, under manufacture the source of profit was recognised to be labour power. However, once production cannot be carried out competitively without machines, production becomes increasingly capital, rather than labour, intensive. As larger and larger sums of money are required to commence production, the money capitalist – Mr Moneybags as Marx calls him – can turn to labour and say, 'Without me there could be no production.' Indeed, assuming capitalist production, this is totally accurate: money capital now appears to be autonomously productive, for, as Cohen suggests, labour power and machines appear productive by being the embodiment of it (Cohen, 1978). These developments Marx called the 'fetishisation' of capital (Grigg-Spall, Ireland & Kelly in this chapter; Cohen, 1978; Sayer, 1979). This is the belief, based on the way things *appear*, that capital is as productive of value as labour; that they are both simply 'factors of production', entitled to their 'fair' share of the proceeds of production. This fetishisation of capital masks exploitation and class division, and provides the basis for treating the exchange between capital and labour as an exchange of equivalents between equals – the basis, that is, for the contract of employment.

Under manufacture, the origins of profit in labour time was apparent. With machinofacture, this connection is lost to consciousness, and capital and labour appear to stand as equals in the production process and to exchange equivalent for equivalent. Workers come to accept as natural, necessary and right the claim of money capital to the profits of production. The hierarchical organisation of the workplace geared to profit-making comes to seem inevitable and necessary. This is reflected in the acceptance by working-class organisations, trade unions and the Labour Party of the 'naturalness' and inevitability of the capitalist market (see John Fitzpatrick in this book).

Elsewhere, this change was reflected in the demise of the labour theory of value and the classical political economy of Smith and Ricardo, and in the rise of neoclassical economics with its concentration (like the modern form of capitalist law) on exchange relations between isolated individuals; on what Marxists would call the fetishised appearances of the market (Fine, 1984; Grigg-Spall, Ireland & Kelly in this chapter). The so-called autonomy of law, the idea that law is unconnected to social and economic relations, and the concept of the rule of law – as expressed in the works, for example, of Dicey and Hayek – is predicated on the same premises (Dicey, 1959; Hayek, 1944).

Machinofacture, and the real subsumption of labour that it engenders, does not, however, entirely eliminate the legal endorsement of and support for managerial authority in the workplace. The contract of employment continues to retain, in the form of implied terms, elements of the old master-and-servant law (Fox, 1974). Thus, for example, the courts imply into the contract non-negotiable duties of obedience, cooperation, fidelity and trust, which employees necessarily owe to their employers (see, for example, *Secretary of State for Employment v. ASLEF* [No 2] [1972] 2 All ER 949). Even the terms 'master' and 'servant', with their implications of unequal status, are still used with great regularity by the judiciary. For some conservative writers, this is a reflection of the 'true nature of the relationship': the new terms 'employer' and 'employee' are simply an attempt to deny reality (Scruton, 1982, p. 293). In Roger Scruton's words, 'capitalist relations of production involve ... the same element of "unfree obligation" that attached to ... feudal relations ... [An] objective of modern radical conservatism [is] ... to endorse the popular sentiment that the relation ... is not and ought not to be, contractual' (Scruton, 1982, p. 222).

Reconsidering Recent Developments in Labour Law

Indeed, in the last 20 or so years (see In Place of Strife, 1969, Cmnd 3888), the need for the legal disciplining of the workforce has been particularly acute in Britain, as a prolonged crisis of profitability has endured. The emergence of labour law as a separate legal category during this period can be largely attributed to the legal and other measures taken in the face of this problem. Certainly, the changing contours of modern labour law can be fruitfully analysed in terms of the twists and turns of the profitability crises of Fordism and Keynesianism and the attempt to resolve them through new regimes of so-called flexible accumulation and post-Fordism (Harvey, 1990). Recent developments in labour law can be seen as part of an endeavour to overcome the problems of profitability by tightening work discipline, weakening trade unions and reinforcing the powers of management.

It is in this context that the legislation of the Thatcher government must be examined. In a series of piecemeal changes embodied in five main acts – the Employment Acts of 1980, 1982, 1988 and 1990, and the Trade Union Act 1984 – the legal position of capital vis-a-vis labour has been greatly strengthened. The internal affairs of unions are now heavily regulated; indeed, many obligations are now imposed on unions which are not imposed on employers, employers' associations, corporations or other organisations of capital. Trade union immunities have been reduced, their political activities regulated (again in ways not applied to companies) and all secondary action declared unlawful. Union members often possess more rights against their union than they do against their employer. At the same time, the ambit of unfair dismissal has been reduced, maternity rights cut back and minimum-wage provisions emasculated. The catalogue of changes is long (Hendy, 1989).

Workers' Rights

In this light the struggle for workers' rights becomes important. If rights are potentially available to clothe bourgeois interests then they should also be available for the working class (see Fine & Picciotto and Peter Fitzpatrick in this book). The terrain must be contested. The struggle for rights has considerable organisational importance and lays the ground for their supercession, but it is a tactical not a strategic struggle. What is necessary for the emancipation of the mass of the people is their effective de facto control of the means of production, distribution and exchange. The struggle for rights is subordinate to that end. As critical lawyers we should be aware of this, and not privilege the legal work that we do.

Constitutional Law
Richard de Friend

Introduction

From everyday political rhetoric and from the accounts given in standard textbooks it would seem that constitutional law is essentially about freedom and empowerment – the basic themes of this handbook. Constitutional law apparently serves as the source of basic rights and liberties, providing each person, no matter what his or her social or material position, with an equal 'civic' capacity, which can be exercised through the political and legal systems and can be asserted against even the most powerful 'others' including, most crucially, the state itself.

The theory that a 'free' society depends upon constitutional law has, of course, been been absolutely central to liberal political philosophy over the last 300 years (Hayek, 1960; Harden & Lewis, 1986; Thomson, 1991). However, it is significant that over the last couple of decades constitutional law has also increasingly been taken seriously by influential sections of the left. This is reflected in: Charter 88; the programme of constitutional reform adopted by the Labour Party; that promoted by *Marxism Today* on behalf of the Communist Party; the more piecemeal changes which, from time to time, are advocated by Liberty (formerly NCCL); and the demands for 'welfare rights' which, since the late 1960s, have been made by groups and organisations seeking to redress the levels of discipline, control and subordination imposed upon those forced to claim state benefits and services. It is also reflected in the proposals for tighter processes of criminal investigation and trial, and for more open and democratic methods of selecting judges, that have been widely canvassed in the wake of recent miscarriages of justice, such as in the cases of the Birmingham Six, the Guildford Four, the Winchester Three and the Maguires.

The central task of any critical constitutional law course should be to evaluate the claims which are made for it, explicitly or implicitly, as a means of empowerment and liberation. More precisely, such a course should seek to establish the kind of justice and freedom which can be realised through constitutional law – and, equally, the kind which cannot. This will involve an analysis, first, of the role ascribed to constitutional law in liberalism (or, as I will now term it, liberal-constitutionalism'); secondly, of how far the legal culture of this country conforms to a liberal-constitutionalist model; and thirdly, of the limits of liberal constitutionalism itself. I will now expand briefly on each of these themes.

Constitutional Law and Liberal-Constitutionalism

As I have been suggesting, the idea that liberty and empowerment are secured through law – and through constitutional law in particular – is part of a much wider system of thought, liberal-constitutionalism. This has aptly been described by Roger Scruton as 'the official ideology of the Western World' (Scruton, 1984, p. 192). Very schematically it can be seen to consist of the following related propositions.

First, a society or total social order is essentially a product of the infinite number and variety of relationships formed by individual human actors on a more or less voluntary basis in pursuit of what they rationally calculate to be their material and non-material self-interests (Arblaster, 1984, Chs. 2 and 3).

Secondly, though a certain basic level of social order has to be achieved through institutions (such as the family), and through an apparatus of state and law, the existence of which cannot be attributed to an act of will on the part of any particular individual or individuals, the 'just' society is one that imposes on individuals as little regulation or government as possible and thus allows them the maximum possible scope to create and recreate their own social and economic orders through the relationships or associations that they form with others.

Thirdly, it follows from this that the state has to be restricted to those governmental functions which help to create or maintain the conditions that permit the exercise of social and economic freedom by individuals.

Fourthly, to this end, the state must itself be subject to law; this will provide the boundaries of what the state can do, and in a sense, establish what the 'state' is. To perform this function 'law' must have a status or authority which is greater than the laws the state produces to govern society; must appear to have been created independently from and antecedent to the state itself; and must serve as the ultimate criterion of the legitimacy of actions taken by the state, its agencies and officials.

In many, though not all, of the countries which, over the past 250 to 300 years, have based their political and legal systems on liberal-constitutionalist principles, comprehensive constitutional instruments have been adopted. These specify first, what the basic institutions or offices of the state are to be, what governmental functions each is to perform, and how those occupying them are to be selected; secondly, how civil society is to be conceptualised for constitutional purposes (normally as formally equal individual citizens, each possessed of certain legal capacities, expressed in the form of basic rights and liberties which are protected against infringement by state action); and thirdly, in which arenas and through which processes the constitution is to be interpreted and conflicts arising under it resolved.

So, to what extent does this country's constitutional law approximate the liberal-constitutionalist model or ideal?

Law and State in the United Kingdom

As writers of standard texts on constitutional law from Dicey to de Smith have emphasised, in the United Kingdom, without a constitution of the kind described above, the common law has served as the source of 'apparently autonomous or antecedent' legal principles and processes that govern the state. However, these principles and processes have hardly comprised a very effective regime for subordinating the state to law.

In the first place, the constitutional law developed by common-law judges contains two core principles, the sovereignty of Parliament and the prerogative powers of the Crown, which taken together provide, formally, an unlimited legislative and an extensive executive capacity to the government which at any time controls Parliament through its majority in the House of Commons. These can and often have been exploited precisely to avoid effective legal challenge to state action. For example, by granting administrators very wide discretionary powers, like those found in the legislation which set up the Social Fund; by introducing broad 'ouster clauses' like those contained in both the Interception of Communications and the Security Services Acts; by claiming 'prerogative' as an authority for action which was seemingly not possible under statute, as in *R. v. Sec. of State for Home Dept. ex. p. Northumbria Police Authority* ([1988] 1 All ER 556) ; or by making extensive use of secondary legislation which can easily and quickly be amended to deal with any defeats that are suffered in the courts.

In the second place, it can hardly be maintained that judges have exercised whatever autonomy they do possess to enhance or even to empower the weak and disadvantaged. Rather, as John Griffiths has argued (Griffiths, 1985), in exercising what is, constitutionally, perhaps their most important jurisdiction of reviewing administrative state action, judges seem consistently to have afforded far greater protection to rights such as private property and freedom of contract which act as the framework for a capitalist economy, than to those, such as communication or association, which could be used to challenge or transform. More generally, they have given much more weight to the claims of order than to those of liberty as a number of recent cases demonstrate.

In *Council of Civil Service Unions and others v. Minister for the Civil Service* ([1984] 3 All ER 935), it was ultimately held that the Prime Minister's assertion of 'national security', widely disbelieved, but untestable in the courts, was sufficient to remove from civil servants even their right to be consulted before the government, exercising a prerogative power, prohibited them from becoming or remaining members of any trade union.

In *R. v. Secretary of State for Home Dept. ex. p. Cheblak*([1991] 2 All ER 319) the Court of Appeal rejected a challenge to the Home Secretary's decision (again on alleged grounds of national security) to detain, with a view to possible deportation, a Palestinian writer who had been lawfully resident in the United Kingdom for many years and who had married and had a family in this country. As the Master of the Rolls put it: 'Exercise of [judicial review] in cases of national security was necessarily restricted by the nature of the subject matter. National security was the exclusive responsibility of the Executive. It was *par excellence* a non-justiciable matter.' (p. 330) The only means of challenge were either through Parliament or through a special 'advisory panel', which required detainees to make their cases without knowing the particulars of the case being made against them, and which denied them the right of legal representation. In any case, the Home Secretary was at liberty to reject the panel's recommendations. To the charge that this amounted to a denial of natural justice, the Master of the Rolls pointed out that 'natural justice had to take account of the realities, and what would otherwise be a breach was not to be so considered in that it was unavoidable' (p. 335).

In *Brind v. Secretary of State for Home Dept.* ([1991] 1 All ER 720) the House of Lords, following both the High Court and the Court of Appeal, unanimously upheld the legality of a ban imposed by the Home Secretary on the direct broadcast of statements made by representatives of proscribed organisations in Northern Ireland. All five judges accepted, almost without question, that the defeat of terrorism had to take precedence over both the right to communicate and the inextricably interrelated right to receive and consider ideas and opinions. Nowhere was this made clearer than in Lord Bridge's judgement where he states: '[I] find it impossible to say that the Secretary of State exceeded the limits of his discretion. In any civilised and law abiding society the defeat of the terrorist is a public interest of the first importance ... The Secretary of State ... decided that it was necessary to deny to the terrorist the opportunity to speak directly to the public through the most influential of all the media of communication ... I do not see how this judgement can be categorised as unreasonable. What is perhaps surprising is that the restriction imposed is of such limited scope. There is no restriction at all on the matter which may be broadcast, only on the manner of its presentation.' (p. 724)

The Limits of Liberal-Constitutionalism

It is hardly possible here to provide a comprehensive critique of liberal-constitutionalism. However, I suggest that the following matters are particularly important to an investigation of its limits.

First, as we noted above, freedom or empowerment is primarily expressed within liberal-constitutionalism in the form of individual 'rights'. Obviously, a person's ability to actually engage in any social, economic or 'politicolegal' activity depends not simply upon their having some formal right to do so, but also upon their material and intellectual resources. To take a couple of well-canvassed examples. The right to communicate may not mean much in practice in a world in which effective communication has to be carried out through the mass media, which requires huge amounts of financial, technological and 'human' capital, and which is owned by large multinational corporations. Similarly the right to natural justice or due process may not amount to much without the resources to purchase the expensive services of the lawyers.

Secondly, the version of freedom which is emphasised most heavily in liberal-constitutionalism is freedom from state and government. However, as political and social theories from the British 'Idealism' of the late nineteenth century (Vincent & Plant, 1984, Ch. 9) to Marxist-Leninism in this century have argued, to achieve substantive or material as opposed simply to formal equality in any complex, industrialised society would necessitate a great deal of sophisticated state activity.

Thirdly, though apparently antithetical to an extensive state, there are certain important features of liberal-constitutionalism which seem to facilitate a strong, *interventionist* state to carry out those functions that this political theory concedes are appropriate for government. Most significantly, as we noted above, corresponding to the notion of society as an aggregate of individuals, vested with rights which formally give them capacity to engage in social, economic or political activity, the state is constituted as a 'bearer' of formal 'capacities' to govern. Unlike most citizens, the state can command the material resources to make full use of its formal capacities, and the legitimacy of its actions tends to be determined by how far they fall within the formal boundaries set by constitutional law. This quite easily then leads to the assumption that *any* state action, no matter how draconian or substantively unjust it may be, has to be accepted as long as it can plausibly be claimed to fall within those boundaries. By the same token, any act of resistance or opposition, no matter how just the cause, has to be rejected if it is illegal. The distorting effect of this formalisation of political action and political discourse can be seen particularly clearly in the 1984–85 miners' strike and, more recently, in the campaign against the Poll Tax.

Finally, and perhaps of greatest significance, is that despite the abstract, general and universal appearance of liberal-constitutionalism, its real history is inextricably intertwined with the development of market capitalism. It has become the official ideology of the West because it has proven to be the most appropriate one for sustaining the legitimacy and authority of capitalist social and economic relations. This alone should give at least some grounds for doubting whether any kind of liberation or empowerment which significantly challenged such relations could ever be secured through existing constitutional law.

Conclusion

This chapter is not meant to induce despair or nihilism, or even to suggest that there is *no* potential for empowering or at least defending the interests of the weak and disadvantaged through a skilled and politically informed use of constitutional law. We have no option other than to exploit it to the maximum extent possible.

My arguments, undoubtedly contestable, are intended, rather, to achieve two things. First, simply to indicate why there are grounds for thinking that only a limited kind of freedom can be secured through the practice of constitutional law. Secondly, to provide some intellectual tools with which to engage critically with the accounts of constitutional law given in standard texts and standard undergraduate courses on the subject, including, I am somewhat ashamed to confess, the one for which I have largely been responsible for the past five years.

European Law
Joanne Scott

Anyone familiar with the common-law system might be surprised when reading the case law of the European Court of Justice (ECJ) by the absence of any attempt to disguise the creative interpretative role of the judges. An examination of the decisions relating to the concept of direct effect (particularly of directives), a topic invariably included in a European law course, illustrates this.

Despite the candour with which the significance of judicial decision-making and the inevitability of interpretation is conceded in the context of the European Community (EC), the role of the ECJ is still presented as a politically neutral one. The choices made by the judges of the ECJ are important but they are not apparently political. It is interesting to ask, very briefly, how this picture of non-political creativity is sustained.

It is made possible by the notion that the judges or their concerns are somehow above politics. The judges are said to favour teleological interpretation – that interpretation which best promotes 'European integration' or 'an ever closer union between the peoples of Europe' (preamble to the Treaty of Rome). Far from taking political decisions, the judges supposedly try to implement a vision of Europe which one can infer is shared by the member states given their accession to the EC. The judges therefore seek to rise above the petty prejudices and anxieties motivated by crude nationalist sentiment of particular governments at particular moments. It is opposition to rather than the promotion of this goal of 'European integration' which should be labelled as political.

In this short contribution I want to suggest that the political implications of this teleological approach are indeed great. In particular I will argue that this approach is significant as it leads to the prioritisation of certain areas of community law and the marginalisation of others. I will illustrate this with reference to the role of international treaties in EC law.

Priorities and Margins in EC Law

Since the emergence of the Commission White Paper in 1985 on the completion of the internal market, the concept of European integration seems largely to be understood through reference to the 1991 programme of attempts to secure an internal or single market in Europe. These political priorities, earlier discussed in terms of a common market, have quickly become legal priorities. As a result many legal norms which apparently form an integral part of community law have been condemned to the margins of the system, unenforceable and largely impotent. One way in which this has occurred is through the application of the legal concept mentioned above, that of direct effect.

This can well be illustrated by reference to international treaties within the community legal order. The EC is a significant world actor. It enters into a myriad of agreements with non-member states and groups of states. With 19 per cent of world trade it is not surprising that many of these concern matters of trade, in particular issues of access to the EC market for goods originating from outside the community. The rules contained in such treaties form an 'integral part of community law'. As such the GATT code containing norms regulating the international trading system constitutes a part of community law (Petersmann, 1983a). Moreover, formally these norms take precedence over both conflicting provisions of community law and the national law of the member state.

This statement of the legal position of the liberal principles of the GATT in community law will be striking to those who know even a little about the operation of the community's Common Agricultural Policy (CAP). The protectionist nature of this policy is well known and there can be no doubt that it operates in contravention of the GATT code.[1] The CAP continues to absorb more than half of the total budget of the EC. Moreover, in an attempt to mitigate the effects of over-production in the community, more than one third of this sum is committed to the payment of export subsidies to farmers seeking to sell on the world market.

The negative impact of this policy on the world's poorest countries is clear. It has contributed to the dramatic reduction in world prices for certain commodities over the last two decades. Even for those countries not competing directly with EC producers the results can be disastrous. Cheap EC food imports can be politically useful for many governments of poor countries. However, these imports tend to undermine the viability of domestic initiatives in food production and thus the possibility of food security in the long term.

It is perhaps less well known that much of the legislation which constitutes the CAP is, according to the GATT and, therefore, according to EC law itself, liable to condemnation. In legal terms and in terms of priorities and margins it is worth inquiring how this situation can exist and persist.

For the answer we must begin by looking more closely at the concept of direct effect. While the GATT, as noted above, forms an 'integral part of community law', it does not form a directly effective part (*International Fruit Company* [1972] ECR 1227). This means that the norms contained in the GATT are not capable of being invoked by individuals before national courts. Moreover a national court is not able to request a ruling, by means of Article 177, from the ECJ in order to question the validity of community law in the light of the GATT. In fact the only route open to individuals seeking to challenge community law on this basis is in a direct action before the ECJ, relying primarily on Article 173 (Hartley, 1981, Chs. 11 and 12). The difficulties involved in bringing such an action are notorious. Thus, while the EC has been careful to confer upon its institutions the means to retaliate against its trading partners who do not honour international law relating to trade,[2] it has been less careful in ensuring its own conformity. It is one thing to declare a theoretical commitment to certain principles, thus gaining political kudos; it is quite another to ensure respect. It is clear then that all community laws are not equal since non-directly effective treaties remain on the margins and are therefore more often honoured in the breach.

The marginalisation of certain areas of community law as a result of a refusal on the part of the ECJ to attribute direct effect forces us to ask questions regarding the criteria invoked in conceding or denying this quality. The question of direct effect has been defined as a question of interpretation and thus a matter to be determined by the ECJ. This court has evolved a test to determine whether a particular provision of EC law is capable of enjoying direct effect. Hartley, in his standard text book on the institutions of the EC, extrapolating from the case law, considers that the following conditions must be satisfied (1981, p. 188): the provision must be clear and unambiguous; it must be unconditional; and its operation must not be dependent on further action being taken by the community institutions or national authorities.

The problems arising are well illustrated by the recent case of (*Demirel v. Stadt Schwabisch Cmnd* ([1989] 1 CMLR 412), which suggests that the accordance of the quality of direct effect is not merely a matter of the objective application of the above criteria but also a question of political priority. Ehlermann, the director-general of the Legal Service of the Commission of the EC, admits that the value of the rule in question is a relevant consideration in determining whether it should be directly effective.

The *Demirel* case concerned a Turkish woman who married a Turkish national who was working in West Germany. Mrs Demirel sought to establish her right to remain with her husband in West Germany. This right was denied on the basis that German law, since 1982, requires a worker to live for eight uninterrupted years in the state before acquiring any right to be joined by his or her family.

Mrs Demirel subsequently sought to rely on EC law, which, given the principle of the supremacy of community law, prevails over inconsistent national law. The relevant international law was in the form of a treaty between the EC, the member states and Turkey. The Ankara Agreement was signed in 1963, its Additional Protocol in 1970. The agreements were concluded in a period of mass labour migration to Europe, and shortly after the building of the Berlin wall stemmed the flow of labour from Eastern Europe. During the post war economic boom years, this migration was encouraged by the governments of the Western European states, as is evidenced by the setting up of national immigration offices. The Ankara Agreement sought (inter alia) to secure the flow of workers from Turkey by guaranteeing certain minimum rights for the migrants. Article 12 of the agreement notes that 'the contracting parties agree to be guided by Articles 48, 49 and 50 of the Treaty establishing the Community for the purpose of progressively securing freedom of movement of workers between them'. Thus it could be expected that Turkish workers would enjoy rights akin to those migrating in an intra-community context, including the right to migrate, to reside, to remain; the right to equal social and tax advantages, and the right to family reunification. These rights were to be secured 'by progressive stages' by December 1986.[3]

However, given the changing labour requirements of European industry during the 1970s and 1980s, the legislative measures to ensure the progressive implementation of these rights failed to emerge. Despite this Mrs Demirel persisted. She sought to establish that Article 12 and Article 36 should be considered directly effective provisions of community law which could be relied on in national courts by individuals seeking to challenge inconsistent national law. Faced with this question (a question of interpretation) the Administrative Court of Baden-Wurttemberg made a reference for a preliminary ruling from the ECJ.

That the ECJ denied the direct effect of these provisions is hardly surprising in the light of the political interests of Western Europe in the late 1980s. However, that this decision is surprising in legal terms becomes apparent when one considers the attitude of the ECJ to the direct effect of 'internal' (that is, not derived from treaties between the EC and non member states) community law. The two cases briefly discussed below should suffice to illustrate this.

Early in the history of the EC, the ECJ determined that Articles 48 to 50 were concerned with the free movement of persons in the community and were capable of conferring rights and obligations on individuals which were enforceable in the national courts (*Van Duyn v. Home Office* [1975] 1 CMLR 1). Given the parallel nature of Article 12 to Articles 48 to 50, this undermines the argument of the ECJ in *Demirel* and exposes its political reluctance to concede direct effect.

The second case, *Defrenna v. SABENA* ([1976] 2CMLR 98), concerned the possibility of Article 119 being directly effective. This article states: 'Each Member State shall during the first stage ensure and subsequently maintain the application of the principle that men and women should receive equal pay for equal work.'

It is clear that this provision required action on the part of the member states to bring the principle into operation. Nonetheless the ECJ concluded in its judgement that given the expiry of the deadline the article was itself capable of direct effect. Given the parallel nature of this article with Article 36 of the Additional Protocol to the Ankara Agreement, Hartley's comment [1981] is worth bearing in mind. He notes that this modification of the original rule to a large extent nullifies it, since almost all community provisions requiring further action contain a time-limit. In such cases the only consequence of the requirement is that direct effect is postponed until the deadline has passed.

Given the case law of the ECJ as exemplified by these two cases, and the obvious attempts of the ECJ to stretch the range of application of the concept of direct effect to its very limits in the interests of the *effet utile* of community law, the legal arguments in *Demirel*, which on their face seem convincing, appear less satisfactory. One might reasonably assume on the basis of such past decisions that the relevant articles of the agreement between Turkey and the EC are capable of direct effect. That this was denied can perhaps best be attributed to the teleological nature of the court's approach to interpretation (discussed above). This results in the court emphasising the context and more particularly the objectives of the provision in question. One result of this approach is that it allows the court to interpret identical words differently if they are placed in different contexts. Thus, in (*Polydor v. Harlequin Record Shops* ([1982] 1 CMLR 677), a provision of the Free Trade Agreement between Portugal and the community was held to be different in its scope from Article 95 which on its surface was identical. After all, the ECJ emphasised, this agreement sought to establish a link between Portugal and the community of a less 'intense' nature than that between the member states themselves. The objectives of the rules, as inferred from their context, could be distinguished.

Thus it is easier to understand the decision of the court in *Demirel* not in terms of an objectively applied legal test, although the ECJ did purport to apply these tests, but in terms of its political context and the changing objectives of the Association Agreement as understood from a Western European viewpoint. By the 1970s immigration had been defined as a problem in Europe, a problem frequently discussed together with drug-trafficking and terrorism.[4] While from a Turkish perspective access for its citizens to foreign labour markets had become of increased importance, the EC no longer welcomed these workers or their family members. Teleological interpretation allows these political needs to be translated, by means of 'context' and 'objectives' or 'value', into legal realities.

The EC as an International Actor

Such a discussion gives rise to questions about the nature of international treaty negotiations. It undermines the picture of these as freely negotiated 'contracts' which lay down fixed and clearly established rights and obligations, the balance of which is mutually satisfactory to all parties. The capacity of the community to devalue the rights accruing to its legal partners, or to render these rights irrelevant in the face of political realities through legal interpretation, demonstrates that recourse to the law does not exclude notions of power in international relations.

This conclusion is perhaps hardly startling. A critic might point out that such a discussion of the interpretative tools of the ECJ is unnecessary. After all one only has to look at the text of an agreement such as the Lomé Convention to be convinced of the significance of political power in the conclusion of international agreements. Lomé IV is an agreement between the EC and 68 African, Caribbean and Pacific states (ACP).[5] It is the showpiece of the community's development policy. It aims, according to Article 1, to 'promote and expedite the economic, cultural and social development of the ACP state ...'.

It seeks to achieve this through a judicial mix of both aid and trade. Given the relatively small scale of the aid package the trade element is of the utmost significance, particularly from an ACP perspective, insofar as it guarantees access to the EC market for ACP products. However, the degree of flexibility surrounding the EC's obligations, and its ability to tailor these to its own changing political and economic needs, is astounding. The development objective of the convention should, it seems, at no time interfere with the operation of the domestic policies of the EC. This is true even of those policies, particularly the CAP, which are in themselves antithetical to the concept of Third World development. Those agricultural products which form part of a common market organisation or regime are excepted from the general principle of free trade on which Lomé is based. Moreover no definitive list of such products was established at the time of the conclusion of the convention. The EC is able to unilaterally extend the scope of this exclusion, as occurred upon Spanish and Portuguese accession to the community. One might expect a broadening of this exception in the light of recent changes in Eastern Europe and in particular the unification of Germany. For certain ACP states whose economies are largely dependent on a few commodities the effect can be catastrophic.

It is, thus, clear that the Lomé Convention, like the Ankara Agreement, does not prevent the preference of EC interests. However, while this is apparent from an analysis of the text of Lomé this is not true of either the GATT or the Ankara Agreement. When the latter was concluded Turkey enjoyed a strong bargaining position. It could offer to the West a commodity which it desperately needed – labour. It was in a position to resist the 'but if' clauses included in Lomé. What is interesting then is the way in which the EC introduced the same insecurity into this apparently stable agreement. This it did through the application of a carefully contrived legal concept, apparently objectively applied and devoid of political significance. What is clear then is that this apparently uncontentious legal tool has accorded to the ECJ the power to render worthless any law which has, in political terms, become an error of judgement.

What is the significance of this? The answer which should surely form a central part of any EC law course is that the EC is a political grouping whose politics do not stop at the door of the ECJ. Underlying, and implicit in, the court's intention to promote 'European integration' are political premises which have a significant and debilitating effect upon non-EC countries. From Turkey to the Lomé countries their very ability to exist and provide for their citizens is affected in a covert and apparently non-political way. Just as the decision in *Demirel* negated a fairly negotiated and apparently binding treaty, so the decisions concerning GATT and the Lomé countries legitimate the maintenance of protectionist measures on the part of the EC. The operation of the CAP not only makes such commodity production in poor countries uneconomic, but also, through the dumping of excess EC subsidised produce, destroys the alternative markets that might exist. EC law is politics and the results are both crucial and devastating.

Notes

1. See Regulation 2641/84 which allows the EC to retaliate against trading partners who engage in 'illicit commercial practices' defined by reference to international law. Also Regulation 2423/88 enables the EC to impose anti-dumping duties in the event of unfair price discrimination. The operation of this law has given rise to accusations that its aim is a protectionist one.
2. See note 1, above.
3. This was laid down in Article 36 of the Additional Protocol which states 'Freedom of movement for workers between member-states of the Community and Turkey shall be secured by progressive stages in accordance with the principles set out in Article 12 of the Agreement of Association between the end of the twelfth and the twenty-second year after the entry into force of that Agreement. The Council of Association shall decide on the rules necessary to that end.'
4. For an example of the amalgamation of these issues see *Completing the Internal Market,* White Paper from the Commission, June 1985, especially paragraphs 47–56.
5. For a critical analysis of the Lomé Conventions see J. Ravenhill (1985) *Collective Clientelism.*

Afterword: Law's (Un)spoken (Pre)sumptuous (Pre)suppositions
Ian Grigg-Spall and Paddy Ireland

In this afterword we seek to excavate the presuppositions about society, people and social relations that underlie law. Our object is simple, to show that the appearances of freedom which are presented by capitalism, and in particular by law under capitalism, depend upon, and mask, conditions of unfreedom and domination which are an inseparable part of capitalist society.

We argue that the extolled liberal elements of capitalist law, which celebrate law as the basis of individual freedom, hinge upon, and obscure, deeply conservative elements which give priority to order, authority and hierarchy; that the free individuals of liberal legal theory are, as Foucault claims, constituted by a highly illiberal network of disciplinary institutions. We move on to suggest that an explanation of the contradiction within capitalism and capitalist law between freedom and domination is to be found in Marx's distinction between the sphere of circulation – the marketplace where freedom reigns – and the sphere of production – where domination and subordination prevail. From this we argue that the freedom which money apparently provides for individuals in the market conceals the role of money as the supreme representation of social power, the foundation of systematic relations of domination and subordination. Finally, we defend the structuralism of our analysis against postmodernism, arguing that the freedoms which postmodernists proclaim – of choice, diversity, individualisation and endless novelty – reflect the surface appearances of capitalist society and its decadent cultivation of imaginary appetites, and conceal the misery and subordination of the vast majority of the world's population upon which they hang.

In short, then, our argument is that each of the different forms taken by freedom under capitalism – liberal freedom, the freedom of money and the freedoms of postmodernism – depends upon the suppression of its own conditions of existence and of the many other forms of freedom excluded by the necessary dominations of capitalist social relations.

Liberalism in Law

Liberal presuppositions in law are most evident in contract, tort, criminal law and constitutional law (see Thomson, Conaghan & Mansell, Norrie, and De Friend in this chapter). One of the defining characteristics of these substantive areas is their individualism, and liberalism (in the political and philosophical sense) is, first and foremost, highly individualistic. It begins with the individual, seeing 'him' – the liberal individual is recognisably male (Gilligan, 1982) – and 'his' rights as taking precedence over society and other collectivities. Individuals are seen as coming before society, both in the sense of having higher moral value attached to them, and in the temporal sense of being seen as existing before society. From this perspective, society is merely an aggregate of individuals. In law this is reflected in the way the world is individualised; both human and corporate bodies are declared 'individual legal subjects' and disputes are treated as purely *individual* affairs between these autonomous persons. The liberal individualism of law in these areas is also expressed in its methodological individualism, in the great emphasis it places on ideas of individual cause, responsibility and culpability (see especially Conaghan & Mansell in this chapter). For most people in our society these presuppositions are simply 'common sense'.

The people who occupy these areas of law also display peculiarly liberal characteristics. They exist as isolated individuals, independent of any social relationships, and are said to possess both a fixed, presocial, self-centred, 'human nature', and natural, equal, inalienable rights which pre-date society and which are in no way dependent for their validity on positive law. In short, liberal law presumes a world of isolated, independent and formally equal individuals. It therefore declares people to be equal in the face of glaring inequalities: social class, gender, education, wealth, race and economic power are proclaimed irrelevant. Individuals are 'decontextualised', abstracted from their real conditions of existence. They are removed from their actual social relations and stripped of most of their distinguishing features. Only the ubiquitous 'A' and 'B' of case summaries and student legal problems remain (see Thomson and Kennedy in this chapter).

The contradiction between these formally equal individuals and their real conditions of existence is most evident in the area of property law. For liberal law above all else secures individual private property rights, and it is, of course, the regular, predictable and formally equal enforcement of abstract private property rights (including rights of inheritance) which underpins the gross inequalities of wealth and power in our society. Property law is, therefore, *par excellence* the domain of liberalism, to such an extent that most liberal philosophers consider private property rights to be more sacrosanct than individual freedom and democracy (Arblaster, 1984).

Abstracted from society, these property-owning, liberal legal subjects stand as essentially unconnected strangers. Strangers who are self-interested and who owe no obligations to one another. As a leading tort textbook says, 'An adult who stands by and watches a child (with whom he has no special relationship) drown in a foot of water may have to answer before some higher tribunal somewhere, sometime, but he is not accountable ... in the English Courts ...' (Rogers, 1979, p. 77). Individuals, in other words, are 'free' to decide for themselves. Here liberal law mirrors not only the liberal view of essential social relations, but also the liberal view of morality: to watch the child drown *may* be, not *is*, morally wrong. For liberals morality is a matter of individual choice, an aspect of individual autonomy, responsibility and freedom. In general, therefore, law should not legislate morality, for this is essentially an individual and private matter. Nor should it intervene when people act in a way that might be morally questionable.

It follows that obligations between these abstract, property-owning individuals will arise principally by contract – by agreement and consent – and that in contractual negotiations these individuals will (naturally) drive the hardest possible bargain, for this is simply to act as a rational, self- interested individual. In short, relations between people are assumed to be essentially competitive and conflicting. Certain crucial characteristics of law follow from this. First, law becomes an affair of individual rights, with legal decision-making turning on who has the better right. And secondly, since rights can only be expressed in rules, law essentially becomes an affair of rules. Under the rule of law – the rule of rules not persons – law appears not merely as an affair of rules but as an affair of abstract rules applied to abstract persons (Gabel, 1980; Pashukanis, 1983).

These liberal presuppositions and their reflection in liberal law and liberal legal process are generally treated not only as unproblematic but as a true representation of social relations and of legal processes in our society (Kairys in this book). They are taken for granted, experienced as natural, as facts, as part of the way things (inevitably) are. They become part of the 'common sense' we have both about ourselves and our relationships with others, and about the role of law, courts and judges. Indeed, even after being confronted with the extensive empirical, sociological, historical and anthropological evidence to the contrary, many students continue to believe that precedents really do determine judicial decisions; that it is 'human nature' for persons to be selfish, egoistic, materialistic and competitive; and that equality, freedom and democracy are the hallmarks of our society.

Conservatism in Law

However, as some of the articles in this book indicate, not all law is underlain by liberal presuppositions. On the contrary, in certain areas of law the underlying ideology is demonstrably *not* one of individuality, freedom and equality. For example, attempts to represent the relations between individuals and state officials, between women and men, between employees and employers, and between students and teachers as essentially contractual relations between free and equal legal subjects simply do not stand close scrutiny (see de Friend, Bottomley, Edie et al. and Kennedy). In many situations law (and judges) simply do not see the world in liberal terms, but rather maintain and express a specific order of hierarchy and authority, of domination and subordination, and of inequality and status. In short, the implicit theory underlying law is often conservative, not liberal. In our view, the conservative philosopher Roger Scruton rightly argues that law, although theorised in liberal terms, is, in fact, predominantly conservative in nature (1984, p. 71).

Conservatism in this political-philosophical sense (which must be distinguished from party political conservatism), rejects the fundamental premises of liberal individualism. For conservatives, individuals cannot be understood in the abstract; they are not intelligible without reference to the social relations of which they are part. Contrary to the liberal view, society and social institutions are antecedent to the individuals which compose them. 'The autonomous individual', Scruton writes, 'is the product of practices which designate him as social. The individual man is the man who recognises that he is no mere individual ... Individual freedom is the great social artifact which, in trying to represent itself as nature alone, generates the myth of liberalism' (Scruton, 1984, p. 73). Individuals are the products of social institutions; they are social 'artifacts'. Therefore, to attack these institutions is to 'assault ... the social order which produced the self' (*Salisbury Review*, July 1985, p. 51). It follows that for conservatives the preservation of social institutions is the supreme political goal. As Scruton writes: 'One major difference between conservatism and liberalism consists ... in the fact that, for the conservative, the value of individual liberty is not absolute, but stands subject to another and higher value, the authority of established government.' He goes on to write: 'In politics the conservative attitude seeks above all for government, and regards no citizen as possessed of a natural right that transcends his obligation to be ruled. Even democracy ... can be discarded without detriment to the civil well-being as the conservative conceives it.' Authority and order are the watchwords of the conservative (Scruton, 1984, pp. 16–19).

For conservatives not only must freedom as a goal be subordinated to the preservation of social institutions and order, it can only be endowed with meaning by them. There is no such thing as freedom in the abstract. Freedom is 'the bequest of institutions ... not the precondition but the consequence of an accepted social arrangement ... Freedom is comprehensible as a social goal only when subordinate to something else, to an organisation or arrangement which defines the individual aim' (Scruton, 1984, p. 19). Thus, 'the conservative philosophy of liberty proceeds from the conservative philosophy of authority, authority which is to be found in the social order.' Scope for individual freedom is only to be found 'in the interstices of social and moral authority' (Nisbet, 1984, p. 19–20). For conservatives therefore, to be 'fit to be free' entails the acceptance and internalisation of the social, political and economic institutions of contemporary capitalist society. Correspondingly, their view of the role and importance of the free market is very different from that of liberals. For conservatives a free market does not suffice to generate social order and adequate social institutions: 'Civil society exists and endures not merely because people associate freely and are guided by negotiation, but also because their lives take place against a backdrop of institutions endorsed and upheld by the law' (*Salisury Review*, July 1986, p. 53). Liberal theory, William Waldegrave asserts, 'is unconvincing ... unless the liberal will say what moral disciplines must be imposed on the individual to make [the liberal's] self-regulating mechanism [the market] work' (1978, p. 52).

The priority given to institutions over individuals has other important consequences. Conservatives see society as essentially composed of a network of these social institutions – the family, the school, the workplace, the nation and so on; institutions in which people submit to the authority of others. Authority of this kind, and the duties and obligations which accompany it, cannot, they argue, be derived from contract or consent. In the conservative view, most social, political and legal obligations are not the product of individual choice and volition. 'It would be absurd', Scruton writes, 'to think of family obligations as in any way arising from a free relinquishing of autonomy ... the language of contract here fails to make contact with the facts' (1984, p. 31). Much the same, they suggest, is true of, inter alia, the employment relation, marriage, and the relationship between state and citizen. In short, people participate in many patently non-contractual relationships characterised by inequality, hierarchy, domination and subordination, with essentially non-negotiable terms. They nevertheless experience them as perfectly legitimate. 'It is a remarkable fact', Scruton says, 'that people recognise authority ... in social arrangements, in institutions, and in the state. It is equally remarkable that this authority can command their allegiance ...' (1984, p. 28). For conservatives, legitimacy is as much a matter of prejudice as it is of reason. (1984, p. 12). 'The condition of society', Scruton argues, 'presupposes this general connivance, and a conservative will seek to uphold all those practices and institutions – among which, of course, the family is pre-eminent – through which the habits of allegiance are acquired' (1984, p. 33).

In our view, de Friend, Bottomley, Edie and Scott demonstrate in different ways the extent to which law and legal practices in certain areas have conservative not liberal presuppositions. It is clear, for example, that in the field of constitutional law the maintenance of a particular version of social order is frequently given a higher value than individual rights and freedoms. In labour law, it is equally clear that the courts view the employment relationship as essentially one of authority and hierarchy despite its liberal contractual form. Employees ('servants') are held to owe implied duties of loyalty, obedience and fidelity to their employers ('masters') which override liberal notions of contract. Similarly, law regularly and predictably conceives of relationships between men and women in marriage as hierarchical and patriarchal. Although marriage is legally theorised in liberal contractual terms, the social practices within marriage are formulated by the courts in terms of masculine authority and female dependence and subordination (O'Donovan, 1985; Pateman, 1988). In all of these legal areas these hierarchies are, for most people, 'common sense', part of the way things necessarily are.

Finally, Kennedy's description of teacher–student relationships in law schools (in this chapter) stands as an example of such relationships in education generally. Up to the age of 18 these relationships are still legally theorised on the basis of the concept of 'in loco parentis', the teacher being granted the authority of the parent over the child. Here again, such hierarchy and subordination is, for most people, natural and inevitable. Yet, as Kennedy shows, hierarchy in schools and universities hinders rather than aids education in a liberal sense. What it does do, most successfully, is to prepare people for the hierarchies and inequalites of the workplace, whether in a City law firm or a factory (Gorz, 1976; John Fitzpatrick, Watkinson in Chapter 3).

This catalogue of areas in which the legal interpretations of everyday practices are based on conservative presuppositions could easily be extended. Foucault in his writings has, of course, made central the prison and the asylum (see Adelman & Foster in Chapter 1). He, like Scruton, is well aware of the contradiction between capitalism's projected ideology of liberalism and its deeply illiberal practices. He writes: 'Historically, the process by which the bourgeoisie became in the course of the eighteenth century the politically dominant class was marked by the establishment of an explicit, coded and formally egalitarian juridical framework ... But the development and generalisation of disciplinary mechanisms constituted the other dark side of these processes. The general juridical form that guaranteed a system of rights that were egalitarian in principle was supported by these tiny, everyday physical mechanisms, by all those systems of micropower that are essentially non-egalitarian and asymmetrical that we call the disciplines.' These disciplinary institutions, he goes on to argue, possess judicial and penal mechanisms which are autonomous of law. There are 'parallel judges' within them (technical experts, teachers, doctors, managers, psychologists, social workers and so on), operating in a sphere 'well protected from judicial or popular intervention'. This is the 'dark' or 'despotic' side of the rule of law – the recognition in and by law of the power and authority of certain persons over others. According to Foucault, the disciplines appear to be an 'infra-law', but are in reality a 'counter-law'. For him the contradiction lies in the opposition between the disciplines and (liberal) legality, rather than, as we have argued, within legality itself (Foucault, 1979, pp. 220–4; Fine, 1979).

Foucault explicitly recognises the non-contractual nature of the disciplinary institutions. Within these disciplinary institutions, people are not classified according to 'universal [liberal] norms'; rather they are 'hierarchically' organised in relation to one another. The disciplines constitute 'the foundation of the formal, juridical liberties'. While 'the contract may have been regarded as the ideal foundation of law and political power; panopticism constituted the technique, universally widespread, of coercion ... The "Enlightenment", which discovered the liberties, also invented the disciplines' (1979, pp. 222–3).

For Foucault, therefore, 'the disciplinary state is placed before the [liberal] constitutional state' (Carty, 1990, p. 25). 'Normalising disciplinary power', says Peter Fitzpatrick, 'provide[s] the conditions for liberal legality ... a constitutive pre-adaption of the individual to freedom' (see Carty, 1990, p. 101). For both Foucaultians and conservatives the disciplinary institutions play a crucial socialising role in society. For Foucault they produce 'useful and docile bodies'; for Scruton they create the 'socialised self', the individual 'fit to be free'. For Foucault the 'free subject' of law, liberalism and democratic politics is 'already in himself the effect of a subordination much more profound than himself'. For Scruton 'the autonomous [liberal] individual is the product of practices which designate him as social' (1984, p. 72–3).

Law, then, is underlain by a mixture of liberal and conservative presuppositions. However, while the principles and values underlying 'liberal law' have received much attention, the same is not true of 'conservative law'. *One* reason for this is that liberal principles, unlike those of conservatism, are both appealing and capable of being spoken at a high level of abstraction. As such they have become the basis for capitalism's abstract claims to securing individual freedom and equality, claims which can only exist by suppressing the realities of the world capitalist order and its everyday practices and institutions. Of the conservative presuppositions which underlie many of our institutions and much of our law we hear very little. As Scruton says, 'The dogma of conservatism ... [is] startling and even offensive to many whose feelings it none the less quite accurately describes' (1984, p. 25).

The liberal elements – individual freedom and equality – constitute the safely spoken, sumptuous suppositions of law. The conservative elements – hierarchy, authority, and domination – constitute law's unspoken presuppositions, spoken only at risk of being declared offensively presumptuous.

Liberalism, Conservatism and Capitalism: A(n) (Im)pertinent Analysis

In this section we rashly consider whether it is possible to account for law's contradictory presuppositions. In our view, the starting point for such an analysis can be found in the separation within capitalism between the sphere of market exchange (circulation) and the sphere of production. 'The sphere of circulation', Marx wrote, 'is a very Eden of the innate rights of man. It is the ... realm of Freedom, Equality,

Property and Bentham ...'. Freedom and equality because in the marketplace buyer and sellers 'contract as free persons, who are equal before the law, ... exchang[ing] equivalent for equivalent'. Property because each disposes 'only of what is his own'. And Bentham 'because each looks only to his own advantage' (Marx, 1976, p. 280). For Marx the market is the exclusive realm and material basis of liberal values. However, when we leave this 'noisy sphere, where everything takes place on the surface' and enter 'the hidden abode of production, on whose threshold hangs the notice "No admittance except on business", a certain change takes place in the physiognomy of our dramatis personae. He who was previously the money owner now strides out in front as a capitalist; the possessor of labour power follows as his worker.' In the factory, 'the capitalist formulates his power over workers like a private legislator ...'; all freedom 'in law and in fact' is ended, for here 'the employer is absolute law-giver ... making regulations at will ...' (Marx, 1976, p. 550). This is a realm of manifest conservative hierarchy and authority.

Capitalism is not merely a market society, but a market society where labour – that is, human beings – are commodities, objects which are bought and sold in the market. From the eighteenth and nineteenth centuries selling oneself for a wage became the usual way to 'make a living' (Malcolmson, 1981). During this period money too came to play an increasingly important role in society, facilitating exchange by representing the value of commodities. In a market capitalist society, therefore, social relationships come to be mediated both by the market and by money. This dramatically affects the way in which individuals see themselves and their relations with others, generating a reification and mystification of the products of labour; what Marx called 'commodity and money fetishism' (Marx, 1976, Sayer, 1987).

The things that people produce – food, clothing, cars and so on - develop a value in money terms – 30p, £50, £6000. In other words, money comes to represent social labour. The products of human labour are 'fetishised' in that these values seem to inhere in the objects themselves. The origin of products in human labour and the connection between that labour and their value (money price) is concealed. As a result the complex social division of labour responsible for the production of commodities, and the many social relationships which make individual existence possible, become lost to consciousness. Social relations take the immediate form not of direct relations between people, but the fetishised form of relations between things – commodities and money. These processes take their most extreme form in the fetishisation of money itself, the process whereby money – which, as has been observed, does not have genitals and can produce nothing (Koffler, 1979) – develops the apparent ability, as interest-bearing capital, to produce more money by itself (Grigg-Spall et al. in this chapter). In short, then, money and market exchange draw a veil over, and mask, social relationships. Harvey explains: 'If I were to trace back where my dinner came from I would become aware of the myriads of people involved in putting even the simplest of meals on the table. Yet I can consume my repast without having to know anything about them. Their conditions of life, their joys, discontents and aspirations remain hidden from me. This masking arises because our social relations with those who contribute to our daily sustenance are hidden behind the exchange of things [one object, money, for another object, the commodity] in the marketplace ... There is no trace of exploitation on the lettuce, no taste of apartheid in the fruit from South Africa.' (1989b, p. 8) As we eat our South African oranges, wear our Thai shorts and watch our Hong Kong TVs and South Korean video recorders, we give not a thought for their producers (and their conditions of life), those upon whom – in reality, if not in liberal fiction – we are totally dependent.

The commodity and money fetishisms generated by market capitalism provide the material basis of liberal thought. As a result of the reification and mystification of labour and the products of labour the dependence of people upon others for their everyday existence is lost to consciousness. People come to appear, and to experience themselves, as essentially unconnected to one another; as 'isolated strangers', as 'others', free of any social and economic ties. Society appears to be the coming together, through market exchange and contract, of these isolated individuals. Indeed, in capitalist society, with the commodification of labour we are, in a certain sense, isolated – made 'others' – even from ourselves, for we are turned into objects for sale, objects whose values are fixed mysteriously in the market. A principle aim in life becomes to sell oneself successfully, to turn oneself into a commodity attractive to prospective employers – something the student seeking a job and worrying about his or her exam results will readily appreciate. Our skill, energy and creativity become just more saleable things and our sense of personal worth becomes largely dependent upon our success or failure as commodities.

In this topsy-turvy world, while people appear to be essentially independent of, and unrelated to, one another, they appear (and in a genuine sense are) totally dependent upon *money* – pieces of paper and lumps of metal! For it is money which enables them to buy commodities, to buy the labour and the products of labour of others. In a capitalist society, therefore, the ability to exercise power over others does not typically take a direct and personal form, but the indirect form of power over a thing – money. This too affects the way things appear, for, as Marx observed, money is a 'great leveller and cynic', an equaliser, which undermines fixed social relations and eliminates many marks of distinction. It is also a form of social power that can be held by private persons – by isolated individuals – without apparent reference to others. As such 'it forms the basis for a wide-ranging individual liberty', for owners of money are 'free, within constraints, to choose how, when, where, and with whom to use that money to satisfy their needs, wants and fancies – a fact that the free market ideologues perpetually dwell upon to the exclusion of all else' (Harvey, 1989a, p. 103; 1989b, p. 168). Therefore, the sphere of market exchange and 'the community of money' are 'strongly marked by individualism and certain conceptions of liberty, freedom, and equality backed by laws of private property ... and freedom of contract' (1989b, p. 168). It is, nevertheless, supremely ironical that in a world in which self-sufficiency is negligible and dependence upon others overwhelming, liberal individualist ideas about the world should be so prevalent. This is not the result of a grand conspiracy by the 'ruling class' to conceal the real nature of capitalism behind illusory notions of freedom, equality and individualism. It is, rather, generated by the realities of market capitalism itself; by the everyday practical activity of market exchange. The liberal elements of both law and 'common sense' reflect the 'fetishised forms of appearance' of capitalist social relations; the superficial 'phenomenal forms' of those relations readily observed in the marketplace.

There is, however, 'a deep tension [in our society] between the individualism, freedom and equality' found in the marketplace and 'implied in the possession of money' and the class relations experienced in the making and distribution of that money (Harvey, 1989b, p. 169), a tension mirrored in the contradictory nature of law. There is much more to capitalism than commodity production, market exchange and money relationships. The social relations which lie beneath the fetishised forms of the market are relations of class, race and sexual division: the systematic inequalities, hierarchies, dominations and subordinations of our society.

In our view the principle source of these hierarchies and inequalities lies in the nature of capitalism as an economic system based not merely on production for market, but on production for private profit. As a result capitalist production is necessarily hierarchical, for as Gorz writes: 'If workers had a say in the goals and arrangement of the work [profit] would cease to be the dominant goal of production. It would be subordinated to or balanced by other aims such as the pleasure, interest, and usefulness of work, the use-value of the products, the increase of free time and so on.' But 'capital's aims are foreign to the worker'; profitability has to be 'imposed on workers as an alien demand to which all others must be subordinated' (Gorz, 1976, p. 56; see also Edie et al. in this chapter). Capitalism inevitably treats workers in instrumental terms, as (reified) 'factors of production', to be exploited as profitably as possible. Indeed, as capitalism develops, moving into the era of 'machinofacture', the grip of the profitability imperative over production tightens. The competitive battle between capitals comes to revolve around technological advances which increase the productivity of labour, reducing the labour time that it takes to produce particular commodities and their cost. Firms *have* to keep abreast of these advances for technologically backward firms, unable to produce at the average socially necessary labour time, will be uncompetitive and forced out of the market. In short, the profitability imperative comes to confront not only capitalists but society as a whole as an external coercive law, for without profit there is no production. Production ceases not when needs have been met, but when profitability ceases. The need for profit comes to be experienced as an imperative inherent in matter itself, as inexorable and incontestable, as the result of the apparently neutral laws of a complex machine, beyond volition and dispute. This has profound consequences both within production and beyond.

Within production people have to be disciplined into accepting the profitability imperative, its requirements and consequences. Historically, central to this disciplining is the wresting from workers of significant control over the work process, through (inter alia) the introduction of factory production and workplace hierarchies. Contrary to the commonsense view, neither of these originally emerged for reasons of technical necessity or productive efficiency, but because of their effectiveness as mechanisms of discipline and supervision, their 'efficiency' 'in the context of alienated and forced labour, [of] work subjugated to [the] alien goal' of profitability. 'Discipline was the essence of the factory' (Gorz, 1976, p. 56; Marglin, 1971). In constituting control as a separate function of managers, technicians and engineers, the factory hierarchy was instrumental in 'denying workers any possible control over the conditions and methods of machine production'. *Technically*, as Gorz observes, the factory could dispense with these functionaries and the hierarchies of which they are part; *politically*, however, they perform a crucial function, 'perpetuat[ing] the workers dependence, subordination and separation from the means and process of production' (Gorz, p. 57).

Capitalism craves more than discipline in production. It needs 'broader social discipline' in society as the basis for discipline in production (Corrigan & Sayer, 1985, p. 184; Kennedy in this chapter). In the eighteenth and nineteenth centuries, the early years of industrial capitalism, this broader disciplining process involved the 'radical restructuring of man's social nature'. As Sydney Pollard says, people who were 'non- accumulative, non-acquisitive, accustomed to work for subsistence, not for the maximisation of income, had to be made obedient to the cash stimulus ...' (1963, p. 254). Wherever people were in control of their own working lives, the work pattern was one of alternate bouts of intense labour and idleness. This had to be changed; so too did cultural traditions and practices and the sense that people had of time itself (Thomson, 1967, p. 73). It was during this period that many of the modern disciplinary institutions emerged, and with them there evolved many of the characteristics now commonly attributed to a universal ('male') human nature. As William Lazonick writes: 'By the 1870's in England, most of the characteristic institutions of the advanced capitalist systems of the twentieth century – the factory, the welfare system, the industrial city, municipal police forces, the dependent family unit, mass public schooling, [trade] unions, electoral democracy – had emerged' (1978, p. 1). It was, Lazonick continues, 'class conflict over the subjection of labour to capital which was [one of] the motivating force[s] in the development of [these] institutions ...'. One of the main spurs behind the development of mass state education, for example, was the desire to 'inculcate and reinforce the norms of capitalist production in the next generation of workers'; it was 'a prime ideological mechanism in the attempt by the capitalist class, through the medium of the state, to continually reproduce a labour force which would passively accept that subjection' (1978, pp. 26–7, 14). As Gorz asserts: 'Teaching is not and has never been the aim of school ... There are many learning methods more fruitful and efficient than schooling ... people are schooled ... because the system is anxious to socialise them in a certain way ... they must be educated into submission, discipline and respect for hierarchy ... [adapted] to the barbarity of the factory, to the hierarchical, fragmented division of labour' (Gorz, 1976, p. 58; Kennedy in this chapter).

Historically, this disciplining took place against the backdrop of preexisting social forms, reminding us that outside of theoretical models there is no such thing as capitalism in general; that real capitalisms only ever exist as particular, historical forms of civilisation. Capitalisms are actively constructed through the transformation of preexisting social forms. For example, although one might imagine a non-patriarchal, non-sexist or non-racist capitalism – patriarchy, sexism and racism cannot be directly derived from the concept of capital – 'all real capitalisms have in practice been constructed through [for example] patriarchal forms of social relationship, which have a history independent of [and prior to] that of capitalism itself' (Corrigan & Sayer, 1985, pp. 189–90). While capitalism certainly invented wage-labour as a dominant form, it did not invent all subordinated groups (or, as postmodernists might say, 'others'). It has, however, 'certainly made use of and promoted them in highly structured ways' (Harvey, 1989a, p. 104).

In this section we have offered the beginnings of an analysis of law's presuppositions. Money – which is a shorthand way of saying capitalist relations, market values and trade and exchange (Macfarlane, 1985) – is the key to both. On the one hand, as we have said, it provides the basis for wide-ranging individual liberty, a liberty which enables us to develop ourselves as apparent individuals without reference to others. On the other hand, in capitalist society it is the supreme representation of social power, conferring upon people the ability to command others. Money enables the building of systematic relations of domination and subordination. As Harvey observes, it 'fuses the political and the economic into a genuine political economy of overwhelming power relations', a problem that 'micro-theorists of power, like Foucault, systematically avoid' (1989a, p. 102). Money unifies precisely through its capacity to accommodate individualism and freedom with hierarchy and domination. It is, therefore, the unification and explanation of the liberal and conservative elements of capitalist society.

Money creates 'a grey world where good and evil are interchangeable; where it is impossible to be certain, to have absolute moral standards; where nothing is entirely black or white'. Money renders 'every moral system throughout the world equally valid', so that *'within* every system whatever is, is right' (Macfarlane, 1985, pp. 69–72). Money, therefore, also enables us to grasp why postmodernists, having acknowledged the authenticity of 'other voices', are unable to distinguish between them. They treat the voices of international bankers 'on a par with' those of 'women, ethnic and racial minorities, colonised peoples [and] unemployed youth' and thereby 'disempower' them (Harvey, 1989a, p. 117). For these reasons the postmodernist concern for the 'signifier' (money) rather than the 'signified' (the commodity), the medium (money) rather than the message (social labour), and emphasis on fiction rather than function, on signs rather than things (see Harvey, 1989a, p. 102) is a reinforcement rather than a transformation of the role of money and, therefore, inevitably of capitalism itself.

Conclusion

This structural account and explanation of liberal and conservative law returns us to some of the theoretical debates raised in Chapter 1 and stands in opposition to postmodernism which is at pains to 'free us from a belief in underlying structures of power' (Thomson in Chapter 1). Postmodernists have attacked 'totalising' 'meta-theories' or 'meta-narratives' (Douzinas & Warrington in Chapter 1) which attempt to connect diverse phenomena, insisting that we cannot aspire 'to any unified representation of the world, or picture it as a totality full of connections and differentiations ...' (Harvey, 1989a, p. 52). The postmodernists insist that the world is a place of 'individualisation' and 'fragmentation' which cannot be understood as a totality. Indeed, they take them at face value and 'actually celebrate the reifications and partitionings, the ... masking and cover-up, [and] all the fetishisms of locality, place, or social grouping' (Harvey, 1989a, pp. 116–17).

The *fact* of individualisation and fragmentation is not at issue. They *are* inevitable features of capitalist society. They are characteristics of a society dominated by commodity and money fetishisms, which thereby seems to be composed of 'others', of millions of interconnecting but fundamentally fragmented social relationships without any structure; aspects of a society dominated by a labour process in which human beings are reduced to mere fragments of persons, to mere 'factors of production'; and of a society ruled by coercive laws of competition which force the 'constant revolutionising of production, uninterrupted disturbance of all social relations, everlasting uncertainty and agitation ...' (Marx & Engels, 1952, p. 25), and the 'melting of all that is solid into air'.

This last point is worth emphasising for it provides the basis for understanding postmodernism's obsession with uncertainty, instability, disconnection, style and fashion. For in the modern era, as Harvey writes, 'the struggle to maintain profitability sends capitalists racing off to explore all kinds of ... possibilities'. In this process, 'new production lines are opened up and that means the creation of new wants and needs in others, thus emphasising the cultivation of imaginary appetites and the role of fantasy, caprice and whim'. The result is to exacerbate insecurity and instability, 'as masses of capital and workers shift from one line of production to another, leaving whole sectors devastated, while the perpetual flux in consumer wants, tastes, and needs becomes a permanent [and personal] locus of uncertainty and struggle' (1989b, p. 106; see Ellis, 1991). The geographical movement of capital and labour in a relentless search for profit adds a further dimension to this. 'If, therefore, the only secure thing about modernity is insecurity, then it is not hard to see from where that insecurity derives' (Harvey, 1989a, p. 107).

While, undoubtedly, meta-theories have often tended to ignore important differences and have given insufficient attention to contradictions and detail, postmodernism fails in losing sight of the determining role played by the imperatives of capitalist production – upon which our material existence depends – and of the 'totalising' role played by state and law in regulating institutions, relations and subjectivities so as to ensure that these imperatives are met.

3
Critical Legal Practice

A first principle of a 'counter-hegemonic' legal practice must be to subordinate the goal of getting people their rights to the goal of building an authentic or unalienated political consciousness. This obviously does not mean that one should not try to win one's cases; nor does it necessarily mean that one should not continue to organise groups by appealing to rights. But the great weakness of a rights-orientated legal practice is that it does not address itself to a central precondition for building a sustained political movement – that of overcoming the psychological conditions upon which both the power of the legal system a:.d the power of social hierarchy in general rest. In fact excessive preoccupation with 'rights-consciousness' tends in the long run to reinforce alienation and powerlessness because the appeal to rights inherently affirms that the source of social power resides in the State rather than in the people themselves.

(Peter Gabel and Paul Harris, 'Building Power and Breaking Images: Critical Legal Theory and Practice of Law', *Review of Law and Social Change*, 1982, vol. II, p. 369)

We will not even adequately defend ourselves in the present, never mind usher in a brave new citizen's world, if we adopt a strategy which is based around the law, constitutional reform and the acceptable face of the market.

(John Fitzpatrick, 'Legal Practice and Socialist Practice', in this chapter.)

Preface

In our view, the practice of law must form an integral part of the critical project and this chapter attempts to bridge the gulf between critical scholars and critical practitioners. We must seek to identify the relationship between critical theory and legal practice and offer not only a critique of orthodox practice but also a discussion of the possibilities and limits of a critical practice.

Views on this subject range from those who see their role as purely defensive – as 'merely' seeking to protect the oppressed against the worst abuses of the system; through those who seek in their practice an extension of rights; those who consider that law offers a range of dramatic 'moments' within which to publicise the oppressive nature of law and legal institutions, to those who would argue for the principle of a counter-hegemonic legal practice – a practice which is power-orientated not rights-orientated – a practice which seeks to build, around legal struggles, a political organisation against the domination of law, legal definitions and indeed lawyers. The important element in all of these positions is the attempt to abstract from the concrete case and consider theoretically the strategy to be followed.

Further, as with legal education, the organisational structures of law centres, solicitors' practices and bar chambers have received little or no attention. As in law schools, we must recognise that organisational changes are crucial to the creation of a new generation of critical lawyers. The traditional forms must be discarded and new democratic working relationships developed. On this issue we have a long way to go.

Critical Legal Practice:
Beyond Abstract Radicalism
Kim Economides and Ole Hansen

Critical legal studies in Britain claims essentially to be a progressive intellectual challenge to the dominant traditions in legal scholarship. It has given a higher priority to the task of integrating legal theory within social theory than to the critical examination of professional legal practice. In other words, it is the activity of the law school, rather than what goes on in the rest of the world, which has been chosen as the principal focus of critical scholarship.

As a result, the relationship between critical legal theory and progressive legal practice appears at best problematical and at worst non-existent. Or, rather, it appears so to critical legal scholars. Most practising lawyers are too busy getting on with their work to notice, let alone worry about, the relationship between their activities and legal theory. While we have a theory in search of a movement, we have yet to identify a movement in search of theory.

In this article we shall argue the need for critical legal scholars to take practice seriously, and the need for progressive practitioners to be equally serious in accepting the contributions that academics can make. The practices of law and the institutional environments which envelop them must become a more important concern to the critical project if it wishes to retain the transformation of legal and social systems as part of its rhetoric. That should be uncontentious – as uncontentious as the statement that theory which places itself in the classificatory category 'legal' must have some point of reference with empirical reality as found in legal practice.

But in the world of critical legal studies it is by no means always so. A significant strand within critical legal thought (particularly that displaying a tendency towards nihilism) emphasises the deconstruction of the discourse latent in existing legal doctrine and practice. The resultant trashing exercise tends to destroy any pretensions that lawyers might have about the compatibility of progressive politics and legal practice. Bankowski and Mungham provided an early example in *Images of Law*:

> First, lawyers, in the long term, can have no material interest in conceding very much to the poor. In other words, the more the client knows, the less the lawyer is able to earn. And second, a significant erosion of the monopoly of legal knowledge is not in the lawyer's interest either, for if this base begins to wither away then so does the claim of the lawyer to power and privileges in society. From this point of view it can be seen that the lawyer has need of the poor, but what we have yet to establish is whether the poor need lawyers. (1976, p. 78).

At another level critical thought actually rejects the notion of rights. Rights are seen as bourgeois myths, empty promises which are part of the existing hegemony and which place individualistic claims above the needs of the community (Gabel & Kennedy, 1984). Yet the assertion and defence of rights is often the main activity of progressive practitioners.[1]

Scheingold (1988) points out that this leads many critical theorists to regard practitioners with a fundamental scepticism – to the extent that 'radical lawyer' is considered to be a contradiction in terms and progressive practitioners are condemned for supposedly adapting their clients to the prevailing system and thereby enhancing the legitimacy of that system. In an attempt to find a way out of the impasse between theorists and practitioners Scheingold examines Campbell's (1983) attempt to formulate a socialist theory of rights. Scheingold finds that it does not work. Campbell's reformulation of bourgeois rights as duties of the socialist state may have internal coherence, but in the transformation, rights have lost their capacity for individual enforcement. Unenforceable 'rights' are simply not rights.

So we are back to square one. A vocal element within critical theorists would say, 'So what?' The postmodernist demolition squad would not consider that it was a matter for them to provide a theoretical basis for practice (Douzinas and Warrington in this book). A wider circle might argue, following the Frankfurt School, that critical theorists have no need to be concerned directly with social change. 'A critical theory', according to Geuss (Geuss, 1981), 'is a reflective theory which gives agents a kind of knowledge inherently productive of enlightenment and emancipation.'

As Cotterrell explains (1986, p. 8) there are clear limits to the scope of a critical theory which

cannot, and has no need to, specify particular social arrangements to be aimed at. Insofar as critical theory offers prescriptions beyond the narrowly methodological these are likely to be moral prescriptions. As such they cannot be turned by logical deduction into a form of specification of practical social arrangements. This can be done only by political calculation in specific historical circumstances.

But radical practitioners know and expect more than that. They know that progressive communities and socialist bureaucracies, as well as bourgeois legal systems, have gaps between their professed norms and their actual behaviour. And they also know that the assertion of an individual's legal rights may not only help that person but may also be a means for the community to ensure that its norms are met. However, they also see in practice how the assertion of individual legal rights may lead to resources being allocated not to those who need them most but to those who have the sharpest elbows.

The use of the Public Health Act 1936 by radical practitioners is a good case in point. That act (like the Environmental Protection Act 1990, its recent and almost identical replacement), among other things, lays down certain minimum standards of housing repair. In particular, if tenanted accommodation is in a state of disrepair which is prejudicial to health, a magistrates court may order the landlord to bring it up to standard (Environmental Protection Act 1990, s79). For the first 35 years or so of the Public Health Act's existence lawyers considered it to be merely part of the regulatory powers exercised by local authorities. Or rather, not exercised. Despite the fact that millions of homes fell below the statutory standard few prosecutions were brought. Left-wing local authorities differed little from the others.

But in the early 1970s the Public Health Act 1936 was developed into an important weapon for tenants. Radical lawyers and environmental health officers, principally in the law centres, discovered that s99 of the Act (now replaced by s82 of the EPA) enabled individuals to bring private prosecutions in the magistrates courts. They also pioneered ways of bringing prosecutions not only on behalf of individual tenants but on behalf of groups too. In many instances, individual court proceedings were part of wider campaigns to improve conditions in the community.

In the meantime, local authorities had themselves become the largest landlords in the country and the private rented market continued to shrink. Because of the appalling quality of much of the local authorities' housing stock and the slowness with which repairs are carried out – if they are carried out at all – most housing disrepair cases under the Public Health Act 1936 (and now the EPA) were brought against local authorities, and among the authorities it is probably the left-wing ones which are on the receiving end of most summonses. In some authorities, repairs are prioritised according to whether a court order has been made or threatened rather than on the basis of need, with the result that those tenants who do not or cannot use the law are unlikely to have repairs carried out however desperate the conditions in which they live, whereas others with access to the legal system will be able to have relatively trivial defects remedied.

The history of s99 (now s82 EPA 1990) shows both the accuracy and the limitations of critical legal theory in relation to contemporary radical practice. First, millions of homes, mostly inhabited by working-class local-authority tenants, fall below the minimum standards of the legislation; to those tenants the law is a myth. Secondly, the law offers no solution to the mass of those tenants: the housing conditions are due to their economic inequality and powerlessness. The legal system is in reality not open to most of them to assert their rights, and if, by some freak of fortune, they were all able to use the system, the substantive law would undoubtedly be changed because the state could not 'afford' the cost of bringing the housing up to standard. Thirdly, it is not necessarily the tenants living in the worst conditions but rather those with the sharpest elbows – time, energy, access to lawyers – who get their homes repaired.

But that is not the whole story. If radical practitioners had not found a means of individual enforcement of the duties imposed by the Public Health Act 1936, its requirements would have been ignored – rather as one suspects would happen to Campbell's 'socialist rights'. At least by their use of s99 radical practitioners have been able in some instances to put flesh on the legal myth. More importantly they have improved the housing standards and, in some cases, saved the health and lives of thousands of tenants. In some localities the impact has gone beyond individual cases; communities have been empowered as a result of campaigns in which s99 proceedings were a central part. And for the local authority which genuinely wants to be responsive to the needs of the local community, s99 proceedings can be a valuable indicator of whether its housing officials are delivering the goods – by no means all housing disrepair is caused by external financial constraints.

If critical theorists are serious about being part of a movement aiming at social transformation they must establish a close and meaningful relationship with radical practitioners. The achievements of the practitioners must be built on rather than sneered at. But at the same time, the practitioners, if they are not to fall into the pit of reformist politics, must accept the value of theoretical insights into the gaps between radical legal practice and the professed politics of the radical practitioners.

The historical obstacles against such a coming together may seem too large. In addition to the specific factors mentioned earlier, it could be said that in many respects the divisions between critical theorists and radical practitioners are simply another example of the general split between academic and practising lawyers, which seems to be deeper in England and Wales than in other jurisdictions and which has existed since the development of law as an academic discipline in the nineteenth century.

Partington (1988) has suggested that legal academics may not be as marginal to mainstream practice as has previously been supposed. While his statistics on academic involvement in practice are now somewhat dated he does show that academics have been more involved with practice than had hitherto been believed to be the case. But his definition of legal practice, which includes involvement in research and development of the law and legal services, is unlikely to be accepted by the mainstream practitioner. Nonetheless, Partington is clearly right in identifying a trend bringing practitioners and academics closer together. At the time he was writing large firms of solicitors were just beginning to recruit specialists to be in charge of in-house education and training. Now, some two years later, more than 40 firms have appointed, under various labels, training managers, most of whom were previously academic lawyers in universities or polytechnics.

In another development, the Law Society has decided to relinquish control of its Finals course to the academic institutions teaching it (Economides & Smallcombe, 1991; Hansen, 1990). Further, the Society has accepted that the institutions should be allowed – and perhaps even encouraged – to offer degrees which provide exemption from the Finals examination. The longer-term implication of that development could be that, for the first time in this country, the working practices of the profession would also become the teaching interests of mainstream academics.

The new educational proposals are a symptom of the rapid technological and economic developments in the profession which are leading to the disintegration of its monolithic structure identified by Abel (1988) and which have already led to the erosion of some of its most prized restrictive practices in the Courts and Legal Services Act 1990.[2] The same developments could lead to the practising profession showing more appreciation for academic values than hitherto. A sharp, critically trained mind and confidence in the use of abstract concepts are likely to prove more important in the marketplace than the details of rote-learnt legal rules.

There is therefore good reason to believe that the historical divisions between academic and practising lawyers in this country may be breaking down, which, in turn, should make it easier for critical theorists and radical practitioners to get together.

At the theoretical level there are also grounds for optimism. A developing strand of critical thought, found particularly in North America, and shared even by Unger (1983), offers a way out of the academic blind alley and tries to connect with praxis. Trubek (see also Garth, 1987) for instance, has castigated 'the error of the cynic' who says that legal rights have no reality except as a smokescreen for oppression. He has called for a 'programme of critical social thought about law' which

> insists on a ruthless contrast of legal ideals with legal and social behaviour, thus embracing the basic empirical programme of the sociology of law. It eschews *naïveté* by expecting that dissonance will be frequent rather than episodic. It refuses to see *only* the gap, or to reduce legal ideals to a mere smokescreen for reality. But it does not embrace the delusion that changes in law and legal institutions alone – without changes in other aspects of society – can resolve the tensions or eliminate the gaps that social research identifies. (1984, p. 575; author's emphasis)

One can quibble with the detail of Trubek's proposals but they do, at the very least, offer an opening towards a politically sophisticated critical theory which has the capacity to take possession of empirical knowledge about the operation and potential of legal services. Such a theory conceives a shift from a rights-orientated to a power-orientated approach to legal practice and would start from the everyday experiences of progressive practitioners rather than from those of the liberal academic. The strategic objective, as suggested by Hunt, would be to build a movement committed to 'counter-hegemonic struggle' (1990, p. 309).

To achieve that objective, critical theory would need to illuminate and inform the work of radical practitioners, a process which could involve much rejection and pain. It would not only be the contradictions of casework, as illustrated by the example of s99, which would come under scrutiny, but also many of the values and much of the common sense of practice. Radical practitioners are likely to share much of this common sense with their more traditional colleagues.

Take, for example, the notion of independence. Few would object to a critical exposure of the 'independent' judiciary and traditional legal profession. But the law centres, with the support of the Law Society and the Bar Council, have used the same notion of independence to resist accountability to their funding bodies. What are the implications of that, and to what extent, if any, have the 'independent' law centres succeeded in empowering their clients and communities? And how would radical lawyers in private practice respond to an independent empirical study evaluating their office organisation, employment practices and client relations? Questions of that sort must be faced or radical lawyering *will* be a contradiction in terms.

But there are also other areas where regular and close collaboration between critical theorists and radical practitioners can be successful without incurring conflict and friction. One example is information technology, which is being introduced by radical practitioners, although at a somewhat slower pace than the mainstream profession (Clarke & Economides, 1989 and 1990). The widespread use of new technologies in the legal profession has encouraged existing tendencies to conceptualise law and legal practice in terms of pure technique and according to narrow criteria of 'efficiency'. Critical theory would help practitioners to take into account the practical political dimensions of the conjunction of law and technology.

Finally, there is likely to be little disagreement between theorists and practitioners about the wider task. That must be to expose the pressure points for structural change which lie buried in legal institutions and the welfare state. If we can link a moral vision and enlightenment which sees beyond the limits of the market mentality with a political realism capable of decolonising law's empire we may then be in a position to glimpse the meaning of truth, justice and democracy.

Notes

1. For recent English examples see H. Kennedy (1990) 'Towards a culture of rights', *Law Society's Gazette;* S. Sedley 'Law and State Power: A Time for Reconstruction', *Journal of Law and Society* and almost any issue of *Legal Action* or *Socialist Lawyer*. And see the discussion of the 'rights-litigation nexus' in A. Hunt (1990) 'Rights and Social Movements: Counter-Hegemonic Strategies', *Journal of Law and Society*.
2. The process began with the Administration of Justice Act 1985 and the Building Societies Act 1986.

Legal Practice and Socialist Practice
John Fitzpatrick

Left-wing lawyers, both academic and practising, have often insisted upon the relevance of their work to the wider project of fundamental social change. They do so now at a time when the traditional agent of change, the working class, is itself marginalised and the left generally is exhibiting a loss of nerve amounting almost to panic. This is the context which now shapes any discussion of the relationship between a legal practice and a socialist practice, and we have to take the weight of it.

The catastrophic failure of the Soviet attempt to construct a new order, the triumphalism of the West and the effective absence of the working class from the political stage have taken a heavy toll on current political thinking (Richards, 1990). The very idea of progress itself is now considered by many to be an undesirable Enlightenment delusion. Marxism is seen as a relic from a time when people naively believed in categories (or meta-narratives) like capital and accumulation, and gullibly trusted in the power of reason to grasp in their totality the laws of motion of the modern world. We now peer darkly through a postmodern pea-souper of pluralism, relativism, difference, consumerism and the politics of identity.

The salient features of the new consensus that is emerging from the fog are an acceptance of the capitalist market and an emphasis on civil society. The market or at least the socialised market, is now confidently embraced by the left as the best form of economic organisation for society (Blackburn, 1991). This is consistent with the growing focus over the past decade on civil society as the most fruitful arena for progressive activity of any sort, well away from the darker realms of power politics and the state. In civil society the participatory citizen of the future will, it is claimed, be enabled and empowered by the exercise of individual freedom and consumer choice and by ever more accountable and democratic institutions and structures.

The model has been described as 'a pluralist civil society guarded by an open and accountable state' (Keane, 1988, p. 238). Notice how the state has crept back into the picture in the guise of a friendly security guard. It would appear that the promise of civil society can only be delivered by substantial reforms of and by the state and its legal system. A bill of rights, a citizen's charter, elected judiciary, community policing, proportional representation, cooperatives, eco-friendly industry, listening banks ... these, we are told, are the way forward.

Inevitably, socialist lawyers are tempted by these ideas to believe that their professional activity can play a major role in achieving social change. As another champion of a 'new settlement' puts it: 'It appears that a plausible resolution of some of the dilemmas of contemporary politics can only be provided if enhanced political participation is embedded in a legal and constitutional framework that protects and nurtures individuals, and other social categories, as "free and equal citizens".' (Held, 1991, p. 23)

Who better then than lawyers to negotiate the new Social Contract with the state, to draft the constitutions which will extend and entrench our liberties, to formulate the ground rules of the new dispensation? Not before time, many will think. After all, didn't Marx always underestimate the importance of rights and the law?[1]

Radical lawyers regard such a deployment of their professional skills as something more than gradual reformism. They see their work as linking up with broader movements of social transformation, as constituting a counter-hegemonic strategy in its own right, as forging one prong of a fork which can still deflate the system altogether. They see themselves as compensating for the failure of the old Marxist left to realise, as Gramsci warned them, that the war against capitalism must first be joined, even won, in civil society, at the level of ideology and culture, before the state and the mode of production can be confronted.[2] This is not the place to defend the Marxist tradition and its project of human emancipation against trends which closely resemble what Marx himself called 'sentimental, socialistic day dreams ... utopian, mutton-headed socialism' (Marx, 1976). It is the place to open the argument that we will not even adequately defend ourselves in the present, never mind usher in a brave new citizen's world, if we adopt a strategy which is based around the law, constitutional reform and the acceptable face of the market.

We should begin by pointing out that the distinction between the state and civil society, in particular as it was first drawn by Marx, is being much abused. Civil society, now referring more to institutions like the family, the church, the supermarket, the hospital, the cooperative and so on than to the capitalist economy, is being represented as a sphere of opportunity where, if state coercion and capitalist excess can be resisted or removed by progressive legislation, freedom can flourish. This is misleading indeed, for it is civil society which is the root cause of our problems (Wood, 1988 and 1990).

To get a better understanding of civil society we have to return to a familiar starting point: the separation of the economic and the political spheres of life which is a distinctive feature of capitalist society. This separation arises because under capitalism the process of appropriation by one class of what is produced by another does not in principle depend upon any juridical or political distinction between capitalist and worker. Nor does the capitalist have to rely in the first instance upon coercion to ensure that appropriation continues.

This is very different from all pre-capitalist societies. Under feudalism, for example, it was broadly accepted that the lord was entitled to appropriate the peasants' surplus, and force was directly applied to that end. The lord's economic power was inextricably bound up with his social status and political power. Under capitalism, however, employer and employee meet as formal equals in the marketplace, exchanging their commodities on an equal basis. The economic relationship does not depend upon rank or any relation of political subordination. The state may be necessary to the capitalist both to assist accumulation and contain the class struggle, but it is not a constitutive feature of the basic process.

We recognise, of course, the discrepancy between the formal equality of these agents and the substantive inequality of the real conditions of their lives. A few privately own the means of production and the rest are free only to exchange their labour power. We recognise that, although everybody does indeed exchange commodities at their value in the market, only those who are in a position to put the commodity labour power to work in production can extract surplus value and exploit the others. Here, at the very heart of civil society, are the mechanisms which will continue to generate exploitation and alienation, crisis and breakdown for as long as they are in place.

We can also see how the various legal and political forms which derive from relations of production based on formal equality and the absence of direct coercion can appear to be independent of that system of production. The institutions of the law and state are distant from the world of home and work, from the world of civil society. It is for these reasons that they can appear to be natural, neutral, and the product simply of the general will of society. This is what Marx called the 'juridical illusion' (Marx, 1973b, p. 81).

Just as important as recognising the juridical illusion, however, and more often overlooked, is the point also stressed by Marx that even though the material basis of our juridical and political relations is obscured and mystified, it nevertheless remains the case that these institutions and ideas are a true and consistent expression of that material basis:

> Equality and freedom are thus not only respected in exchange based on exchange values but, also, the exchange of exchange values is the productive real basis of all *equality* and *freedom*. As pure ideas they are merely the idealised expressions of this basis; as developed in juridical, political, social relations they are merely this basis to a higher power. (Marx, 1973a, p. 245)

Both the form (free and equal) and the content (exploitative and coercive) of the freedom and equality of capitalist society are an expression of the way in which civil society, the world of production and the market, of unequal ownership and equal exchange, is organised (see Grigg-Spall and Ireland in this book). Marx emphasised the restricted nature of any freedom in a civil society dominated by commodity production and exchange where the only commodity that matters to most people is their own labour power:

> This kind of individual freedom is therefore at the same time the most complete suspension of all individual freedom, and the most complete subjugation of individuality under social conditions which assume the form of objective powers, even of overpowering objects – of things independent of the relations among individuals themselves. (Marx, 1973, p. 652)

It is extraordinary how left wing commentators today can celebrate this sphere, drawing an imaginary line between freely associating individuals and the social conditions that reproduce and shape them. Blackburn (1991), writing recently in defence of the socialised market, states: 'The imposition of narrow commercial criteria menaces the integrity of civil society, and hands the initiative to rapacious commercial interests, such as the media empires of Rupert Murdoch and Robert Maxwell.' Civil society is built on narrow commercial criteria and rapacious commercial interests, never mind menaced by them. Rapacious commercial interests hardly develop from the personalities of media moguls. This has the same analytic grasp as Ted Heath's 'the unpleasant and unacceptable face of capitalism'.[3] Furthermore, integrity is a strange word to describe a system which is spreading degradation and decay around the world: famine and war abroad, unemployment and homelessness at home.

Marx, unlike many since, did not flinch from the logical conclusion. To gain real freedom would require more than political and legislative reform, it would require the transformation of civil society itself. Marx did not underestimate political and legal structures, but always emphasised the dual nature of the task, referring to the 'fight for the abolition of the state and of bourgeois society' (Marx, 1845). It is a matter of record not interpretation that for Marx this meant among other things a political and a social revolution, involving both the destruction of the state machine of the old order and the abolition of private property (Freeman, 1988).

The terms in which Marx argued against those who thought that somehow the existing civil society could be successfully reformed, and the state used to reform it, are remarkably apt to the debate today:

> Assume a particular civil society and you will get particular political conditions which are only the official expression of civil society.

M. Proudhon will never understand this because he thinks he is doing something great by appealing from the state to civil society – that is to say, from the official résumé of civil society to official society ... They all want competition without the lethal effects of competition. They all want the impossible, namely, the conditions of bourgeois existence without the necessary consequences of those conditions. (Marx, 1976)

The quarrel between Marx and Proudhon has echoed in many subsequent debates. Even those who have accepted that the bedrock of civil society, the capitalist relations of production, have to be replaced, still argue that this may be achieved simply by passing the appropriate laws in the very institutions thrown up by those relations. Here again is a promising opening for lawyers. Perhaps the most famous exchange on this point was that between Eduard Bernstein and Rosa Luxemburg at the turn of the century. Bernstein counterposed legislative reform to revolutionary politics: 'Whether the legislative or the revolutionary method is the more promising depends entirely on the nature of the measures and on their relation to different classes and customs of the people.' (Bernstein, 1961, pp. 218–19) So far as Bernstein was concerned either reform or revolution could deliver socialism; circumstances would dictate the best route, and he was in no doubt that they dictated the path of reform. It is worth quoting extensively from Luxemburg's famous reply:

That is why people who pronounce themselves in favor of the method of legislative reform in place of and in contradistinction to the conquest of political power and social revolution, do not really choose a more tranquil, calmer and slower road to the same goal, but a different goal. Instead of taking a stand for the establishment of a new society they take a stand for the surface modification of the old society. Is it possible that now, as a result of the development of the bourgeois juridical system, the function of moving society from one historic phase to another belongs to legislative reform, and that the conquest of state power by the proletariat has really become 'an empty phrase,' as Bernstein puts it? The very opposite is true. What distinguishes bourgeois societies from other class societies – from ancient society and from the social order of the Middle Ages? Precisely the fact that class domination does not rest on 'acquired rights' but on real economic relations – the fact that wage labor is not a juridical relation, but purely an economic relation. In our juridical system there is not a single legal formula for the class domination of today. (Luxemburg, 1988 pp. 49–50)

Socialists today, and particularly socialists who are also lawyers, would do well to heed Luxemburg's warning and resist the invitation to make the surface modification of the old civil society the centre of their political work.

But if they eschew the task of reforming the market or trying to legislate it out of existence, what then can lawyers, as lawyers, do for socialism? The problem is that socialist lawyers tend to answer that question by adjusting political priorities to fit their legal skills, rather than the other way around. It is one thing for lawyers to make their legal skills available, and to help individuals and groups to make the best use of the law. It is quite another for them to suggest that their work in itself constitutes a socialist political practice or to argue that the law in itself offers a strategic route to social change.

Most lawyers carry out their work in order to live. Their services are retained by the state or private individuals to operate a legal system which functions within strictly defined codes and procedures. Lawyers may expect to get other things out of their work but its prime purpose for them is as a livelihood, and its prime purpose for their employer is to ensure that the wheels of the legal system run as smoothly as possible, to deliver what they want.

Nevertheless, encouraged no doubt by prevailing ideas about how social change may be effected, socialists entering the law often assume that they will be able to integrate political activity with their wage labour. Any solicitor or barrister operating within the financial, professional and political restraints of the real world will soon be disabused of any such idea. Even so, many lawyers who are socialists do try to arrange things so that their legal work, so far as possible, helps workers defend their jobs and housing conditions, helps women and black people resist harassment and discrimination, helps the victims of police repression and so on. They try, too, from the confines of their employment, to press for improved legal services and progressive legislation.

It is no slight on the value of any of this work to say that much of it can be, and in practice is, undertaken by lawyers who have no commitment to socialism. That is so because it is an essentially technical activity in which expertise is usually more useful to the client than political or personal sympathy. Furthermore, at present the state ensures that, at some level, a legal service of this sort is available. It is needed to reinforce the legitimacy of the legal system as a whole and in particular to prevent the aggrieved from taking matters into their own hands. It is the reason for all public legal services, from legal aid to the network of law centres.

Outside work, lawyers use their experience and skills in a wide variety of ways from campaigning on specific cases and issues to lobbying for wide-scale legal reform. Socialists as well as lawyers will always want to fight for the best structures and services, and the widest possible rights. So too will many liberals and conservatives who fully accept the existing order. The struggle for such measures, like the struggle for decent living conditions as a whole, is essentially defensive and tactical in character, even though it can often be conducted creatively and offensively. It is an inevitable response to given conditions, and of course it can never be ignored.

It is misleading, however, to claim that such work constitutes a socialist practice simply because it seeks to enhance the material circumstances of workers, or has a counter-hegemonic quality because it challenges the state to make concessions, and so exposes and undermines it. Only when demands for reform are firmly set in the context of an openly anti-capitalist movement can they have this effect. Such claims also misrepresent the way in which improvements and concessions actually occur.

Reforms are not produced out of a hat by reformist politicians and campaigners, but are the consequence of wider objective and subjective factors, such as the ability of an economic system to afford them (as in the postwar boom) and the strength of the working class at any given time (as in the early 1970s). If there is sufficient working-class pressure the state will find their own lawyers quickly enough to make the necessary adjustments, as they did in 1972 when the Official Solicitor released five docker shop stewards from Pentonville prison. It is often forgotten that as a direct result of collective action in this and other disputes, a British court, the National Industrial Relations Court, was effectively destroyed, and the government's employment policies rendered inoperative.

On the other hand, over the last decade or so, with the working class in retreat, we have witnessed the steady erosion of both trade union and wider civil liberties. It did not matter that after the upsurge in militancy in the early 1970s a new government arrived (Labour, 1974–9) and better trade-union laws were passed, consolidating some of the gains that had been made. What mattered was that this government soon coordinated a counter-attack on the working class which was taken up by Margaret Thatcher and continues to this day. The working class suffered considerable defeats, and it was not long before new employment legislation, aggressive policing and a steady loss of rights reflected the new balance of power.

Of course there is a dialectical relationship between legal rights and social power. We have to identify the force for change. The lesson here is not to make a campaign for new trade union laws the new priority. The lesson is surely that we have to rebuild and maintain a strong, combative and independent working class movement – just to hold our current position. The urgency of the task is shown by the fact that we are still going backwards: in social security, housing, employment, immigration, censorship, secrecy, police powers, legal aid – the state marches on, at our expense. The recent decision to deprive immigrants and their families of free legal advice and assistance is another straw in the wind.

We will only build a new movement if we win the battle of ideas across a wide range of social and political issues. We have a long way to go. We will have to take on, for example, the absurd argument that the market is the best regulator of resources that humanity is ever likely to devise. We have to take on the argument that the rule of law and the state are neutral institutions. We have to argue with those who would embrace rather than explode the contradictory features of these and other social institutions.

We are not going to win many of these arguments if we encourage individuals and groups to define their problems in the context of the legal remedies available to them. We are hardly going to encourage a broader view of the possibilities for change if we suggest that the real power in the land lies with the honourable members of Parliament, the judiciary and committees of civil servants and professionals. At the first sign of trouble trade-union leaders have for generations reached for their MPs and their lawyers rather than their members. Now more than ever they are happier with an injunction than a strike. Shop meetings and branch meetings are dominated by the question 'Is it is legal?' rather than 'Will it be effective?' Yet there are still those who encourage trade unionists to take Parliament and the courts more seriously.

We need at this time to develop, amongst socialist lawyers in particular, a culture of politics more than a culture of rights, a political culture rather than a legal culture. We need a culture in which the full determinations of every relationship and conflict are readily explored and not channelled down the narrow corridors of the law. We need a culture which not only contests every instance and every inch of our oppression but always does so in the context of our ultimate aim. We need a culture which is not embarrassed to state that aim: a society in which every person gives according to ability, and receives according to need, in which the condition for the free development of each individual is the condition for the free development of all.

Lawyers are well placed to help build such a culture. As Marx said, 'the really difficult point to discuss here is how relations of production develop unevenly as legal relations' (Marx, 1973a). There is a lot of difficult but exciting work to be done in teasing out the mediating structures and ideas which carry power and dominion to every corner of society (Grigg-Spall, Ireland & Kelly in this book). Lawyers observe these processes at close hand, and so have a unique opportunity to help clarify the way in which society works. We have to leave the old quarrels behind, for that is what we have been discussing. We have to develop a new, dynamic analysis which captures in thought the real movement of capitalism today, and does so as part of the task of reconstituting the working class as a political force.

Notes

1. Marx was not in fact dismissive of rights under capitalism. His oft-quoted reference in the 'Critique of the Gotha Programme' to 'the old democratic litany familiar to all: Universal suffrage, direct legislation, popular rights, a people's militia, etc.' as 'pretty little gewgaws' was, in context, dismissive only of the view which 'sees the millenium in the democratic republic'. Less often quoted is his complaint that the programme, in its immediate demands, should specify the length of the working day and the age limit for child labour (Marx & Engels, 1968, pp. 315, 330).
2. In fact Gramsci never elaborated a consistent conception of civil society, although it should be noted that, unlike many of his followers, he set out to do so as part of developing a strategy of revolutionary overthrow (see Gramsci, 1971).
3. Edward Heath, Conservative Prime Minister, replying to a question in the House of Commons, about the Lonrho affair, 15 May 1973.

Critical Legal Practice and the Bar
Michael Mansfield Q.C.

Critical legal practice requires definition. There must be a clear set of principles which govern it and which thereby provide a target for the practitioner. I suggest:

1. The enactment of legislation that ensures social and economic justice, particularly in relation to employment, housing, education and health.
2. The preservation of fundamental human rights and freedoms, particularly speech, assembly, association and movement.
3. The provision of means to allow equal access to legal remedies and protections.
4. The construction of a legal process in which issues are fully and thoroughly investigated and tried.
5. The development of a judicial and legal profession which is independent of vested interest and reflects the matrix of the society which it serves.

There is now an even greater need at the Bar for entrants who have these aspirations. The past decade has witnessed wholesale erosion and destruction of social and economic welfare such that there is now a sub-stantial number of people who are vulnerable and disadvantaged in the face of an authoritarian state. At the same time there has been a relentless and coordinated attack on every fundamental freedom, part of which has emanated from and found support in the courts themselves.

The most notable examples have been these: decisions restricting the right to collective protest and demonstration followed by the draconian measures ontained in the Public Order Act 1986; the proposal to abolish the right of silence; the endorsement of the broad-casting ban and the requirement that journalists be forced to reveal their sources and, under PACE (the Police and Criminal Evidence Act 1984), to give up photographic and film material to the police; the abolition of the 'public interest' defence under the Official Secrets Act 1989; the trade union and employment legislation (Employment Acts 1980, 1982, 1988 and 1990; Trade Union Act 1984) which effectively emas-culates any attempt at independent trade unionism; increasing limitations on the right to jury trial and legal aid; and endorsements of the government's Poll Tax philosophy which will eventually reverse the time-honoured maxim of 'no taxation without representation'.

Almost in the same breath, support is professed for the struggle by Solidarity and Lech Walesa's shipyard workers in Gdansk (Poland); for Civic Forum and the force of mass demonstration led by Vaclav Havel in Wenceslas Square, Czechoslovakia; for the resilience of the young people of the Intifada, Palestine; and for the young people of the townships in South Africa who struggle to penetrate the emergency leg-islation and media censorship.

Mining communities in Yorkshire; print workers in Wapping; seafarers in Dover; black communities in Notting Hill, Tottenham, and Liverpool; nationalist communities in West Belfast; nurses, students and Poll-Tax protesters in Trafalgar Square will all recognise the familiar symptoms.

Bearing such an onslaught in mind, the critical lawyer who comes to the Bar must be prepared to speak out, preferably in a collective fashion, to halt the demolition of rights that have taken hundreds of years and lives to develop and sustain. It is instructive to note that the only time that many members of the higher judiciary and the Bar have been impelled to take a public and collective stand was not in relation to the erosion of these freedoms but in relation to the perceived threat to their territory posed by the Lord Chancellor's Green Paper on the legal profession. Then it was that reference was made for the first time to oppressive and authoritarian government and to little men sporting armbands and toothbrush moustaches.

In terms of collective action and analysis, the Critical Lawyers' Group provides the broadest forum for lawyers from many different fields and is to be encouraged to the full. To date there has been too much fragmentation of effort and too much division between academics and practitioners. Members of the Bar must be prepared to create close links with law departments at universities and colleges so that the problems may be jointly addressed.

Those within the profession must then actively endeavour to apply the critical principles to their work. There are numerous ways in which this can occur.

The casework undertaken should have particular regard to the needs of those who are least able to articulate or protect themselves, such as those subject to the complexities and arbitrariness of social security or immigration law; those intimidated by the police station interview; those victimised by corporate intransigence, and those isolated by racial prejudice.

The preparation of cases should disregard the traditional view of minimising contact with the client. It is essential that understanding and trust become the hallmark. In this way, much can be done to restore public confidence in a profession commonly seen to be Dickensian and obsessed with fees. Close cooperation with solicitors, early delivery of papers, careful research, collaboration with colleagues on approaches and points of law, regular in-house seminars on the latest developments in the law (such as the growth of judicial review): all are equally important.

These initiatives should help to overcome the traditional attitude at the Bar of insular individualism. The structure, method of working and organisation of the profession all contribute to this attitude, which gives rise to misjudgement, misunderstanding, pomposity and jealous competition. It is for these same reasons that, from a personal standpoint, I favour fusion, multidisciplinary partnerships and direct access.

There are other pressing reasons for currently examining how barristers operate. The main one is the recently reiterated threat to the provision of legal aid. This has been the hidden agenda in both the Green and White Paper proposals, which talk of flexibility and greater recourse to the private and voluntary sectors. Essentially, this heralds the importation of market forces and privatisation into yet another area of human welfare which is clearly unsuitable for measurement on the profit gauge.

It has to be remembered that there are already considerable areas where there is no legal aid in any event, areas which touch upon what is most important for most people and where they are most vulnerable – social security tribunals, industrial tribunals, sex and racial discrimination, inquests, planning and other forms of public enquiry.

The advent of new technologies allows for a reappraisal of chambers and the traditional working base. I would like to see the growth of consortia or amalgams, comprising barristers, solicitors, researchers, para-social workers and forensic science consultants, who through computerisation, fax and DX (document exchange) facilities would be able to establish branches in major cities. This is akin to the way some group medical practices have developed. Such ideas are sturdily resisted by the Bar at present and there is no prospect of implementation.

Without these options there are decreasing avenues open to the critical lawyer with limited financial resources. Deregulation may allow practice on a temporary basis from a library. The emergence of the mega-set (40–50 counsel) may give safety in numbers and commercial work may subsidise welfare work. Neither of these is palatable. The first merely reinforces individualism, while the second produces massive problems of internal management, identity and unity. Both options deflect energy from the task of persuading central Government to fund an adequate national service for legal welfare.

All of this has to be set alongside the real and similar difficulties facing organisations with related aims: Liberty (formerly NCCL), LAG, Amnesty, Justice, lCCJ, Interrights, Haldane Society, FRU, Community Law Centres and CABs. This should be a time for combination rather than a narrowing concentration on specialities.

It is also coincident with the imminence of new legal frontiers in 1992. There has been hesitancy, reluctance and resistance by British courts and lawyers to adopt the principles and codes of international status. This has been most obvious in the field of human rights. A deaf ear is turned in domestic courts to references to UN charters or European conventions. Few make use of channels of appeal at Strasbourg, but when they do, often from the North of Ireland, they frequently succeed. Britain has the worst human rights record at that court. Such cases have far-reaching effects in exposing serious abuse, particularly in the treatment of Irish issues. In one recent incident, the British government disgracefully used derogation to escape the consequences of a ruling (Brogan, December 1988).

Another important example which merits legal action both in the UK and Europe is the appalling conditions in British prisons and the utter disregard for prisoners' rights. We have one of the highest pro rata prison populations in Europe, with consistent overcrowding above certified levels and lack of integral sanitation, combined with arbitrary internal discipline and absence of effective channels of communication and of discussion of grievances. Successive governments have steadfastly refused to invoke an enforceable code of minimum standards, despite its adoption by the United Nations in 1955, the Council of Europe in 1973 and the representations of the present HM Inspector of Prisons, the Prison Reform Trust, the Prison Officers' Association, the Prison Governors' Association, NACRO, the House of Commons All Party Committee on Prisons and the Howard League for Penal

Reform. The courts have likewise rejected arguments derived from such sources as the European Standard Minimum rules. We now await with interest action on the recommendations of the Woolf enquiry on prisons.

To facilitate these legal battles, it is essential to have association and cooperation with European critical lawyers who can assist with cases here and in the European Courts. Chambers should have links in Europe and reciprocal arrangements with European lawyers.

Even more intractable than the development of Chambers is the problem of access to the Bar in the first place. There has only been a slight change in the numbers and composition over the last 10–15 years. It remains a small, tightly organised coterie of white middle-class males. Because the judiciary are drawn mainly from the Bar, the same observation applies there.

This has serious repercussions for clients and cases. One fears that Lord Denning's recent pronouncements about capital punishment being the antidote to miscarriages of justice are not merely a reflection of his age but also of his class. At the root of some of the most recently cited examples of miscarriages of justice have been the strongly held beliefs and directions of the original trial judges and of those judges who have heard the subsequent appeals.

Two alterations far beyond those contemplated by the Lord Chancellor are required. First, a separate career structure via a judicial college for judges under the auspices of a Ministry of Justice. This would be a job on offer to school-leavers like any other. Secondly, the rationalisation of legal education and training so that students are not dependent on the chance of a pupillage and still more a pupillage grant or loan.

Qualification, however, is by no means the most serious hurdle. The present system permits only slow and limited expansion. Sets of chambers are over-crowded and normally only accept one or two new tenants per year.

The CLG might consider promoting workshops for critical lawyers to discuss the ways in which assistance with accommodation, libraries, finance and management might meet the challenge of the 1990s, and ways to ensure the application of an equal opportunities policy for women and black entrants and for all those with limited resources.

The Politics of Law Practice
Paul Harris

The politics of law practice is both a critique and the subject of a course taught at New College of Law in San Francisco. The critique is derived from the view that legal culture encompasses different areas of struggle, ranging from the internal structure of the office all the way to legal arguments raised in a brief before the Supreme Court (see Kennedy in this book, Watkinson and John Fitzpatrick below in this chapter). In each area political choices are made, that is, choices which demystify images and build power, or which increase alienation and powerlessness. Even decisions such as the physical location of a law office have an impact on clients, peers and the public. To pretend such choices are private and have no political consequences is to reinforce the existing legal system and its dominant culture.

Unfortunately, the 1980s was a decade of spiralling business costs, political fragmentation and preoccupation with material desires. The legal system in the United States was marked by the entrenchment of conservative courts and the staffing of government agencies by Reagan appointees. The result was an unconscious retreat by progressive attorneys. This retreat was marked by workplace elitism, personal caution and legal cynicism. Legal cynicism, like political cynicism, exaggerates the strength of the state and underestimates the potential of the people. It rationalises the failure to include clients in the decision-making process, the failure to use one's practice to build power among indigenous communities, and the failure to break away from practising in traditional forms.

Two examples may help to illustrate this analysis. The first example is a simple one, revolving around money and drugs. The epidemic of rock-cocaine use ('crack') has infected every criminal law practice. Most criminal lawyers, due to economic considerations, are now representing crack dealers. The more successful lawyers have represented the more successful dealers. Many progressive trial lawyers are spending an inordinate amount of energy and time defending major cocaine smugglers and dealers while crack is ripping apart the fabric of minority communities. Ironically, some lawyers have thus not only maintained their standard of living, but have improved it.

The justification for their drug caseloads is that they are defending civil liberties against a government 'war on drugs' which is allowing the state to make serious inroads on all constitutional rights. This is the traditional liberal response, and it contains much truth. But it avoids facing the depth of the destruction wrought by their clients, and it avoids developing a radical alternative to the present practice of criminal law.

There is precedent for wrestling with the conflict between rights and justice. The women's liberation movement educated us to the dangers of defending rapists. Out of the conflict between ensuring a defendant's rights and achieving justice for the victims, new evidentiary laws were passed protecting the rape victim, and procedures were established to stop police abuse at the investigative stage.

There is also precedent in the area of drug defence. Years ago, when heroin flooded poor communities in San Francisco, the Community Law Collective refused to defend heroin dealers. They volunteered their services to a community anti-drug group, and released a legal worker to spend almost all her time organising against Methadone maintenance programmes. These positions were taken after difficult internal debate and in spite of detrimental economic consequences.

Today, in their general political retreat, left lawyers seem to have lost the will to step outside the financial confines of their offices. Without criticism and self-criticism they have fallen prey to the seduction of the glamorous case which brings notoriety and money. Consequently, there has been almost no discussion of confronting this most crucial problem of present-day criminal practice.

The second example involves the sometimes false dichotomy between winning more rights and building power. Two legal aid lawyers brought a suit on behalf of Mexican-American farmworkers to improve working conditions. The day of the trial, the farmworkers filled a bus and travelled 150 miles from the fruit orchards in which they worked to San Francisco's imposing federal court building. When the liberal judge took the bench and saw the courtroom filled with farmworkers he asked all counsel to come into his spacious chambers. He then proceeded to have discussions in chambers, making it evident that he wanted a settlement. Soon it was clear that the judge was hammering out a settlement favourable to the farmworkers, and that he intended to keep counsel in chambers all day while facilitating that settlement. Understanding what the judge was doing, the two legal aid lawyers made no effort to have the hearing taken back into court. The negotiations dragged on all day, and except for the lunch break, the lawyers had no contact with their farmworker clients who continued to sit in the majestic, marbled courtroom. At the end of the day a settlement was signed. It was not all that legal aid wanted but, realistically, it was the best they could have got. They could justify having had the proceedings out of the presence of their clients by the winning of rights for those clients.

Critical legal practice should not have been satisfied with only this legal victory. We must ask what did the parties learn from this conflict pitting the growers and the state labour agency on one side, against the workers on the other. On the positive side, the workers saw that the law can be used to enforce some of their rights. They also learned that their presence had an impact on their adversaries as well as on the court. But on the negative side, they once again were taught that they must rely on professionals, and in this instance, white, male professionals. Furthermore, the dynamics of the entire day reinforced their beliefs in the mystique of the legal system. They left court not understanding the law's process, remaining ignorant of the pragmatic dealing in chambers and still conditioned to put their faith in an apparently objective legal system and its professional manipulators. On the long bus ride home they had, in actuality, less power than when they began their trek.

The state learned that the legal aid lawyers are skilled advocates. Most importantly, the state learned that the farmworkers still know their place! The legal aid lawyers proved that they know what is best for their clients. They learned that filling a courtroom with workers has a powerful impact. But they never experienced the exhilarating, though at times frightening, power of liberated clients. They missed out on the experience of merging their knowledge with the wisdom of the farmworker. They returned to their offices with a legal victory (which was to take other suits to enforce) but without having grown as political lawyers.

Critical legal practice does not advocate losing cases. In this instance, we do not suggest that the lawyers should have refused the session in chambers. We do suggest that the lawyers could have won a favourable settlement without leaving their clients in an alienated subordinate situation. The attorneys had three viable options: 1) to ask the judge that two representatives of the workers be allowed in chambers; 2) if the judge refused, to request ten minute breaks every hour to inform their clients; 3) if the judge refused, to demand that at critical junctures in the negotiations they be allowed to consult with their clients. These options were realistic. The lawyers were sincere, liberal people; why didn't they make any of these requests? It is because lawyers are taught to keep decision-making vested in themselves, not their clients. And because lawyers are so intent on winning rights, they fail to think of ways in which to build power among their clients.

The final example shows the erroneous way in which many progressive lawyers view the law itself. They simply try to use existing rules and precedents to win cases and expand their clients' rights. This approach assumes that law is basically a tool that can be used by both the powerful and the powerless, and that their job is to use it to serve progressive causes.

The problem with this approach is that it focuses almost exclusively on the results of cases while paying little attention to the ideological framework that judges use to reach those results. Over the last 15 years, writers associated with the critical legal studies movement have shown the limitations of this exclusively result-orientated approach. For example, they have shown the way that the United States labour movement was partially co-opted by the body of labour law that emerged from it. While workers originally sought to bring about genuine workplace democracy and worker control over all aspects of work (a first step towards which was winning the right to form unions and engage in collective bargaining), the Supreme Court gradually 'interpreted' the main goal of labour law to be that of assuring 'industrial peace' by creating a labour–management partnership that would increase workers' wages and provide somewhat safer working conditions. Workers won many rights that they did not have before, but the ideological framework that defined the meaning of these legal victories actually helped to undercut the deeper political aims of the movement. Many workers today see their union as a way to protect wages and benefits but not as a community seeking an egalitarian society, and this is, in part, a result of how their legal victories have tended to narrow their aspirations and objectives.

The implications of this kind of analysis are that progressive lawyers cannot be satisfied with just making good legal arguments that they think will work under existing law. They must also find ways to make sure that their arguments express the vision of social change towards which they are working.

The dynamics of a daily law practice result in lawyers submerging their ideals to economic considerations and pragmatic results. It is a sad fact that office meetings are concerned mainly with management and case flow; there is rarely time to analyse the political consequences of the practice. Even firms doing progressive cases rarely have the energy to measure their actual work against the philosophical priorities upon which they first organised their law practice.

Although progressive lawyers have been successful, winning many cases in court and legitimising public interest legal work, there is a frustration and dissatisfaction among them. There is a malaise, a conscious feeling of lack of fulfilment, a need to be part of something more than the isolated and traditional practice of law.

As teachers at New College of Law we felt there was an opportunity to reach many of these lawyers through a new type of clinical programme. We also felt a responsibility to help our students build a career orientated to effecting social change. Peter Gabel, a founder of the Critical Legal Conference, conceived of a course which we hoped would address these issues. The course is entitled the Politics of Law Practice. In it, Peter and I have tried to merge critical legal theory and actual law practice. It is based on the dialectic of the lawyer's desire for politically meaningful work and the law student's uncynical vision of what the legal system should be.

The course deals with the following thematic questions essential to critical law practice:

1. How does our practice expose the law for its temporary political existence instead of its image as being eternal?
2. How do we raise demands that cannot be easily co-opted by the state?
3. How do we develop the power of our clients, not increase their isolation and weakness?
4. How do we sustain internal office structures that are a model of a more egalitarian society?
5. How can we strengthen our commitment to radical law practice?

The course begins by placing students in public and private law offices. The lawyers are committed not only to supervising the students' work, but also to meeting one hour a week with the students to discuss the political implications of the work. In other words, the *key* to this course is not the actual legal work, rather it is the dialogue between the lawyer and law student (and where possible, the legal workers). All areas are open to question.

The class sessions dissect legal culture. We teach students to observe lawyer–client relationships, salary and decision making structures in the offices, community-legal organising, and the limitations legal doctrine seems to put on the lawyers. The students are taught that in each area there are choices which are being made. They are to reflect on whether those choices build power or increase powerlessness. Later, the students discuss these questions and critiques with the lawyers and legal workers.

We also urge the participants to consider such questions as: is a legal response to the client's problem the most productive way to proceed? are the goals of the client being redefined by the legal process? is there an empowerment of the client or a inforcement of patterns of authority and mystification?

Finally, we urge students and lawyers to develop a vision of their own practice. At the end of the semester the lawyers come to the class and discuss the following topic: what are the goals and vision of your law practice and how did the student placements impact on them? The results of what we call 'compelled articulation' are fascinating. One attorney joked that her goal was to get to the office each morning and try to make it through the day. In fact, this had become the 'goal' of many attorneys who once considered their practice to be a way to bring about social change. A legal worker at a once politically active firm said: 'The student placed in our office asked us to discuss how the cases effect social change. This blew my mind; we hadn't discussed that for years.' Most of the lawyers felt the discussions with the students and the final presentation stimulated them to think about their practice in a politically conscious manner. For some of them, it became a real opportunity to re-evaluate their practice, testing it against the vision of social change they once embraced.

The class has been taught for three years, and in a small way it has helped bridge the gap between critical legal theory and law practice. Hopefully, we can train and encourage students and lawyers to transform the oppressive legal culture, and to build a practice consistent with the dreams that brought them to law school.

Radical Chambers, Wellington Street: A Personal View
David Watkinson

The Themes

This article is concerned with the barristers' chambers established at 6 Bowden Street in Lambeth, London and then at 35 Wellington Street in Covent Garden between 1974 and 1988. The experience of those chambers provides two themes: first, the practicability of a barristers' chambers being committed to working in the social-welfare areas of the law with inevitable concentration on legal aid and less financially productive cases; secondly, how during those years, and particularly recently, various aspects of the practice of Wellington Street have been adopted or recognised as a model to be followed by the establishment of the Bar.

The Beginning

The chambers grew out of the political climate of the late 1960s. Trends were the rejection of political activity through established organisations such as Parliament and local government; and the opposition to dominant forces in the workplace, in the home, in housing distribution and welfare benefits, and to racial and sexual stereotyping. Our ideology was fundamentally against hierarchy and for equality, democracy and respect for the individual (see also John Fitzpatrick's second article in this chapter and Kennedy in the previous chapter). It is noteworthy that four out of the six barristers who were the founder members of Bowden Street qualified between 1971 and 1974. (The sixth, Lord Gifford, QC from 1982, qualified in 1961.) It is also noteworthy that four out of the six either trained or practised at the chambers of John Platts-Mills QC (one of the founders of the

Haldane Society of Socialist Lawyers in the 1930s) and probably the only chambers in the early 1970s to have any form of left-wing identity.

The Original Aims

The law-centre movement, having started with North Kensington in 1971, took off in 1972–4 with the establishment of centres in Islington, Camden, Paddington and Lambeth. Despite some closures (and re-openings) and financial difficulties, local law centres, remarkably, continue to be founded and are now approximately 35 in number. The essence of a law centre is to provide at least a full-time, first point of call for legal advice and assistance from lawyers or legally trained personnel to people in a particular, usually local authority, area, without the constraint of profit-making. They have the capacity to concentrate on legal abuses affecting large numbers of people, which a private firm of solicitors would be unable to do.

It was the aim of the founders of Bowden Street (later Wellington Street) to offer a service to the law-centre movement in particular. The law centres concentrated on crime, housing, industrial tribunals, immigration, social security and, in some cases, domestic violence. The Bowden Street chambers' barristers were specialists or developing as specialists in those areas (except industrial/social-security work which came later). They made a deliberate choice to locate the chambers outside the area of the Inns of Court and take up the opportunity of Lambeth instead, where a new law centre had recently been founded. There were a number of reasons. First, the founders wanted to emphasise that this was a different sort of chambers, not identified with the intimidating Inns with their air of distance, formality and wealth, but rather identified with the same or similar locality as the client. Secondly, some had the notion of a local barristers' chambers to complement the local law centre, and the new Lambeth Law Centre seemed an ideal opportunity to put that to the test. The internal organisation of the chambers represented a reaction against the system from which the founders had come as well as an attempt to put shared ideals into practice. Internally, there was no head of chambers. Decisions were made collectively, by voting if necessary. Initially meetings were held weekly. The chambers clerk (of which more later) had a voice in the decision-making on an equal basis with the barristers (see also Kennedy and John Fitzpatrick in this book).

The most radical part of the internal organisation was the system for distributing the income of the barristers. Traditionally, each barrister keeps the fees he or she earns on his or her cases. Up to 10 per cent is deducted to pay the clerk. Up to about another 10 per cent is deducted to pay the rent and other expenses of the administration of chambers. Depending on the particular chambers the percentage is decided by the head of chambers, by the senior members or by chambers meeting. That system favours the more senior barristers (and still does) and also helps to make the clerk or senior clerk a powerful figure. It was obviously in his direct interest to maximise the amount of financially productive work in chambers. Since the clerk controls the distribution of work to the barristers, at least until the barrister's reputation is established, the clerk is the person who can make or break a starting barrister's career. To insist on a particular area of work in preference to others is not welcome.

No clerk's percentage was included in the Wellington Street system, and so the incentive to concentrate only on the more lucrative work was removed. The income of all barristers was pooled, and after deduction for the rent and administration expenses, the income was divided between barristers and clerk in previously agreed shares. For a short period there was an equal distribution of income to all parties, but this method of division altered from time to time. Sometimes the division was weighted in favour of those who were in their first years of practice. This acted as a corrective to the traditional system in two ways. First, the lack of payment during training and the number of years before a living income was earned were a bar to those without financial resources becoming barristers. Secondly, important but less lucrative areas of work, for example legal aid, family, or industrial tribunals, were neglected as areas of practice, particularly by more senior and experienced barristers. With the fee-sharing system, the faster-paying areas, particularly crime, no longer imposed a disincentive on the slower-paying areas.

As a further reaction against the prevailing clerk system, neither the first clerk, nor any of the later additional clerks, came from a background or training in the Inns of Court. The first clerk was a former law-centre worker, and was expected therefore to be able to understand and prioritise law centre requirements. That she was a woman was also unusual for the time (and still is today).

Finally, the chambers agreed that pupils should be guaranteed an income and receive a training in every area of work. The presumption was that any person who completed pupillage would become a full member of chambers immediately. This was an attempt to alter a number of elements of the traditional system: first, the financial barrier to becoming a barrister; secondly, the haphazard nature of the training which traditionally depended on the area(s) of work practised by the pupil master and what he was engaged in during the pupillage; thirdly, the uncertainty as to the future after the completion of pupillage. Many pupils did their pupillages in two six-month periods in different chambers. Bowden Street felt that its training required a year and therefore only offered one-year pupillages. The result of this pupillage system was that pupillage selection was a serious decision never taken until after the pupil had been interviewed by the full chambers.

How it Worked Out

These features of the chambers substantially remained until its dissolution in spring 1988. The commitment to social-welfare areas of law did not change. This did not exclude private paid work, particularly from local authorities, for example on issues in which they were in dispute with central government, or in introducing measures for the benefit of their tenants. Nor as the reputations of members of chambers grew, and as law centre solicitors left to set up their own private firms, did it exclude an increasing proportion of work, though still basically legal aid, from private firms of solicitors.

In 1976 the move to Wellington Street took place. The prime reason was the need for more space in order to take on more people. Very shortly afterwards four barristers and another clerk joined the chambers, effectively in a merger. They greatly strengthened the family, industrial-tribunal and social-security aspects of the chamber's work. However, the chambers never developed a strong practice in immigration work, nor in mental health tribunals, though it did some of that work.

The move to Wellington Street marked the end of the idea of a locally based barristers' chambers. Work came to be accepted from law centres and solicitors from all over London and, as the reputation of chambers spread, from all over England and Wales. The chambers would not have had enough work to maintain an income if it had not done so. Perhaps the idea of being locally based was incompatible with the intention that members develop individual areas of expertise, for success meant that expertise could only be put to use by offering it over as wide a geographical area as possible.

Expansion meant the weekly meeting became an unwieldy vehicle for attendance, clarity and implementation. At first, an administrative committee was chosen to carry out chambers decisions and the number of full meetings reduced to twice a month. Later, sub-groups of those who practised in particular areas were formed. They met once a month to exchange news of cases, swap information and, at times, to discuss particular issues. They were found to be useful, even enjoyable, by those who attended them, but may have contributed to a lessening of the feeling of collectivity between members. The full chambers meeting was reduced to once a month. All final and all major decisions continued to be made by the full chambers meeting.

From 1978, paid paternity (one month) and maternity leave (initially four months increased to six with unpaid leave thereafter) were introduced. These changes coincided with an increasing number of members becoming parents and were intended to remove, so far as possible, the financial disincentive.

The fee-sharing system required regular revision. The parity system was abandoned as it became apparent that it bore unfairly on members who had heavier financial and other commitments and who had worked longer or more intensively on a particular case or cases. Indeed one member always contributed a far higher proportion of his or her income to the system than any other. Eventually a system was agreed by which there was a base rate for all but pupils, who received a proportion, with 'weighting' for age and experience. Starting members were still advantaged, especially starting members older than average who received a 'weighting' for their greater commitments. The system continued to require refinement, and a considerable quantity of chambers time was devoted to its working. However its particular strengths were shown at the time of the miners' strike 1983–4. Many cases were first heard and many completed in the magistrates court. In a lot of cases legal aid was not obtained, either because it was refused or because the alleged offences were not those for which legal aid was normally granted (even though the defendants were facing conviction for the first time). Chambers members were able to represent a substantial number of such cases without the concern that their incomes would be adversely affected in comparison with other members.

A considerable quantity of time was also devoted to the pupillage selection system. The ethos that it was potential members being sought remained, though modified by the recognition that the pupil could be rejected as a full member at the end of training. The increase in the members of chambers led to increasingly unwieldy interviewing by the full group, and eventually chambers divided for the purposes of interview into two or three groups, each asking different questions of the applicant, and then joining up again for the final decision. In practice the chambers took on few pupils, at most four in one year, and usually one or two. Selection became more difficult as the number of members increased with the consequent need for the applicant to impress, or at least not offend, more people. The commitment in terms of finance and training also pointed in the direction of taking on only a few, particularly after the chambers decided not to be bound by the traditional twelve-month period for pupillage but to continue as long as was necessary for the pupil concerned. In retrospect, it may have been too rigid to require all training to be carried out at Wellington Street, and it would have been an advantage to the pupil and to the chambers for there to be experience in other chambers. The insistence that a pupil be trained in all areas of work was probably over-rigid both for the pupil's and the chambers needs.

How it Collapsed

From the beginning of 1987, chambers realised that it faced a severe financial crisis, and for a year members attempted a variety of measures to promote economies and increase income. There was not agreement about every measure. By January 1988, a number of members, principally those with criminal practices, decided to leave the chambers and set up elsewhere. This led to the dissolution of the whole chambers, and, in a process lasting until the summer, members gradually found other chambers to go to. The chambers had no constitution and so no previously agreed means of dissolution. An agreement as to the distribution of the assets and liabilities had to be negotiated and arrived at from scratch, which took until April 1990. The chambers formed of those members who had originally decided to leave itself dissolved two years later in the spring of 1990.

Retrospect

Could Wellington Street or a similarly based chambers have survived or was its collapse inevitable? Its dissolution can perhaps be seen in the context of the number of solicitors' firms which were in financial difficulties in the 1980s, and which dissolved, merged, or abandoned legal aid work. However, other firms took steps in time to ensure their survival, and it was Wellington Street's failure to maximise its possible sources of income and make economies that was the ultimate cause of its demise. In my view there were too many mechanisms which reduced the incentive to maximise income and too few to encourage it, and the fee-sharing system could have been made more acceptable with a greater weighting for experience or productivity. Finally the absence of a written constitution (despite the attempts to produce one) led to time-consuming debate, particularly at the time of dissolution, which could have been avoided.

The Bar Changes

During Wellington Street's history at least three other chambers were founded with a commitment to the social-welfare areas of law. One of those was established outside the Inns of Court and, in the past three years, a number of other chambers have moved to Fleet Street and further afield. The traditional financial incentive to remaining within the Inns is disappearing as the administration moves closer to charging market rents (95 per cent for the year 1991–2). There has even been an out-of-London, locally based annexe opened.

More significantly, the Bar establishment, in response to the government's legislative proposals to extend rights of advocacy to solicitors, has supported a series of reforms to encourage barristers to adopt some of Wellington Street's practices. A commitment to legal aid work was announced in November 1990 by the newly elected Chairman of the Bar, Anthony Scrivener QC, who declared that his first objective was 'to fight to maintain the Bar's principle that those on legal aid have as equal access to the best barristers as the well-off' (*Bar News*, December 1990). The new Code of Conduct (effective from 31 March 1990) acknowledged 'a public obligation based on the paramount need for access to justice to act for any client (whether legally aided or not) in cases within his field of practice'. That was backed by an amendment (22 October 1990) to the Bar's Code of Conduct forbidding the refusal of a legal-aid brief because the fee was insufficient (para. 502 (b)). In October 1990, the Bar Council Strategy Group recommended that pupils be paid 'between £12,000 and £18,000 per year'. (*Bar News*, November 1990). Even fee-sharing was sanctioned by the 1989 rules. These permitted barristers to share their professional receipts or a proportion of them in such manner as they think fit (para. 8.3 – subsequently withdrawn from the 1990 rules, as was the absolute prohibition of partnership, para 211. (2)).

Although Wellington Street's practices could not claim to be more than a factor in the changes that are occurring at the Bar, they did show ways in which the Bar could attempt to alter its remote and moneyed image. How far they go remains to be seen but it seems to have become a permanent feature that at least a minority are committed to many of the essential aims.

Collective Working in Law Centres
John Fitzpatrick

The two distinctive features of law-centre organisation are management committees which include elected representatives of the users of the service, and collective working among the staff. Despite the many problems associated with both of these structures, I believe they have served those who need law centres well, which is of course how they should be judged. For that reason they are preferable to the likely alternative of appointed civil servants and lawyers directing hierarchies of staff (see Kennedy in this book; Watkinson in this chapter). There has recently been renewed discussion within law centres about collective working and some moves to dispense with it. This will seem to some an arcane debate, but it is in fact quite instructive about law centres generally. After all, it is impossible to discuss ways of organising without considering the aims and objectives of the organisation.

First, a description. Collective working means that the staff employed at a law centre are not organised in a hierarchy under a manager or director, but work as a team in which each person not only collaborates closely with the others but also participates in decision-making. This is usually done at a weekly staff meeting which proceeds by way of consensus, or failing that by majority vote with each member of staff having one vote.

It should be emphasised that collective working refers to how the staff operate. It does not mean that law centres themselves are cooperatives or collectives. Law centres are generally limited companies (by guarantee) whose directors form their management committees. This body employs the staff and is responsible, among other things, for directing the work they carry out and for internal discipline. It stands in a hierarchical relation to the staff as a whole.

It will be apparent that for collective working to succeed all the staff must have a shared understanding of and commitment to the goals and working methods of the organisation. Further, each person must make an equal input and take equal responsibility for the work that is carried out.

The fact that strict equality in these matters is obviously impossible, if not meaningless, does not mean that it is at all difficult to get a workable sort of equivalence. This is certainly much easier to achieve if differences in pay and the division of labour among staff are both minimised. This is why pay parity and self-servicing are the usual concomitants of collective working.

If staff are prepared to take equal responsibility and make an equal effort it is not unreasonable for them to expect an equal reward. If staff of widely differing skills undertaking very different functions are employed (lawyers and secretaries) then it will be more difficult for them to work effectively in a collective way. For example, staff undertaking only clerical work will find it more difficult to contribute to discussions about legal strategies, and staff undertaking only legal advocacy will be at sea about the problems confronting clerical staff. This is not to suggest that the only successful collective is a homogenous one, but simply that the more the members of the collective are involved in broadly similar work the easier it will be for them to pull together, and for each person to make a useful contribution to collective decision-making.

Some differences in both pay and work are inevitable. For example, at some law centres all staff begin at the same rate but receive annual increments thereafter. Over the years this can lead to substantial differences, although nowhere near as big as those in private practice or local authorities. Also, everybody has the same prospect of achieving the top rate simply by remaining in post. This system is adopted to encourage staff to stay in what for many of them is a relatively low-paid job. The most obvious example of differences in work undertaken is to be found in the many law centres which have a bookkeeper who does no other work at all. It is generally accepted that this task is sufficiently specialised to justify a separate post.

Nevertheless, the wider the pay differentials and the more advanced the division of labour (into, for example, receptionist, caseworker, project worker, bookkeeper/administrator, lawyer, secretary, fundraiser), the more difficult it will be to sustain a collective approach.

A proper understanding of the role of the staff meeting is important. The staff meeting, in addition to being the focal point for combined effort and cooperation, is also the collective middle manager or line manager between the management committee and the individual staff. The staff, when they come together in the meeting as the collective manager, must have a very clear idea about the nature and extent of their managerial function: how far they can direct individual staff, when they can delegate, when they must report to the management committee and so on.

Practice varies, but given the small size of law centres and the proximity of working, the staff meeting usually has no formal disciplinary function, although it may make recommendations to the management committee. The meeting must exercise the considerable power it does have in a sensitive way, but it must have authority. It must not be oppressive in the use of the majority vote, but neither must it allow individuals or groups the power to veto its decisions in an irresponsible way.

The staff meeting is to be sharply distinguished from the union meeting. Staff meetings are management meetings, whose prime purpose is to manage the service efficiently. Union meetings are workers' meetings, whose sole purpose is to advance the interests of the staff as employees. The fact that the same people, as employees and collective managers, attend both meetings obviously complicates matters, but for that very reason it is important for the distinction to be observed. If, for example, it is convenient for union meetings to follow staff meetings, they should have a different chair or convenor to mark them out. In this way it is much easier to identify the inevitable conflicts of interest which arise between the roles of manager and worker, and to deal with them properly. It also helps clarify the relationship of employer and employee, between the staff and the management committee, which is easily obscured by the close working partnership that usually exists between them.

There may not be any one law centre which operates collective working according to the model described here. Many would no doubt dispute the description itself. The majority, however, have largely subscribed to something like this in spirit, if not to the letter, for the past 20 years, and usually operate it in some form. Adjustments will always have to be made to fit local conditions, financial constraints and the particular skills and predilections of the team in post. In any event, it is a mistake to approach the matter in a rigid way. Concentrating on keeping a balanced, team approach is much more important than worrying about literal infringements of the principle, many of which will, in any case, inevitably result from outside pressures.

This leads us to the question: why bother with collective working? Is it not a nightmare to operate – difficult to get staff, fraught with tensions and, above all, inefficient? There is certainly ample evidence of self-indulgence and ill-discipline in its operation, particularly in terms of the hobby-horsing, guilt-tripping and personal-politicking to which staff meetings, the central mechanism of collective working, are vulnerable, especially given the generally libertarian temper of law-centre staff. On the other hand, there is no reason to suppose that a more hierarchical structure would operate any better in these respects. There is no shortage of examples from other organisations of lazy, oppressive, self-indulgent and corrupt hierarchies.

More importantly, the central charge of inefficiency usually begs the question as to what law centres should be efficient at. They do not, for example, have the same aims as a legal aid practice, where a sharp division of labour and a clear command structure are probably necessary to get through as many cases as profitably as possible while at the same time providing a good legal service.

Law centres, however, are trying to deliver something more than that. Good legal advice and representation are, of course, crucial, especially in those areas where for want of legal aid or private practice expertise many people would receive no legal service at all. But law centres are also more ambitious: addressing policy issues in the delivery of legal and public services generally; enabling local organisations to flourish with advice on constitutions, incorporation, charitable status; undertaking group work with tenants' associations, planning groups, women's groups; responding to local issues which affect many people, such as a planning redevelopment or rehabilitation programme; campaigning on specific cases (for example, deportations) or specific pieces of legislation; informing and educating the public about a wide range of procedures and entitlements.

Law centres try to stretch available resources to help as many people as possible. This involves undertaking individual reactive casework along well-established tracks. It also involves deploying a variety of methods of working: researching, lobbying, negotiating, publicising, organising, campaigning, as well as the fresh application of traditional legal skills. It involves developing new strategies and remedies which are apt to improve the quality of life for people in their localities.

It is in this context that both a mixture of skills and a team approach are vital. Most law centres employ not only lawyers but people with other skills and experience, for example in local or national government, race relations, community organisations, languages, education, journalism, trade unions, women's groups etc. They also try to ensure that women and black people, for example, are properly represented on the staff, not only as a good employment practice, but also to include on the team those who have a fuller understanding of the problems facing users.

A team of this sort will find it easier than a team of lawyers to address the problems of a locality in a creative way. It will be able to consider legal, quasi-legal and other strategies, and will be less constrained by consideration of the existing legal remedies. For example, an increase in the number of applicants declared intentionally homeless may be dealt with by way of renewed attention to judicial review proceedings or by representations to local councillors and participation in a local campaign or a combination of these.

If the team is dominated by a lawyer, and it is usually a lawyer at the top of a hierarchy when one is introduced, there is a real danger that the formulation of policy and priorities will be dominated by a legalistic approach. As it happens, this is the trend already in law centres, where traditional legal casework and routine legal-aid gap-filling work now squeezes out more experimental approaches.

Whether a lawyer is head of the hierarchy or not, the dictum that several heads are better than one is particularly apposite in the case of law centres. Staff have to address problems of considerable social complexity, and to do so from several perspectives; the idea that one person is likely consistently to reach better decisions than a group is not very convincing.

Each member of a hierarchy has a role which is defined firstly in terms of their position within the organisation. Each member of a collective, by virtue of their joint responsibility, takes a more proprietorial interest in the organisation and is more likely to look outwards. More traditionally organised offices, therefore, tend to be more insular and present a more formal face to the public. As a result they are not only less accessible to those who need to use them, but also less sensitive to their problems and needs. The more relaxed, informal atmosphere of law centres and their external orientation not only offers a more sympathetic service, but also narrows the distance between expert and client. This encourages understanding and cooperation on both sides and can lead to very fruitful joint work (see Ritchie, 1991).

It may be objected that it is the job of the management committee to formulate policy, and for the staff to carry it out. This is true, but it does not follow that the way staff are organised is simply a technical matter. Committee members obviously bring their own agendas to the task of developing policy and allocating resources. They can only do the job properly, however, if they are presented by staff with the information necessary to complement their own knowledge, and given the opportunity to make real choices between competing strategies and between areas of work which the staff could undertake. It will be apparent that the role of the staff is crucial, and so it will be equally crucial how they carry it out. It should also be apparent that the work and experience of a collectively organised staff is more likely to be fully available to management committee members than if it were funnelled through a single director.

There is no doubt that collective working is attractive to many individual members of staff, simply in terms of pay and working conditions. After all, it offers a greater degree of control over work, a greater level of participation in the decision-making process, and greater cooperation with others in the planning and execution of tasks than is normally available to many employees. Some staff (especially those who were around at the time that collective working and elected management committees developed in the early 1970s) feel that these structures, imperfect as they are, represent in embryonic or prefigurative form the way workers should organise in the future, and see themselves as setting an example and paving the way in that direction. It is not necessary to embrace such utopianism to welcome new and improved ways of organising our wage-labour.

Collective working, however, will be judged mainly on whether it has delivered the goods to the people who need them. Law centres are justly criticised for the conduct of some of their internal problems and for the consistency and quality of some of their work. On the other hand, given their pitiful resources and their constant funding struggles, they can also boast a formidable list of achievements in terms of court victories, successful campaigns, policy issues raised, procedures developed and very substantial and tangible gains won for their clients. More than anything else, they have proved that there are ways of delivering legal services which are much more flexible and responsive to the needs of ordinary people than anything we have seen before.

The contribution of both elected management committees and collective working to that success is much underestimated. Law centres continue to face problems of recruitment, of organisation and of the allocation of skills and time in the office. The biggest problems they face, however, concern a crisis of clarity and confidence about their aims and potential, and, indeed, about their achievements. That is another discussion, but adopting hierarchies and renouncing collective working would, I believe, compound rather than resolve those problems.

Socialism, Liberation Struggles and the Law

Bill Bowring

Is it just fantasy to suppose that there is an international 'critical legal practice' in which lawyers and law students can engage? Public international law tends, in Britain at least, to be taught as the law of states and their treaties; no struggles, please.

On the contrary: in this article, I argue: 1) that there are live contemporary legal issues concerning liberation struggles which are not simply of academic interest; and 2) that there are concrete, vital practices (some of which I mention below) to which socialist lawyers and law students can contribute.

Socialism

Very few people now believe that the socialist future has been built in any part of the world. Stalinist regimes fall, or carry out radical, market-orientated reforms which have all the appearance of the restoration of capitalism. In postcolonial Africa, one regime after another faces a rising tide of demands for political pluralism. Is it surprising that socialism itself is subject to critical challenge?

This is not the place to seek to define socialism. But Joe Slovo of the South African Communist Party, himself no stranger to liberation struggles, puts it this way:

> Humankind can never attain real freedom until a society has been built in which no person has the freedom to exploit another person. The bulk of humanity's resources will never be used for the good of humanity until they are in public ownership and under democratic control. The ultimate aim of socialism, to eliminate all class inequalities, occupied a prime place in the body of civilised ethics even before Marx. The all-round development of the individual and the creation of opportunities for every person to express his or her talents to the full can only find ultimate expression in a society which dedicates itself to people rather than profit. (1990, p. 28)

Not every lawyer identifying him or herself as a socialist would agree with every word. But I suggest that a commitment to socialism means orientation and engagement. Orientation to liberation from oppression and exploitation. Engagement, as lawyers, using legal skills and knowledge, in the service of organised, collective struggle against those evils.

Liberation Struggles

Academic lawyers are locked in fierce debate as to the juridical nature of national liberation struggles; and even as to whether 'peoples' exist in law. Wilson, in her very useful *International Law and the Use of Force by National Liberation Movements*, defines a national liberation struggle as 'a conflict waged by a non-state community against an established government to secure the right of the people of that community to self-determination' (1988, p. 1). 'Self-determination is now a legal principle', says Brownlie (1981); but it is a legal principle with a real historical content.

The first postwar liberation struggles were concentrated in Britain and France's African colonies. The great war of liberation waged against France by the Algerian movement FLN from 1954 to 1962 gave birth, in 1960, to the crucial UN General Assembly resolution 1514 (xv): the Declaration on the Granting of Independence to Colonial Countries and Peoples, which declared:

1. The subjection of peoples to alien subjugation, domination and exploitation constitutes a denial of fundamental human rights, is contrary to the Charter of the United Nations and is an impediment to the promotion of World peace and co-operation.
2. All peoples have the right to self-determination; by virtue of that right they freely determine their political status and freely pursue their economic, social and cultural development.

The resolution, initiated by the socialist countries, was adopted in the Afro-Asian countries' draft by 89 votes to none, with nine abstentions (including Portugal, Spain, South Africa, the UK and the US). Adoption of the resolution would not have been possible without radical changes in the composition of the UN. From 1946 to 1956 ten new states joined the UN. From 1956 to 1960 17 new states joined, 16 of them African. In 1955, 13.2 per cent of members had achieved independence since 1945; by 1966 45 per cent had done so.

Progressive and socialist lawyers also played a key role in developing these new principles. One such, Cassesse, notes that:

Along with the gradual expansion from Africa to other continents, liberation movements also broadened their objectives: in addition to colonialism, new goals were invoked by liberation movements, namely the struggle against racist regimes and alien domination. (1986, pp. 90–1)

It is in this manner that apartheid has been declared a crime (see the UN document, *International Convention on the Suppression and Punishment of the Crime of Apartheid,* November 1973, New York); and the ANC and PLO have received international legal and political legitimation.

The law, too, has continued to develop. Cassese was one of the authors (as were Rigaux, Salmon & Falk) of the 1976 Universal Declaration of the Rights of Peoples, the 'Algiers Declaration' (see Crawford, 1988), which, although 'unofficial', has had a profound influence in shaping the concepts of international law. It states that:

5. Every people has an imprescribable and unalienable right to self-determination. It shall determine its political status freely and without any foreign interference.
6. Every people has the right to break free from any colonial or foreign domination, whether direct or indirect, and from any racist regime. (Crawford, 1988, pp. 187–9)

That influence was felt in the African Charter on Human and Peoples' Rights (adopted by the Organisation of African Unity in Nairobi in June 1981; entered into force on 21 October 1986 with 30 African States parties); its controversial Article 20 states:

1. All peoples have the right to existence. They shall have the unquestionable and inalienable right to self-determination. They shall freely determine their political status and shall pursue their economic and social development according to the policy they have freely chosen.
2. Colonialised or oppressed peoples shall have the right to free themselves from the bonds of domination by resorting to any means recognised by the international community.(Crawford, 1988, pp. 193–202)

The international community recognises that self-determination cannot always be won peacefully. Wilson concludes:

In this post-colonial world, the denial of self-determination is generally considered to be an evil of such magnitude that the use of force to secure it may be justified. Wars of national liberation are now widely considered to be international wars to which international law must apply. (1988, p. 187)

AM Babu, who was Minister for Development in Nyerere's Government in Tanzania, argues that:

an entirely new outlook is essential, one which recognises the need for a complete break with imperialism and its economic hegemony, as a precondition for a viable and self-sustaining development. (1989, p. 7)

Law

Many British lawyers doubt whether any of the above really constitutes law; and there is much useful work to be done on the academic front. But I propose to describe four (but by no means the only) ways in which lawyers may actively engage themselves, as lawyers, in solidarity with liberation struggles.

First, the UK organisation Lawyers for Palestinian Human Rights (LPHR),[1] not only campaigns for those rights but has, for example, been working on a petition to the Permanent Peoples Tribunal (PPT) (whose President is Professor Rigaux) on the question of breaches by Israel of human rights in the occupied territories.

The inauguration of the PPT in Bologna on 24 June 1979 was inspired by the Algiers Declaration. Its mission (set out in Article 2 of its statute) is 'to promote universal and effective respect for the fundamental rights of peoples by determining whether these rights have been violated, by examining the causes of such infringements, and by pointing out to world public opinion the authors of these violations'. It has been petitioned to rule, among others, on Western Sahara (1979), Argentina (1980), Afghanistan (1981 and 1982) and Guatemala (1983). In September 1988 the PPT was convened in Berlin to coincide with the IMF Congress, and considered complaints of violations by the IMF and the World Bank of the international law of the self-determination of peoples. They were found to be in breach of the UN Charter and of their constitutions, and to have acted negligently.

Secondly, LPHR, along with Al-Haq, the West Bank Affiliate of the International Commission of Jurists, has been investigating the enforcement of international law in relation to the Israeli-occupied territories, particularly as regards 'grave breaches' of the IV Geneva Convention of 1949, which are war crimes (see Stephens, 1989); for example, by invoking the UK's Geneva Conventions Act 1957. LPHR are currently campaigning to stop the separation of Palestinian families.

Thirdly, another UK organisation, Lawyers Against Apartheid,[2] campaigns on a number of international law issues, for example, ratification by the UK government of Protocol I Additional to the Geneva Conventions of 1949 (on international armed conflicts, signed by 102 states and three national liberation movements on 10 June 1977), as part of the campaign for prisoner-of-war status for combatants in the struggle against apartheid. In autumn 1991, LAA launched their 'Vote for Democracy in South Africa' campaign, to show that the people of Britain support democracy in South Africa.

Fourthly, many of the lawyers mentioned above are activists in the International Association of Democratic Lawyers,[3] whose British section is the Haldane Society of Socialist Lawyers,[4] and which comprises sections representing progressive lawyers in South Africa, Palestine and over 70 other countries. Its journals include the *International Review of Contemporary Law*,[5] and *Palestine and Law*. The Haldane Society has an international sub-committee which works closely with solidarity and liberation movements.

Notes

1. Lawyers for Palestinian Human Rights, PO Box BMJP1, London WCIN 3XX.
2. Lawyers Against Apartheid, PO Box 353, London WC1R 5NB.
3. International Association of Democratic Lawyers, 263 Avenue Albert, B 1180 Brussels, Belgium.
4. Haldane Society of Socialist Lawyers, Panther House, 38 Mount Pleasant, London WC1X OAP. The Haldane Society was founded in 1930, and provides a forum for the discussion and analysis of law and the legal system from a socialist and internationalist perspective. It has mobilised and organised effective lawyers' solidarity with mineworkers, printworkers at Wapping, seafarers and Trafalgar Square defendants, among others. It is independent of any political party. Its membership of about 1,200 comprises individuals who are lawyers, academics, students, legal workers and others with interests in and against the law. It also has trade-union and labour-movement affiliates. The journal *Socialist Lawyer* appears three times a year; and the Society's work is enriched by active Lesbian and Gay, Women's, Northern Ireland, Employment, Crime, Mental Health and International Sub-Committees.
5. Two recent articles of importance to appear in the *Review* are: Christos Theodoropoulos, 'The Character of the War in South Africa', *IRCL* 2/1989, p. 53; and Kader Asmal, 'The Illegitimacy of the South African Apartheid Regime', *IRCL* 1/1990, p. 21.

The Politics of Legal Aid
Kate Markus

Legal aid in many countries means the provision of legal assistance through a variety of means (voluntary work, grant-aided or charitable legal-service bodies, *pro bono*) to the poor. In Britain the term legal aid is used more specifically to mean the provision of legal advice, assistance and representation through the legal aid scheme, which was first established by Parliament in 1949 and is now governed by the Legal Aid Act 1988.

Under the scheme those who fall within the prescribed limits of income and capital obtain the services of solicitors and barristers in private practice. The legal aid committees, which administer the scheme, also have to be satisfied that the applicant has a reasonable case on its merits. The services to the client are either free or relatively cheap, the state paying the fees to the lawyers. Over the years the financial eligibility limits have become so low that many people are excluded from the scheme even though they clearly cannot afford to pay lawyers' fees. As a result, many people are effectively excluded from the courts.

Superficially, the history of legal aid has been that of a public service development in the interests of the community and, in particular, those of the poor and disadvantaged. It is, however, more accurately seen as a historical struggle between the professional concerns of private legal practice and the government, and between public service and the private market. In 1949, when the scheme was founded, the Law Society battled with the government to keep legal aid in the hands of private practice and out of the hands of salaried lawyers. The Law Society won, using arguments about the need for lawyers to be independent. Paradoxically, the fact that legal aid has thereby remained in the hands of private practice has led to an undermining of the independence upon which the Law Society so strongly relied. Rather than responding to need, legal aid practitioners must respond to the requirements of running businesses in a highly competitive market place. This severely limits the range of services that legal aid lawyers can offer to their clients. More seriously, it is the cause of the current decline of the legal aid scheme. When the public purse is constrained by central government spending policies, it cannot compete with commercial concerns and is inevitably squeezed out of the market. Legal aid practitioners are finding it increasingly difficult to make ends meet, and are simply pulling out of the scheme.

The Problems with Legal Aid

The legal aid scheme was limited from the outset. It was developed under a Labour government which was clearly hostile to the intervention of lawyers in the new welfare state. Legal aid was, therefore, generally made available only in those areas in which lawyers had always functioned and not in the area of so-called welfare law. The areas in which private lawyers operated were extended only as a by-product of the development of law centres and of welfare law (for instance, on issues of state support for women and children after divorce).

These limitations of the scheme meant that, as well as being under-funded, it was and still is inherently defective. Although in the criminal courts, in personal injury and in family matters, a large number of people have obtained the services of lawyers through the scheme, legal aid has nevertheless failed to provide the services that are most suited to the needs of vast numbers of people, especially the needs of the working-class, poor or disadvantaged sections of society. These are some of the main problems with our legal aid scheme :

1. Private practitioners have to make a profit, even where paid by the Legal Aid Board, and very often they feel, therefore, that they cannot afford to spend the time that may be required on legal aid cases. As legal aid rates fail to keep up with private rates of pay, practitioners do decreasing amounts of legal aid work. Political, social and economic rights of individuals and sections of society must be enforceable regardless of financial resources, yet a system based on profit in a competitive market cannot achieve this.

2. The attitudes and experiences of most lawyers are quite alien to the majority of poorer clients. The orientation of legal services to money and property matters has led to the development of expertise in areas which, in general, are not those affecting the poor or working class. Lawyers are drawn mainly from relatively well-off backgrounds, are often public-school educated, white and male and have a very different set of social, personal and financial expectations to many of their clients. There is surrounding lawyers an aura of mystery, tradition and wealth that puts many people off approaching them.

3. The cost associated with lawyers is also a factor that deters many potential clients. Even if they have the benefit of legal aid , they may have to pay contributions.

4. Private practice is mainly geared to litigation as the solution to problems and as a result individualises problems. However, very often solutions are found in a combination of legal argument and expert evidence, and in the unity and organisation of people

involved. Often decisions made by unaccountable authorities and organisations cannot be challenged in the courts. Providing more of the traditional lawyers' skills, as under legal aid , does not alleviate those problems.

5. Rich and corporate clients have always required and had access to the services of many different types of professionals – not only lawyers, but also accountants and financial advisers, public relations consultants, media advisers, personnel advisers, management consultants, and many more. The poorer clients also require a similarly diverse service (although the specific skills may be different to those required by the commercial clients). Legal aid has not provided it and, based as it is on the private-practice model, will never do so.

6. Legal aid is centrally controlled and so is bureaucratic, inflexible, unresponsive and inaccessible. It does not allow for sufficient variation in provision in different areas of the country to account for different needs. There is very little avenue for those dissatisfied with it to complain or challenge it.

7. There is widespread ignorance of legal rights and the means of enforcing them. Legal aid does not aim to overcome this and consequently has little or no preventative effect. Nor does it encourage self-help and independence. It also fails to counter the low take-up of legal aid due to this ignorance.

Legal Services and Political Change

These flaws in the legal aid scheme were becoming apparent within 20 years of its inception. At the same time, in the late 1960s and early 1970s, political activity and awareness were burgeoning after the long and relatively passive period since the end of the war. The decline in industrial relations led to an upsurge in trade-union activity and new repressive industrial-relations legislation generated yet more militancy. Black consciousness was also rising. The massive growth of immigration into Britain meant that there was a new political and economic concern about its impact on the country and a concern among many to ensure proper protection of the rights of these new minorities.

The growth in the social and political movements stimulated by these concerns was particularly obvious in the inner cities, where living conditions for the poor, black and working-class residents deteriorated. These movements challenged the very legitimacy of authoritarian power. The challenge they made was not just to the rights over which courts had jurisdiction but also to decisions of government, authorities and large corporations which remained relatively unaccountable and unchallengeable within the legal system. There was a demand for services that could operate in a non-litigation-orientated and socially responsive manner.

It was in this context, along with the popular discontent with legal aid and the developing role of lawyers in new forums such as local government, that law centres in England and Wales developed.

Law Centres

In the last 20 years and more, a wide variety of methods of work has been developed by law centres. Since the first law centre in 1970, they have sprung up in many, mainly inner-city, areas of the country, initiated by local community activists and lawyers as a result of perceived local needs for adequate legal services which private practice was failing to meet. Law centres have become popular and much in demand.

Despite the diverse nature of their services, there are common threads running through all law centres:

1. Their services are usually free, thus overcoming many of the problems associated with the means-testing of legal aid or the Law Society charge.
2. Law centres are run by locally elected management committees, which employ the staff of the centres. The management committee decides on the centre's policies and priorities, ensuring that as far as possible each centre responds to local demands and is accountable to their users.
3. The traditional hierarchical structures of solicitors' offices serve to deny access to lawyers. Law centres have, in various ways, found alternative structures (see Kennedy in this book, and John Fitzpatrick's second article in this chapter).
4. Law centres do not employ lawyers alone. Because of the wide range of services they offer, and their innovative methods of working, they rely on diverse resources. Apart from the lawyers, there are specialists in various aspects of community work, and those with expertise ranging from local government administration to trade unionism, education and housing. Many centres offer a range of languages appropriate to their locality.
5. There are no predetermined limits on their work (other than professional limits) so law centres can work creatively and innovatively in a wide range of issues thus exposing need that would not otherwise be apparent. It was mainly through law centres' prioritising immigration and nationality casework that that area became one of growth and resulted in the establishment of local agencies around the country providing specialist immigration and nationality advice and representation services.

6. They aim to direct their resources to best effect, providing the most needed and popular service for the community in which they operate. This often involves determining priorities and setting criteria by which work is or is not undertaken.

7. Law centres encourage self-help, and aim to provide people with sufficient information to deal themselves with actual or potential legal problems without unnecessary dependence on lawyers. They produce leaflets, posters and other publications that are easy to understand and often in languages other than English. They give talks, explaining to people what their rights are and how they can enforce or defend them. They work with local groups and organisations, providing them with the necessary information and support so they can put forward their own views and demands to their local authority, employer or landlord.

8. They deliberately set out to attract and encourage users who would not normally approach lawyers in private practice. Generally they are in shopfront, high-street premises or other offices designed to attract such people. However, the more important aspect of the law centre approach is the way in which they target the working-class, disadvantaged or vulnerable people in their areas, providing them with information and encouraging them to exercise their rights. The centres will often have to make a commitment to give quite long-term support to growing organisations and campaigns to achieve this.

9. Law centres have also found that needs for legal services are often concealed and need to be deliberately searched out. So in an area with no agency providing advice on schools and education, very few problems of that nature will come to the attention of local lawyers. Parents, teachers and pupils become more frustrated with the inadequacies of the local education scheme and respond in a haphazard and individualistic way – for instance, parents may remove their children from the school, which in turn results in further degeneration of the abandoned schools. However, the provision of specialist advice on education issues will result in a growth of awareness of the real problems and possible means of tackling them. In many areas where law centres have recently begun to provide such advice, parents have organised themselves for the first time into effective groups which make unique and valuable contributions to the development of their local education systems.

10. The function of law centres is therefore very different to that of Citizens' Advice Bureaux and other generalist advice agencies, which tend to offer an open door to all requiring advice and operate on an individual case-by-case level. Law centres have developed close working relationships with these other agencies

at a local level, referring cases to each other, often jointly identifying and tackling issues, and pressing for further advice and
legal services in areas of still unmet need.

The Legal Services Debate Today

The Legal Aid Board, which was invested with duties under the Legal
Aid Act 1988 to run the legal aid scheme and ensure other forms of legal
advice, assistance and representation, is currently engaged in two
major exercises in the reform of the policy and practice of legal services.

First, in the name of efficiency, it is experimenting with a reform
of the green form scheme (by which eligible individuals obtain a
limited amount of legal advice and assistance). Solicitors' firms and law
and advice centres which participate will obtain a franchise to deliver
these services. They will have to conform to a range of criteria imposed
by the Board, and will be subject to close review and monitoring. In
return, there will be some small improvements in the system of
payment for these services. It remains to be seen whether this scheme
will have any significant impact on services or practice.

Secondly, the Board is considering its future role in relation to the
funding of law centres.

These areas of activity are closely linked. Each arises from the
endeavours of the Board to find a cheaper means of being seen to meet
the ever-increasing demands for effective legal services.

The issues involved in many respects mirror transactions between
local authorities and their grantees, all of which are part of the
deepening contract culture. Contracts are seen by many as attractive
because they can provide a degree of financial security. However, they
also carry the grave dangers of increased control by the funder, and loss
of flexibility and responsiveness.

The contract approach is not surprising. Major industries are being
privatised, local authorities are required to tender competitively, public
services generally are obliged to compete with the private sector in cost-
efficiency and profit-making, and representatives of financial and
industrial concerns are now running the health service and other
public services. Decisions which ought to be made according to need
and social welfare are now being made so as to enable big business to
continue to reap vast profits, and to prepare commercial concerns for
the European marketplace. At the same time, any democratic control
of, or participation in public service provision is being stamped upon
systematically. The Poll Tax with, worse, the capping of many authorities, is the most recent example of the atrocities being committed in
the name of accountability and improved services.

Starting with the Lord Chancellor's Department's Legal Aid Efficiency
Scrutiny report of 1986, the proposals to cash-limit legal aid and to drive

law and advice centres into competitive bidding provoked widespread opposition. Despite superficially abandoning those proposals in the subsequent Legal Aid Act, the government and the Board have so far failed to produce any satisfactory proposals as to the development of non-profit legal services and have, instead, set an agenda which has focused attention increasingly on contracts and the supervision or control which accompanies them.

Most recently, the Lord Chancellor's Department has published its 'Review of Eligibility for Legal Aid ' in which the main proposal is that litigants only become eligible for legal aid once the costs of a case exceed a level determined according to the litigant's means. This will mean that all but the very poorest will have to pay substantial sums, possibly thousands of pounds, towards the costs of litigation before they receive any legal aid at all. The effect will be to deter litigants through cost. The proposals have attracted widespread opposition. Nevertheless, the review does provide considerable opportunities for the reform of legal services. It represents an acknowledgement of the deep problems within the legal aid scheme and the need for reform of legal services, including the development of alternatives to legal aid .

Containment of costs will always be a requirement of central government. However, the starting point for determining provision should not be primarily a financial exercise. The fundamental issues of the different roles of the law in society – as the arbiter of business disputes on the one hand, and as a framework for securing democratic rights on the other – must underpin any programme for meeting unmet legal need. The financial questions can be answered by ensuring that legal services are deployed as effectively as possible to relieve the greatest needs.

There is a great deal of discussion to be had on how to resolve this in practice. There are already models on which to base legal services reform and development. Law centres and advice agencies could be developed to carry out casework and provide advice and information in the context of an overall strategic plan for the delivery of legal services. In this way they would tackle underlying problems in a manner that is responsive to the particular concerns of the poor and working class. With adequate resources, they could handle the majority of non-commercial cases. They could also, with far greater expertise and authority than the Legal Aid Board could ever have as a central government body, monitor those that participate in any legal services scheme and make sure that their work is of the highest quality.

4
Critical Lawyers' Groups
Richard Carroll, Ian Grigg-Spall and Lorraine Talbot

To achieve major changes in legal education and practice, critical students, academics and practitioners must, in our view, work closely together. Until recently, the critical legal studies movement had failed to pursue this objective. In the last few years, however, Critical Lawyers' Groups have successfully been formed in a number of polytechnic and university law departments. They have received wide support not only from students and academics but also from many practitioners. Our hope is that this handbook will contribute to the formation of many more of these groups.

Organising Critical Lawyers' Groups

In our experience student-run CLGs have shown the greatest energy and commitment and have been the most successful in drawing in academics and practitioners. In a way, therefore, this chapter is addressed principally to the new generation of law students whom we would like to encourage to establish CLGs in their own institutions. The following points may be helpful to students organising CLGs.

If possible you should establish your CLG as a student union society. This enables you to ask the Student Union for money to pay for speakers (normally a meal and travelling expenses), stationery, postage and telephone costs. You will need to draft a constitution. As a guide, the constitution of the CLG at the University of Kent reads:

> The CLG is open to all students and staff with a critical approach towards law, legal education and practice. The CLG will seek: (a) To develop a theoretically grounded critique of orthodox legal studies; (b) To foster debate on the role and limits of law in a capitalist society and to consider the potentiality of a legal education and practice in the interests of the disadvantaged and oppressed; (c) To provide a discussion forum for organisations and campaigns concerned with struggles around law, legal education and practice; (d) To initiate and to support progressive struggles around law, legal education and practice; (e) To encourage and to initiate alternative forms of legal education and practice; (f) To these ends to invite speakers, engage

in critical debate and undertake practical work; and (g) To affiliate to the National CLG and assist in its organisation and activities.

Local 'critical' practitioners should be invited to attend meetings (see Chapter 5) and to sit on your committee. You should approach your law department for assistance. This is useful as it will encourage staff to become actively involved in the CLG. Student Union rules allow staff to be members of student societies but not to hold office. To launch the group you might, perhaps, hold an open meeting on legal education. The editors can supply speakers for this or you might ask contributors to visit you. Further regular open meetings should be organised. This last point is crucial for it is the basis for meeting and working with people from all over the country.

In recent years CLGs have welcomed a wide range of persons and many of these have become active supporters. They include Michael Mansfield QC, who has spoken on the Irish cases, the miners' strike, and 'Suspect Confessions'; Ed Rees (barrister) on the Tottenham Three and the Orgreave 'riot' trial; Tanoo Mylvaganam (barrister) on 'Racism and Sexism at the Bar'; Maggie Monteith, the Director of the Women's Legal Defence Fund; John Fitzpatrick (solicitor) on 'Law Centres and Critical Practice' and 'Imperialism, Palestine and the Gulf War'; Stephen Sedley QC on 'Judicial Review – A Weapon for Socialists?'; Kate Markus, the Secretary of the Law Centres Federation, on 'The Politics of Legal Aid'; Geoffrey Bindman (solicitor) on 'South Africa and the Rule of Legal Terror'; John Hendy QC on 'Anti-Union Laws – How They Work'; Tony Jennings (barrister) on 'The Abuse of Civil Liberties in Northern Ireland'; Andrew Puddefat, General Secretary of Liberty (formerly NCCL), on 'Rushdie – To Ban or Not to Ban'; Terry Munyard (barrister) on 'The Legal Oppression of Gays and Lesbians'; Mike Anderson (lecturer) on 'The Bhopal Litigation – How Lawyers Ensure Clients Don't Have To Pay'; Nick Blake (barrister) on 'Irish prisoners and British judges'; Tim Gopsill, editor of the *Journalist*, on 'Censorship and the Gulf War'; Paul Rawlinson (solicitor) on 'City Lawyers – Acting in Whose Interest?'; Sinn Fein on 'Legal and Illegal Repression in Northern Ireland'; Richard Schwartz (researcher) on 'Human Rights and Palestine', and Bill Bowring, Chair of the Haldane Society, on 'International Law and the Gulf War'.

Free Legal Advice Centres

At a number of educational institutions (for example, at Coventry and Kent) the CLG committees have established free legal advice centres on local housing estates. Not only do these provide much-needed assistance to local communities, they are also a very useful way of bringing together practitioners, academics and law students and of encouraging cooperation, discussion and the development of a critical approach to law and legal practice. For students in particular the experience of the legal problems of the poor and disadvantaged has been a powerful antidote to the orientation of many law courses as currently taught.

Readers may find useful some detail on the operation of one of the centres.

The Canterbury centre (known as Canterbury Community Aid – CCA) is responsible to the CLG executive committee and organised by a student coordinator. Its main objects are to establish a free legal advice and action centre and to consider the possibilities and practicalities of a legal eduation and legal practice relevant to the needs of the disadvantaged and poor. The centre operates every Monday evening from a local community social club on one of the council estates in Canterbury. It is staffed by a rota of volunteer solicitors and legal executives who work with a team of law students. The qualified legal adviser is there in a supervisory capacity, the students interview the clients, take notes, do any necessary legal research, write letters (although all letters are checked by a legal adviser before posting) and, where possible, represent clients before tribunals and courts as 'McKenzie friends'. Students have appeared in the magistrates', county and crown courts as well as before social security appeals and legal aid tribunals.

Richard Carroll, the student coordinator for 1990/91, indicates in his annual report that over 150 persons sought advice, principally in the following areas: Poll Tax, consumer problems, employment (including change of contract, underpayment, unfair dismissal, tribunal representation, temporary lay-offs and holiday entitlements), social security and housing problems (including notice to quit, eviction, rent, repairs and easements).

The centre has not only been involved in individual casework, but has also participated in a number of political campaigns, notably that against the Poll Tax, becoming one of the Kent Anti-Poll-Tax Union's legal advisers. The centre published leaflets on legal resistance to the Poll Tax and took part in many media presentations. In Poll Tax cases student advisers were initially allowed by magistrates' courts to represent persons as 'McKenzie friends'. However, the success of their efforts in raising procedural and substantive issues led the court to remove this 'right' and to refuse all further applications. This became the policy of magistrates across the country as they sought to process the huge number of Poll Tax resistors. The centre worked with the NCCL on a judicial review of one of the McKenzie refusals which was heard by the High Court in November 1990. The High Court declared that the McKenzie friend had never been a 'right', merely a privilege which might be allowed by magistrates using their 'discretionary' powers. This flew in the face of authorities dating back 150 years and, for blatant political manipulation, must stand on a par with the courts' judgements during the miners' strike! Comment on this case and other breaches was published in the *Legal Action Bulletin*. The case is now on appeal.

A further development in 1990 was the establishment by CCA of links with the Women's Legal Defence Fund. A new Canterbury Employment Discrimination Clinic has been handling sex-discrimination cases since October 1991.

The centre has had many successes and students have gained a considerable amount of knowledge about, and insight into, the operation of the legal system. These insights have led to proposals for changes in the way that law is taught at Kent and in the content of specific law courses. The Kent law school now recognises work in the centre for degree assessment purposes. A new course on legal process will actively encourage students to participate in the centre.

If you would like further details on Canterbury Community Aid, contact Richard Carroll, 42 Ulcombe Gardens, Canterbury, Kent CT2 7QZ, or telephone the CCA 24-Hour Help Line on (0227) 475435.

The National CLG Committee

Since February 1989 there has been a National CLG Committee to coordinate the activities of the local CLGs. This committee organised the first CLG Annual Conference at Coventry Polytechnic in November 1990 under the title, 'What's Left in the Law?'. It also jointly published with the editors of the journal *Law and Critique*, an article on the concerns and objectives of CLGs (vol 1, spring 1990, pp. 121–6). Readers may be interested in some further details of both the conference and the article.

The conference was attended by over 150 law students, practitioners and academics, including a majority of the contributors to this handbook. The theme of the conference was the prospect for the legal left of developing a liberating legal education, campaigning for legal freedoms and humanising legal practice.

At the plenary session, Sol Picciotto (former Chair of the University of Warwick Law School) spoke about the past failures of left legal groups in education and how CLGs must become involved in issues that affect all students as well as seeking to overcome traditional 'black-letter' law teaching, now bolstered and distorted by private finance. Mike Mansfield QC surveyed the state attacks on fundamental freedoms since the mid-1970s and insisted that socialist lawyers must unite in public condemnation of these developments and in fighting for a platform of rights firmly anchored in popular support. John Wadham (the Legal Officer of the NCCL, now Liberty) further detailed the assaults on civil liberties and outlined a view of the priorities for campaigning in the 1990s.

The plenary session was followed by student-chaired workshops in which discussion focused on developing specific campaigns against the Poll Tax, Third World debt, the abolition of the right to silence and for the release of the Birmingham Six and the Tottenham Three; proposals for transforming both academic and vocational legal education; whether law centres are central to socialist struggle; how to radicalise the practice of solicitors and barristers; and what contribution feminist, Marxist and/or poststructuralist theory might make to developing CLG analysis and policy.

The article in *Law and Critique* took the form of an interview with the student members of the NCLG. We reproduce extracts here as it reflects *some* of the continuing concerns and objectives of the CLGs.

Editors One of the themes which has emerged as pivotal for this issue is the very question of the relationship between students and teachers in the (legal) academic enterprise. To the extent that the editors of this issue are all poachers turned gamekeepers, ex-students left simply with memories of student life, it seemed to us important to try to elicit student views and to record what students, today, might understand by the 'critique of law'. If the questions which follow seem at times forced or contrived, this is probably the result of the distance between the academic and the student. But it seems to us that law and critique can provide a forum for students as well as academics to engage in the development of the critique of law.

NCLG Before attempting this questionnaire on, as you say, a broad assessment of the relationship between students and teachers, we feel it is important to comment on your attitude to this relationship as illustrated by your use of the poacher-turned-gamekeeper analogy.

This presumption of students as poachers implies that in order to equip oneself with the intellectual means to survive in a non-student world, we must first steal fragments of information from another's land. With this part of the analogy we find ourselves in certain sympathy; the academic game park is essentially 'theirs' and not 'ours'. In order to 'get on' we are obliged to make this arena our own and if you like we steal a degree on this basis.

The part of the analogy that really worries us is that of teachers as gamekeepers. Is it too simplified to say that the role of a gamekeeper is to restrict by any means the poacher's access to the benefits of the park? Is this really how you perceive yourselves? Are we labouring under a rather naive illusion that the role of a 'critical' teacher is more that of the highly skilled poacher indicating to her less experienced colleagues where the best game is to be had and not a structurally bound role to cast the poacher from the park in utter disgrace, without considering the starvation that might have brought this poor soul to such a way of life!

As critical lawyers we do not accept that these divisions are insurmountable or even real. The CLG is based on 'egalitarian', anti-hierarchical principles; we are all, if you like, 'poachers', bound by a common cause.

The fence that you feel on the other side of is not one necessarily constructed by the division between students and teachers. Political differences can be the only relevant and real fence; in the CLG teachers and students find themselves on the same side of the fence.

It is a mistake to define yourselves primarily by a role enforced from above and not of your own creation. As to the question of students acting as a 'crucial instrument in the games which teachers play', we do not accept this role as passive legitimators of others' positions.

Editors   How would you place yourselves? Who are you? Where would you say you are 'coming from'? You have taken the trouble of setting up groups not only on individual campuses but at national level. How uniform or consistent would you say the goals are that fuel what you are doing?

NCLG   The CLGs have been formed as a response to the failure of the law to tackle a profoundly oppressive and unequal society. There are structural relations of exploitation and domination which the legal system reflects both externally and internally. The eradication of these relationships internally can only be a positive step towards change. The law, like other bourgeois ideologies, is taught as if it is just another set of facts, a manifestation of a 'natural' form of order emanating from a free society of individuals interacting as they choose. As critical lawyers we view this concept as inherently fallacious. For us, law must be viewed historically as it has developed to legitimise capitalism. We reject the 'autonomy of the law' ideology, and its implicit premise of a world consisting of competitive individuals engaged in isolated and intricate power games.

These are the shared premises of the critical lawyers' group, or, if you prefer, 'where we are coming from'! The goal of the national group is a demystification of the individualistic ideology that the law seeks to perpetuate. We seek to expose the gender, race and class conflict and exploitation which constitutes the law's raison d'etre.

Editors   How would you describe the relationship of your movement to politics, at either the national or student level? To what extent are you concerned with the politics of vocationalism, professionalism, with especial regard to the politics of legal professionalism and vocationalism?

NCLG   Our relationship to politics is not an interesting appendage to the movement but is central to all our analyses and activities. Obviously law students tend to look towards the legal profession. In order to build a critical perspective we must develop an understanding of the nature of that profession and its potential relationship to the struggle for social change. To this extent the issue of legal professionalism and vocationalism is a focus of debate. This has centred on the possibilities of a legal practice that may be a force for social change and in finding political rather than legal solutions to the problems that the legal profession attracts.

These questions have constantly cropped up in the activities of student-run law centres in which many members have invested much time and energy. There has been a tendency to search for exclusively legal solutions, thus reproducing the individualistic power relation between those with 'the knowledge' and those without; there is a danger that this can become a patronising philanthropic exercise. We are presently rethinking this approach with a view to greater involvement in campaigning around issues which the state seeks to submerge in legal definitions but which are in reality issues of class, race or gender.

Editors   How do you see yourselves in relation to the legal profession, to the extent that this is the dominant relationship with which and against which law students tend to define themselves?

NCLG   The legal profession is clearly hierarchical. There is both the obvious stratification within the professional hierarchy and the underlying stratification along class, gender and racial lines. The former category pertains to the alienated roles which we are invited to adopt. These roles are defined by relationships of dominance and subordination. The latter category uses these personal characteristics to provide a so-called rational basis for social subordination. We do not define ourselves negatively in these terms but turn the definitions outwards to understand and clarify the dynamics of the world we live in.

Editors   How do you see your position in relation to that of other law students, critical or otherwise, and in relation to other student bodies?

NCLG   Our relationship to other student bodies depends on common political ground. For example, we have little contact with groups such as the Young Conservatives. The structure of the CLGs is genuinely democratic. Communication between members on a local and national basis is of primary importance. Students, practitioners and lecturers are incorporated on this basis. We do not act within the confines of state requirements and as such we have often found ourselves in confrontations with other student bodies. This was clearly illustrated by Kent's experience with the Student Union when providing a platform for a Sinn Fein speaker last February. Under the guise of bureaucratic requirements the University sought to censor the title of the talk, 'Legal and Illegal Repression in Northern Ireland', to restrict the numbers of persons attending, to supervise publicity and stewarding and to inhibit the use of the student radio station to broadcast the talk. The SU was prepared to accept these rules and was less than sympathetic in challenging the University's authority. Most of these 'requirements' were fought off and served to clarify the non-compromising position of the CLGs.

Editors   What do you think of the current attempts at critical legal education? Do you think it is possible, or desirable, or important to get away from the sorts of hierarchical relations and effects Duncan Kennedy talks about?

NCLG   We accept much of Duncan Kennedy's analysis of how traditional legal education is both a training in subordination and a training for subordination. We must, as critical lawyers, seek in every possible way to 'subvert' this dominant tradition – to 'subvert' the law school if you like and to put at the centre of legal education (as with legal practice) the questions of Whose law? Whose values? Whose hierarchy?

Editors   Do you think 'academic freedom' is important or 'meaningful' in faculties of law? Does it matter to students?

NCLG   Obviously the quality of our education is an important issue for students. When academic freedom is directly restricted by right- or left-wing state control, critical education has been forced backwards. However, we are aware that academic teaching is dominated by bourgeois ideology and that academic freedom may serve as a guise for promoting reactionary ideologies and so called liberal or even radical educators may in reality act as 'soldiers with typewriters'.

Editors   How far do students take account of the internal politics of law departments? Are students pawns in others' games?

NCLG If by internal politics you are referring to the formulation of academic courses, we strongly believe that students and teachers should involve themselves in a constructive dialogue, exploring the possibilities that each course may offer. As to students being 'pawns in others' games', again you have assumed a strict division between student and teacher. If you believe this to be the case, is this questionnaire an example of such a game?

Editors How can issues of race, gender and class be tackled within law departments?

NCLG If legislation is conveyed to students on a neutral basis as just another poachable fact then issues of race, gender and class are not tackled. However, if placed in sociopolitical context, the purpose of such legislation is clarified. The law has failed to prevent racism. Anti-discrimination laws have been imposed on a structurally racist society. The law plays a dual and a contradictory role in legitimating this. The law's formal rejection of racism stands in stark contrast to the increasingly tighter immigration laws it institutes. In 1981 the Nationality Act restricted the residential rights of 'new' Commonwealth citizens in Britain. In 1988 the right to appeal against deportation for residents of less than seven years was abolished. In 1985 Winston Silcott was convicted of PC Blakelock's death without the usual prerequisite of evidence and without reference to the intense police harassment and murder of Mrs Cynthia Jarratt that preceded the Tottenham riots. By isolating the case from its social context the state was able to name its victims.

The 'radical' approach to tackling the recession has meant that in real terms the working class has paid. This has meant increased repression facilitated by new legislation. Four anti-trade union laws have been instituted since 1979 and the Police and Criminal Evidence Act of 1984 has extended police rights to stop and search. In 1985 the police gained the right to use CS gas and plastic bullets and the Public Order Act of 1986 extended police rights to restrain protesting individuals 'for the public good'. In reality this was instituted as a direct reaction to the miners' strike of 1984–5. The abolition of the right to strike is firmly on the agenda as is the abolition of the right to silence. The state's use of the law is clearly seen in its repression of Irish republicans. In 1988 the Prevention of Terrorism Act was made permanent and Sinn Fein was banned from the airwaves. We are increasingly policed. The Security Services Bill means that M15 may 'legally' tap our phones and the Official Secrets Act obliterates public access to information.

Gender discrimination is opposed by the law in the Sex Discrimination Acts but inequality is substantially upheld through the marriage relationship and property rights. The women's movement has tended to focus on radicalising the law without always being aware of the law's function in perpetuating a structural patriarchy.

The law is political and must be tackled with that knowledge. Class, race and gender are the categories that must be central to any teaching of the law.

Editors   How should and how can students take issue with doctrinal teaching?

NCLG   Doctrinal teaching may be tackled firstly by our political approach which must by now be clear. Secondly, students must attempt to bridge the gap between doctrinal teaching, critical discourse and legal practice. They must link 'education, agitation and organisation', a marriage of theory and practice, in order to be a potent force for social change. The 'truth' about the law cannot emerge from an inward looking analysis of legal discourse and the contradictions therein. (*With thanks to* Law and Critique *for their permission to publish this extract.*)

The Need for More CLGs

We hope that this account will convince our readers of the need to expand the CLG network and encourage them to do so.

If you would like our help, do get in touch. For further information, contact Ian Grigg-Spall, Rutherford College, University of Kent, Canterbury, Kent CT2 7NX, tel. (0227) 764000 ext 3425 or fax (0227) 475473.

5
An Alternative Guide to Solicitors' Firms and Bar Chambers
Ian Grigg-Spall and Mollie Roots

As we indicated in the introduction, this chapter is intended to serve two purposes: first, to identify some of the practitioners who may be willing to be associated with local CLGs and CLACs. Secondly, to provide an alternative guide to firms and chambers for students seeking placements and legal training.

We also include at the end of the chapter the addresses of all law centres in Britain. We suggest that they be represented on the executive committees of local CLGs.

Solicitors' Firms

Needless to say, guides to practice opportunities in the City and in large practices serving private clients are readily available. This is not the case for firms which have a commitment to legal aid practice and to dealing with the problems of the poorer sections of the community. This problem is exacerbated by the fact that law centres, where many students would ideally like to serve their training period, are hindered by funding problems and the training regulations from taking 'trainee solicitors'.

We thought, therefore, that it would be worthwhile attempting to compile an alternative guide to law firms to assist students. To do this we sought the help of the law centres.

We thank the firms listed for their help in compiling this guide. Obviously, inclusion does not indicate that firms subscribe to the views of the CLGs or the views expressed in this book. Equally, we are aware that there will be many other firms who would, no doubt, have liked to have been included, but whom we failed to reach.

The guide identifies firms by geographical area and areas of work.

These firms are willing to consider applications for trainee solicitors, vacation placements, and outdoor court clerks. *Only a firm's major areas of practice are listed.*

Outside London

Belfast
Norman Shannon & Co., 28 Donegal Street, Belfast BT1 2GP
  All areas of legal aid.

Birmingham
Robin Thompson & Partners, The McLaren Building, 2 Masshouse
  Circus, Queensway, Birmingham B4 7NR
  Trade union, employment and personal injury.
George Jonas & Co., 190 Corporation Street, Birmingham
  Crime.
Tyndallwoods & Millichip, King Edward Building, 205 Corporation
  Street, Birmingham B4 6QB.
  Fifty percent of work is legal aid in the areas of community law (i.e.
  housing, welfare benefits, civil liberties, employment) immigration
  and nationality, family and matrimonial, 'trouble with police' and
  all criminal matters and civil litigation (including personal injury).
Glaisyers, 10 Rowchester Court, Printing House Street, Birmingham B4
  6DZ
  Crime and civil litigation.

Bristol
Bobbetts Mackan, 20A Berkeley Square, Clifton, Bristol BS8 1HP
  Crime, childcare and matrimonial, housing, civil litigation.
Douglas & Partners, 115 Grosvenor Road, St. Paul's, Bristol BS2 8YA
  Crime, childcare, mental health, race and civil liberties.

Canterbury
Harman & Harman, 10 Station Road West, Canterbury, Kent.
  Crime, family, childcare, personal injury and housing.
Jane Hinde, 59 Dover Street, Canterbury, Kent CT1 3HD
  Crime and matrimonial.

Cardiff
Robin Thompson & Partners, 1 Fitzalan Place, Newport Road, Cardiff
  CF2 1US
  Trade union, employment and personal injury.

Hayes, Middlesex
Desmond Wright & Co., 1094A Uxbridge Road, Hayes, Middx. UB4 8QH
  Crime, childcare, civil action against the police and matrimonial.

Hove, Sussex
Keith Arscott & Co., 48 Albany Villas, Hove, E. Sussex BN3 2RW
  Crime, litigation and matrimonial.

Hull
Robin Thompson & Partners, Jarratt House, 10 Jarratt St, Hull HU1 3HB
Trade unions, employment and personal injury.

Leeds
Ruth Bundey & Co., 37 York Place, Leeds, LS1 2ED
Immigration, crime, child care and civil litigation (medical negligence and suing the police).
Victor D. Zermansky, 10 Butts Court, Leeds, LS1 5JS.
Matrimonial, personal injury, medical negligence and crime.

Leicester
Greene D'sa, 1 Halford Street, Leicester, LE1 1JA
Crime, personal injury, medical negligence, housing, children, matrimonial.
Harts, 146 Melton Road, Leicester, LE4 5EG
Crime, housing, family, personal injury, welfare.

Liverpool
Brian Thompson & Partners, Richmond House, Rumford Place, Liverpool L3 9SW
Trade unions, employment, personal injury.
R. M. Broudie, 1–3 Sir Thomas Street, Liverpool L1 8BW
Civil liberties and crime.

Macclesfield
Andrew Fitzpatrick, 59 Park Green, Macclesfield, Cheshire SK1 17N
Crime.

Manchester
Brian Thompson & Partners, Acresfield, 8 Exchange Street, Manchester M2 7HA
Trade unions, employment, personal injury.
John Pickering, Old Exchange Buildings, St Ann's Passage, 29–31 King Street, Manchester M2 6BE
Personal injury, medical negligence, trade unions, employment.
Rhys Vaughan, 382 Dickenson Road, Manchester M13 0WQ
Crime, matrimonial, civil liberties, personal injuries.
Robert Lizar & Co., 2 Woodcock Square, Hume, Manchester M15 6DJ
Crime, housing, family and childcare.

Newcastle upon Tyne
Brian Thompson & Partners, 2 Kentle Street, Newcastle upon Tyne NE1 5XN
Trade unions, employment, personal injury.

David Gray & Co., 17 Elswick Road, Newcastle upon Tyne NE4 6ER
  Crime, family, immigration, employment, housing, personal injury,
  welfare, mental health.

Nottingham

Gregsons, The Old Milton's Head, 84 Derby Road, Nottingham NG1
  5FD
  All female firm. Crime, personal injury, actions against police,
  family, childcare, employment, immigration.
Robin Thompson & Partners, Price House, 37 Stoney Street, The Lace
  Market, Nottingham NG1 1LS
  Trade unions, employment, personal injury.

Oldham

Dunderdale Wignall, 5 Union Street, Oldham OL1 1HA
  Crime, family, personal injury and welfare.

Salford

Herwald Seddon & Co., 306 Great Cheetham Street East, Salford M7
  0UJ
  Crime, childcare, mental health.

Sheffield

Brian Thompson & Partners, Arundel House, 1 Furnival Square, Sheffield
  S1 4QL
  Trade unions, employment and personal injury.
John Howell & Co., 427–431 London Road, Sheffield S2 4HJ
  Crime, family, personal injury, immigration, childcare, housing,
  welfare, employment and mental health.(Other offices in London
  and Spain)

Southampton

Bernard Chill & Axtell, The First House, 1a, The Avenue, Southamp-
  ton S09 1NA
  Crime, matrimonial and personal injury.

Uxbridge, Middlesex

Booth Bennett, The Market House, High Street, Uxbridge, Middx. UB8
  1AQ
  Crime, childcare, family and personal injury.

Walsall

Geffens, Malvern House, 62 Bradford St, Walsall, WS1 3QD
  Crime,family and divorce, general civil litigation (personal injuries)
  housing (some immigration and mental health).

London

Alan Edwards & Co., 36A Notting Hill Gate, London W11 3HX
  Housing (tenants association and homeless), crime, family, personal
  injury and action against police.

B. M. Birnberg & Co., 103 Borough High Street, London SE1 1NN
  Crime, immigration, employment, civil liberties.

Bindman & Partners, 1 Euston Road, King's Cross, London NW1 2SA
  Family, housing, criminal litigation, immigration, defamation, discrimination and personal injury.

Bradburys, 119 Camberwell Road, London SE5 0HB
  Crime, personal injury, family and housing.

Brian Thompson & Partners, 102 St George's Square, London SW1V 3QY
  Trade unions, employment and personal injury.

Christian Fisher & Co., 18 Russell Street, Covent Garden, London
  WC2B 5HP
  Crime, civil liberties, immigration and housing.

Clinton, Davis, Cushing & Kelly, 26 Lower Clapton Road, Hackney,
  London E5 0PD
  Crime, family and all legal aid.

Daniel & Harris, 338 Kilburn High Road (off Iverson Road), London
  NW6 2QN
  Family, personal injury and housing.

Darlington & Parkinson, 78 Pitshanger Lane, Ealing, London W5 1QX
  Crime, family, childcare and mental health.

David Levene & Co., Tottenham Enterprise Centre, 560–568 High
  Road, London N17 9TA
  Personal injury, immigration, housing, crime, employment and
  family.

Dowse & Co., 23–25 Dalston Lane, London E8 3DF
  Crime, housing, employment (and discrimination), medical
  negligence, action against police, immigration and family.

Dundons, 261 Lavender Hill, London SW11 1JD
  Crime, childcare, personal injury, action against police and civil
  liberties.

Evill & Coleman, 113 Upper Richmond Road, Putney, London SW15
  2UD
  Personal injury, medical, negligence, employment and family.

Fisher Meredith, 2 Binfield Road, London SW4 6TA
  Crime, family, medico-legal (specialising in large and complex
  cases) and libel.

G. L. Hockfield & Co., Etna House, 350 Kennington Road, London SE11
  4LD
  Personal injury and housing.

Glazer Delmar, 223–229 Rye Lane, Peckham, London SE15 4TZ
  Personal injury, family housing, crime and mental health.

Goodman Ray, 450, Kingsland Road, London E8 4AE
  Family, crime and housing.
Hallmark Atkinson Winter, 379–381, Brixton Rd, London SW9 7DE
  Crime, housing, family, childcare, civil injunctions and personal
  injuries.
Harter & Loveless, 398 Caledonian Road, London N1 1DN
  Family, crime and housing.
Hodge Jones & Allen, 148–150 Camden High Street, London NW1 0NG
  Crime, matrimonial, housing and general litigation.
Hornby & Levy, 2 Acre Lane, London SW2 5SG
  Crime, civil liberties and family.
Howard Pallis & Co., 128 Upper Clapton Road, London E5 9JY
  Crime, matrimonial, housing and general litigation.
Jane Coker & Co., 523–525 High Road, Tottenham, London N17 6SB
  Immigration and family.
J. B. Wheatley & Co., 64–70 Denmark Hill, London SE5 8RZ
  Crime, childcare and general litigation.
Lawrence & Co., 194 North End Road, Fulham, London W14 9NX
  Crime, family, housing, personal injury and employment.
Leigh Day & Co., 37 Gray's Inn Road, London WC1X 8PP
  Environmental, medical negligence, pollution and nuisance action.
McGoldrick & Co., 124 Deptford High Street, London SE8 4NS
  Crime, family and actions against police.
Nash & Dowell, 246 Hornsey Road, London N7 7LL
  Crime, civil liberty, personal injury and family.
Offenbach & Co., 60, Great Marlborough St, London W1V 2BA.
  Crime, family and all litigation
O. H. Parsons, Sovereign House, 212-224 Shaftsbury Avenue, London
  WC2H 8PR
  Trade unions, employment and personal injury.
Pattinson & Brewer, 30 Great James Street, London WC1N 3HA
  Branch Office: 8–12 New Road, Chatham, Kent ME4 4QR (also
  branch offices in Bristol and York)
  Trade unions, employment, personal injury, litigation, discrimi-
  nation, crime and defamation.
Peter Kandler & Co., 50 Goldborne Rd., London W10
  Crime, childcare and wardship
Philcox Gray & Co., 92 Camberwell Road, London SE5 0EJ
  Housing, consumer credit, crime, family and personal injury.
Powell Spencer & Partners, 290 Kilburn High Road, London NW6
  2DB
  Crime, family, personal injury and civil liberties.
R. R. Sangvi & Co., 32 Watford Road, Wembley, Middlesex HA0 3EP
  Crime, matrimonial and all legal aid work.

Robin Thompson & Partners, Bainbridge House, Bainbridge Street, London WC1A 1HT
Trade unions, employment and personal injury.

Rowley Ashworth, 247 The Broadway, Wimbledon, London SW19 1SE
Trade unions employment and personal injury.

Saunders & Co., 413–419 Harrow Road, London W9 3QL
Crime and civil litigation.

Simons Muirhead & Burton, Lading House, 10–14 Bedford Street, Covent Garden, London WC2E 9HE
Crime, immigration, Privy Council, media, matrimonial and civil litigation.

Stennett & Stennett, 274 Seven Sisters Road, London N4 2HY
Crime and family.

Taylor Nichol, 3A Station Place, London N4 2DH
Crime, immigration, civil liberties and medical negligence.

Winstanley-Burgess, 378 City Road, London EC1V 2QA
Immigration, crime, family and housing.

Barristers' Chambers

We are indebted to the Haldane Society for their list of chambers in which there are a number of members of the Society. All these chambers are willing to receive applications for placements and pupillages.

14 Tooks Court, Cursitor Street, London EC4A 1JY. Tel: 071-405 8828

Cloisters, 2nd Floor, Temple, London EC4Y 7AA. Tel: 071-583 0303

Doughty Street Chambers, 11, Doughty Street, London WC1N 2PG. Tel: 071-404 1313

23 Mitre House, 2nd Floor, Mitre Court, 44 Fleet Street, London EC4Y 1BN. Tel: 071-583 8233

2 Garden Court, 3rd Floor, Middle Temple, London EC4 9BL. Tel: 071-353 1633

8 Kings Bench Walk, 2nd Floor, Temple, London EC4Y 7DU. Tel: 071-353 7851

4 Verulam Buildings, Ground Floor South, Gray's Inn, London WC1R 5LW. Tel: 071-405 6114

2 Plowden Buildings, 2nd Floor, Middle Temple Lane, London EC4Y 9AS. Tel: 071-353 4341

15 Old Square, Ground Floor, Lincolns Inn, London WC2A 3UE. Tel: 071-831 0801

11 Kings Bench Walk, 3rd Floor, Temple, London EC4Y 7EQ. Tel: 071-353 4931

Addresses of all UK Law Centres

Adamsdown Law Centre, 15 Splott Road, Splott, Cardiff CF2 2BU. Tel: 0222 498117

Avon & Bristol Law Centre, 62 Bedminster Parade, Bristol BS3 4HL. Tel: 0272 667933

Belfast Law Centre, 7 University Road, Belfast BT7 1NA. Tel: 0232 321307

Bradford Law Centre, 31 Manor Row, Bradford BD1 4PX. Tel: 0274 306617

Brent Community Law Centre, 190 Willesden High Road, London NW10 2PB. Tel: 081-451 1122

Brent Young People's Law Centre, 190 Willesden High Road, London NW10 2PB. Tel: 081-451 2428

Brighton Law Centre, 36a Duke Street, Brighton BN1 1AG. Tel: 0273 29634/5

Brixton Law Centre, 506/508 Brixton Road, London SW9 8EN. Tel: 071-733 4245

Camden Community Law Centre, 2a Prince of Wales Road, London NW5 3LG. Tel: 071-485 6672

Carlisle Law Centre, 43 Cecil Street, Carlisle CA1 1NS. Tel: 0228 515129

Castlemilk Law Centre, 30 Dougrie Drive, Glasgow G45 9AD. Tel: 041-634 0313

Central London Law Centre, 47 Charing Cross Road, London WC2H 0AN. Tel: 071-437 5854 (Entrance: Little Newport Street)

Chesterfield Law Centre, 70 Saltergate, Chesterfield S40 1JR. Tel: 0246 550674

Coventry Legal and Income Rights Service, The Bridge, Broadgate, Coventry CV1 1NG. Tel; 0203 223051/3

Ealing Borough Law Centre (Ealing branch), 2 The Green, High St, London W5 5DA. Tel; 081-579 5340

Ealing Borough Law Centre (Southall branch), 11b King Street, Middlesex UB2 4DF. Tel; 081-574 2434

Gateshead Law Centre, Swinburne House, Swinburne St, Gateshead, Tyne & Wear NE8 1AX. Tel: 091-477 1109

Gloucester Law Centre, Widden Old School, Widden Street, Gloucester GL1 4AQ. Tel: 0452 423492

Greenwich Law Centre, 187 Trafalgar Road, London SE10 9EQ. Tel: 081-853 2550

Hackney Law Centre, 236/238 Mare Street, London E8 1HE. Tel: 081-985 8364/Emer. 081-986 9891

Hammersmith & Fulham Law Centre, 142/144 King Street, London W6 0QU. Tel: 081-741 4021

Handsworth Law Centre, 220 Soho Road, Birmingham B21 9LR. Tel: 021-554 0868/551 1969

Harehills & Chapeltown Law Centre, 263 Roundhay Road, Leeds LS8 4HS. Tel: 0532 491100

Hartlepool Law Centre, The People's Centre, Raby Road, Hartlepool, Cleveland TS24 8LA. Tel: 0429 861333

Highfields and Belgrave Law Centre, Seymour House, 6 Seymour St, Leicester LE2 0LB. Tel: 0533 532928

Hillingdon Legal Resource Centre, 12 Harold Avenue, Hayes, Middlesex UB3 4QW. Tel: 081-561 9400

Hounslow Law Centre, 51 Lampton Road, Hounslow, Middlesex TW3 1JG. Tel: 081-570 9505

Humberside Law Centre, Centre 88, Saner St, Anlaby Rd, Hull, HU1 2PG. Tel: 0482 211180

Hyson Green Law Centre, 65 Birkin Avenue, Nottingham NG7 5AW. Tel: 0602 787813

North Islington Law Centre, 161 Hornsey Road, London N7 6DU. Tel: 071-607 2461

South Islington Law Centre, 131/132 Upper Street, Islington, London N1 1QP. Tel: 071-354 0133

North Kensington Law Centre, 74 Golborne Road, London W10 5PS. Tel: 081-969 7473

Leicester Rights Centre, 6 Bishop Street, Leicester LE1 6AF. Tel: 0533 553781

North Lambeth Law Centre, 381 Kennington Lane, London SE11 5QY. Tel: 071-582 4425/4373

North Lewisham Law Centre, 28 Deptford High Street, London SE8 3NU. Tel: 081-692 5355

Liverpool 8 Law Centre, 34/36 Princes Road, Liverpool L8 1TH. Tel: 051-709 7222

Luton Law Centre, 2a Reginald Street, Luton LU2 7QZ. Tel: 0582 481000

North Manchester Law Centre, Community Services Centre, Paget Street, Manchester 10 7UX. Tel: 061-205 5040

South Manchester Law Centre, 584 Stockport Road, Manchester 13 0RQ. Tel: 061-225 5111

Middlesborough Law Centre, Saint Mary's Centre, 82/90 Corporation Road, Cleveland TS1 2RW. Tel: 0642 223813/7

Newcastle Law Centre, 279 Westgate Rd, Newcastle upon Tyne NE4 6AJ. Tel: 091-230 4777

Newham Rights Centre, 285 Romford Road, Newham, London E7 9HJ. Tel: 081-555 3331

Oldham Law Centre, Prudential Buildings, 2nd Floor, 79 Union Street, Oldham OL1 1HL. Tel: 061-627 0925

Paddington Law Centre, 439 Harrow Road, London W10 4RE. Tel: 081-960 3155

Plumstead Law Centre, 105 Plumstead High St, London SE18 1SB. Tel: 081-855 9817

Rochdale Law Centre, Smith Street, Rochdale OL16 1HE. Tel: 0706 57766

Salford Law Centre, 498 Liverpool Street, Salford M6 5QZ. Tel: 061-736 3116

Saltley Action Centre, 2 Alum Rock Road, Saltley, Birmingham B8 1JB. Tel: 021-328 2307

Sheffield Law Centre, 1st Floor, Waverley House, 10 Joiner Street, Sheffield S3 8GW. Tel: 0742 731888

Southwark Law Centre, 2 East Dulwich Grove, London SE22 8PP. Tel: 081-299 1024

Springfield Law Centre, Springfield Hospital, Glenburnie Road, London SW17 7DJ. Tel: 081-767 6884

Stockton Law Centre, 76 Norton Road, Stockton on Tees, Cleveland TS18 2DE. Tel: 0642 605060

Stockwell & Clapham Law Centre, 57/59 Old Town, Clapham, London SW4 0JQ. Tel: 071-720 6231

Thamesdown Law Centre, 26 Victoria Road, Swindon SN1 3AW. Tel: 0793 486926/7

Tottenham Law Centre, 15 West Green Road, London N15 5BX. Tel: 081-802 0911

Tower Hamlets Law Centre, 341 Commercial Road, London E1 2PS. Tel: 071-791 0741

Vauxhall Law Centre, Multi-Services Centre, Silvester Street, Liverpool L5 8SE. Tel: 051-207 2004/3502

Warrington Law Centre, 64/66 Bewsey Street, Warrington, Cheshire WA2 7JQ. Tel: 0925 51104

West Hampstead Law Centre, 59 Kingsgate Road, London NW6 4TD. Tel: 071-328 4501/4523

Wytheshawe Law Centre, Fenside Road, Sharston, Manchester M22 4WZ. Tel: 061-428 5929/8739

References and Further Reading

Chapter One

Alan Thomson: Foreword: Critical Approaches to Law

Bankowski, Z. and Mungham, G. (1976) *Images of Law* (London: Routledge & Kegan Paul)

Berger, P. and Luckmann, T. (1967) *The Social Construction of Reality* (London: Allen Lane)

Critical Legal Studies Symposium (1984) *Stanford Law Review*, vol. 36

Fine, R., Kinsey, R., Lea, J., Picciotto, S. and Young, J. (1979) *Capitalism and the Rule of Law* (London: Hutchinson)

Fine, R. (1984) *Democracy and the Rule of Law* (London: Pluto Press)

Fitzpatrick, P. and Hunt, A. (eds) (1987) *Critical Legal Studies* (Oxford: Blackwell)

Foucault, M. (1979) *Discipline and Punish* (Harmondsworth: Penguin)

Gabel, P. and Harris, P. (1982) 'Building Power and Breaking Images: Critical Theory and the Practice of Law', *Review of Law and Social Change*, vol. II, pp. 369–411

Goodrich, P. (1986) *Reading the Law* (Oxford: Blackwell)

Hunt, A. (1986) 'The Theory of Critical Legal Studies', *Oxford Journal of Legal Studies*, vol. 6, pp. 1–45

Hutchinson, A.C. (1988) *Dwelling on the Threshold: Critical Essays on Modern Legal Thought* (London: Sweet & Maxwell)

Hutchinson, A.C. and Monahan, P.J. (1984) 'Law, Politics and the Critical Legal Scholars: The Unfolding Drama in American Legal Thought', *Stanford Law Review*, vol. 36, pp. 199–245

Kairys, D. (1982) *The Politics of Law: A Progressive Critique* (New York: Pantheon)

Kelman, M. (1987) *A Guide to Critical Legal Studies* (Cambridge, Mass: Harvard University Press)

Lukacs, G. (1968) *History and Class Consciousness* (London: Merlin)

Pashukanis, E. (1983) *Law and Marxism* (London: Inklinks/Pluto Press)

Smart, C. (1989) *Feminism and the Power of Law* (London: Routledge)

Trubek, D. and Esser, J. (1988) *Critical Empiricism*, University of Wisconsin Working Papers, nos 3–4

Unger, R. (1983) 'The Critical Legal Studies Movement', *Harvard Law Review*, vol. 96, pp. 561–75

Robert Fine and Sol Picciotto: On Marxist Critiques of Law

Althusser, L. (1965) *Reading Capital* (London: New Left Books)

Arthur, C. (1977) 'Towards a Materialist Theory of Law', *Critique*, vol. 7, pp. 31–46

Balbus, J. D. (1977) 'Commodity Form and Legal Form', *Law and Society Review*, vol. 2, pp. 571–88

Beirne, P. and Sharlet, R. (1980) *Pashukanis: Selected Writings on Marxism and Law* (New York: Academic Press)

Binns, P. (1980) 'Law and Marxism', *Capital & Class*, vol. 10, pp. 100–13

Bottomore, T. and Goode, P. (eds) (1978) *Austro-Marxism* (Oxford: Oxford University Press)

Clarke (1982) *Marx, Marginalism and Modern Sociology* (London: Macmillan)

Colletti, L. (1972) *From Rousseau to Lenin* (London: New Left Books)

Colletti, L. (1975) *Introduction to Marx: Early Writings* (Harmondsworth: Penguin)

Dewar, J., Paliwala, A., Picciotto, S. and Ruete, M. (1986) *Nuclear Weapons, the Peace Movement and the Law* (London: Macmillan)

Draper, H. (1977) *Karl Marx's Theory of Revolution* (New York: Monthly Review Press)

Fine, R. (1984) *Democracy and the Rule of Law* (London: Pluto Press)

Fine, R., Kinsey, R., Picciotto S. and Young J. (eds) (1979) *Capitalism and the Rule of Law* (London: Hutchinson)

Fine, R. and Millar, R. (eds) (1985) *Policing the Miners' Strike* (London: Lawrence & Wishart)

Habermas, J. (1974) *Theory and Practice* (London: Heinemann)

Holloway, J. and Picciotto, S. (1977) 'Capital, Crisis and the State', *Capital and Class*, vol. 2, pp. 76–101

Holloway, J. and Picciotto, S. (1978) *State and Capital: A Marxist Debate* (London: Edward Arnold)

Kay, G. and Mott, J. (1982) *Political Order and the Law of Labour* (London: Macmillan)

Keane, J. (1988) 'Despotism and Democracy', in *Civil Society and the State* (London: Verso)

Marx, K. (1954) *Capital: Volume I* (London: Lawrence & Wishart)

Marx, K. (1975) 'Economic and Philosophical Manuscripts' in L. Colletti, *Introduction to Marx: Early Writings* (Harmondsworth: Penguin)

Marx, K. and Engels, F. (1989) *Selected Works of Marx and Engels* (London: Lawrence & Wishart)

Neumann, F. (1957) *The Democratic and Authoritarian State* (Glencoe, Ith.: Free Press)

Neumann, F. (1986) *The Rule of Law* (Oxford: Berg)

Norrie, A. (1982) 'Pashukanis and the Commodity Form Theory: a Reply to Warrington', *International Journal of the Sociology of Law*, vol. 10, pp. 419–37

Norrie, A. (1990) 'Locating the Socialist Rechtsstaat: Underdevelopment and Criminal Justice in the Soviet Union', *International Journal of the Sociology of Law*, vol. 18, pp. 343–59

Pashukanis, E. (1983) *Law and Marxism* (London: Inklinks/Pluto Press)

Poulantzas, N. (1978) *State, Power, Socialism* (London: New Left Books)

Redhead, S. (1978) 'The Discrete Charm of Bourgeois Law: A note on Pashukanis', *Critique*, no. 9, pp. 113–20

Renner, K. (1949) *The Institutions of Private Law and their Social Functions* (London: Routledge & Kegan Paul)

Rose, G. (1981) *Hegel contra Sociology* (London: Athlone)

Sayer, D. (1987) *The Violence of Abstraction: Analytical Foundations of Historical Materialism* (Oxford: Blackwell)

Sharlet, R. (1974) 'Pashukanis and the Withering Away of Law in USSR' in S. Fitzpatrick (ed.) *Cultural Revolution in Russia 1928–31* (Bloomington, Ind.: Indiana University Press)

Thompson, E.P. (1977) *Whigs and Hunters* (Harmondsworth: Penguin)

Thompson, E.P. (1978) *The Poverty of Theory* (London: Merlin)

Thompson, E.P. (1980) *Writing By Candlelight* (London: Merlin)

Williams, M. (ed.) (1988) *Value, Social Form and the State* (London: Macmillan)

Wood, E. (1990) 'The Uses and Abuses of "Civil Society"', *Socialist Register* (London: Merlin)

Anne Bottomley: Feminism

Bottomley, A.B. (1987) 'Feminism in Law Schools', in S. McLoughlin (ed.), *Women and the Law*, University College London working papers no. 5

Bottomley, A.B. et al. (1987) 'Dworkin; which Dworkin? Taking Feminism Seriously' in P. Fitzpatrick and A. Hunt (eds), *Critical Legal Studies* (Oxford: Blackwell)

Braidotti, R. (1991) *Patterns of Dissonance* (Cambridge: Polity Press)

Brennan, T. (ed.) (1989) *Between Feminism and Psychoanalysis* (London: Routledge)

Dahl, T.S. (1987) *Women's Law* (Oslo: Norwegian University Press, distributed by Oxford University Press)

Delphy, C. (1984) *Close to Home* (London: Hutchinson)

Eisenstein, Z. (1988) *The Female Body and the Law* (Berkeley, Calif.: University of California Press)

Gibson, S. (1990) 'Continental Drift: The Question of Context in Feminist Jurisprudence' in *Law and Critique*, vol. 1, no. 2, pp. 173–200

Jardine, A. (1987) *Gynesis: Configurations of Women and Modernity* (Ithaca, N.Y.: Cornell University Press)

Jardine, A and Smith, P. (1987) *Men in Feminism* (London: Methuen)

MacKinnon, C. (1987) *Feminism Unmodified* (Cambridge, Mass.: Harvard University Press)

Olivier, C. (1989) *Jocasta's Children* (London: Routledge)

Pateman, C. (1988) *The Sexual Contract* (Cambridge: Polity Press)

Rifkin, J. (1985) 'Teaching Mediation: A Feminist Perspective on the Study of Law' in M. Culley and C. Portuges (eds) *Gendered Subjects* (London: Routledge & Kegan Paul)

Smart, C. (1976) *Women, Crime and Criminology* (London: Routledge & Kegan Paul)

Smart, C. (1984) *The Ties that Bind* (London: Routledge & Kegan Paul)

Smart, C. (1989) *Feminism and the Power of Law* (London: Routledge)

Smart, C. (1991) 'Feminist Jurisprudence' in P. Fitzpatrick (ed.) *Dangerous Supplements* (London: Pluto Press)

Young, A. (1990) 'Of the Essential in Criticism: Some Intersections in Writing, Political Protest and Law' in *Law and Critique*, vol. 1, no. 2, pp. 210–18

Costas Douzinas and Ronnie Warrington: Postmodernism

Callinicos, A. (1989) *Against Postmodernism: A Marxist Critique* (Cambridge: Polity Press)

Davidson, D. (1984) *Inquiries into Truth and Interpretations* (Oxford: Clarendon Press)

Derrida, J. (1976) *Of Grammatology* (Baltimore: Johns Hopkins University Press)

Goodrich, P. (1990) 'We Orators', *Modern Law Review*, vol. 53, no. 4, pp. 546–63

Habermas, J. (1987) *The Philosophical Discourse of Modernity* (Cambridge, Mass.: Harvard University Press)

Harvey, D. (1989) *The Condition of Postmodernity* (Oxford: Blackwell)

Heidegger, J. (1968) *What is Called Thinking?* (New York: Harper & Row)

Lyotard, J.F. (1984) *The Postmodern Condition: A Report on Knowledge* (Manchester: Manchester University Press)

Marx, K. (1954) *Capital: Volume I* (London: Lawrence & Wishart)

Nietzsche, F. (1961) *Thus Spake Zarathustra* (Harmondsworth: Penguin)

Sammy Adelman and Ken Foster: Critical Legal Theory

Davidoff, H. (1952) *The Pocket Book of Quotations* (New York: Pocket Books)

Fitzpatrick, P. (1987) 'Racism and the Innocence of Law' in P. Fitzpatrick and A. Hunt (eds) *Critical Legal Studies* (Oxford: Blackwell)

Foucault, M. (1971) *Madness and Civilisation* (London: Tavistock)

Foucault, M. (1979) *Discipline and Punish* (Harmondsworth: Penguin)

MacKinnon, C. (1987) *Feminism Unmodified* (Cambridge, Mass.: Harvard University Press)

Marx, K. (1989) *Selected Works of Marx and Engels* (London: Lawrence & Wishart)

Smart, C. (1989) *Feminism and the Power of Law* (London: Routledge)

Peter Fitzpatrick: Law as Resistance

Baxi, U. (1985) 'Popular Justice, Participatory Development and Power Politics: the Lok Adalat in Turmoil' in A. Allott and G. Woodman (eds), *People's Law and State Law: The Bellagio Papers* (Dordrecht: Foris)

Delgado, R. (1987) 'The Ethereal Scholar: Does Critical Legal Studies Have What Minorities Want?', *Harvard Civil Rights – Civil Liberties Law Review*, vol. 22, no. 2. pp. 301–22

Derrida, J. (1976) *Of Grammatology* (Baltimore: Johns Hopkins University Press)

Donzelot, J. (1980) *The Policing of Families: Welfare versus the State* (London: Hutchinson)

Fitzpatrick, P. (1987) 'Racism and the Innocence of Law' in P. Fitzpatrick and A. Hunt (eds) *Critical Legal Studies* (Oxford: Blackwell)

Henry, S. (1982) 'Factory Law: The Changing Disciplinary Technology of Industrial Social Control', *International Journal of the Sociology of Law*, vol. 10, no. 4, pp. 365–83

Hutchinson, A.C. and Monahan P.J. (1984) 'Law, Politics and the Critical Legal Scholars: The Unfolding Drama in American Legal Thought', *Stanford Law Review*, vol. 36, pp. 199–245
Marx, K. (1954) *Capital: Volume I* (London: Lawrence & Wishart)
Miller, E.J. (1986) *Conflict and Reconciliation: The Newham Experiment*, Occasional Paper 9 (London: Tavistock Institute)

Chapter 2

Alan Hunt: Legal Education and Practice

Barnett, H. & Yach, D. (1985) 'The Teaching of Jurisprudence and Legal Theory in British Universities and Polytechnics', *Legal Studies*, vol. 5, pp. 151–71
Hunt, A. (1986) 'The Case for Critical Legal Education', *The Law Teacher*, vol. 20, pp. 10–20
Kennedy, D. (1981) 'Rebels From Principle: Changing the Corporate Law Firm From Within', *Harvard Law School Bulletin*, vol. 33, pp. 36–40
Thomson, A. (1987) 'Critical Legal Education in Britain' in P. Fitzpatrick and A. Hunt (eds) *Critical Legal Studies* (Oxford: Blackwell)
Twining, W. and Miers, D. (1982) *How To Do Things With Rules* (London: Weidenfeld & Nicolson)

Alan Thomson: Law of Contract

Adams, J. and Brownsword, R. (1987) 'The Ideologies of Contract', *Legal Studies*, vol. 7, pp. 205–23
Atiyah, P.S. (1979) *The Rise and Fall of Freedom of Contract* (Oxford: Clarendon Press)
Collins, H. (1986) *The Law of Contract* (London: Weidenfeld & Nicolson)
Dalton, C. (1985) 'An Essay in the Deconstruction of Contract Law', *Yale Law Journal*, vol. 94, pp. 997–1114
Feenman, J. M. (1985) 'Critical Approaches to Contract', *UCLA Law Review*, vol. 30, pp. 829–49
Gabel, P. and Feinman, J. M (1982) 'Contract Law as Ideology' in D. Kairys (ed.) *The Politics of Law: a Progressive Critique* (New York: Pantheon)
Gabel, P. and Harris, P. (1982–83) 'Building Power and Breaking Images: Critical Legal Theory and the Practice of Law', *Review of Law and of Social Change*, vol. 11, pp. 369–411
Horwitz, M. (1977) *The Transformation of American Law* (Cambridge, Mass.: Harvard University Press)
Hunt, A. (1986) 'The Theory of Critical Legal Studies', *Oxford Journal of Legal Studies*, vol. 6, pp. 1–45
Hutchinson, A.C. and Monahan, P. J. (1984) 'Law, Politics and the Critical Legal Scholars: The Unfolding Drama in American Legal Thought', *Stanford Law Review*, vol. 36, pp. 199–245
Kelman, M. (1981) 'Interpretive Construction in Substantive Criminal Law', *Stanford Law Review*, vol. 33, pp. 591–631
Kennedy, D. (1982) 'Distributive and Paternalistic Motives in Contract and Tort Law with Special References to Compulsory Terms and Unequal Bargaining Power', *Maryland Law Review* vol. 41, pp. 614–24
Kronman, A. (1985) 'Contract Law and Distributive Justice', *Yale Law Journal*, vol. 89, pp. 472–511

Unger, R. (1983) 'The Critical Legal Studies Movement', *Harvard Law Review*, vol. 96, pp. 561–675

Alan Norrie: Criminal Law

Clarkson, C.M.V. and Keating, H. M. (1984) *Criminal Law: Text and Materials* (London: Sweet & Maxwell)

Foucault, M. (1979) *Discipline and Punish* (Harmondsworth: Penguin)

Glazebrook, P. (1960) 'Criminal Omissions', *Law Quarterly Review*, vol. 76, pp. 386–411

Griffiths, J. (1985, 2nd edn) *The Politics of the Judiciary* (London: Fontana)

Hale, M. (1971) *Pleas of the Crown* (London: Professional Books)

Hay, D. (1977) 'Property, Authority and the Criminal Law' in D. Hay et al., *Albion's Fatal Tree* (Harmondsworth: Penguin)

Kelman, M. (1980–1) 'Interpretative Law Construction in Substantive Criminal Law', *Stanford Law Review*, vol. 33, p. 591–673

Lacey, N., Wells, C., Meure, D. (1990) *Reconstructing Criminal Law* (London: Weidenfeld and Nicolson)

Moore, M. (1984) *Law and Psychiatry* (Cambridge: Cambridge University Press)

Nelken, D. (1987) 'Criminal Law and Justice: Some Notes on Their Irrelation' in I.H. Dennis (ed.), *Criminal Law and Justice* (London: Sweet & Maxwell)

Norrie, A. (1989) 'Oblique Intention and Legal Politics', *Criminal Law Review*, vol. l, pp. 793–807

Norrie, A. (1990) *Law, Ideology and Punishment* (Dordrecht: Kluwer)

Smith, J. and Hogan, B. (1988) *Criminal Law* (London: Butterworth)

Williams, G. (1983, 2nd edn) *Textbook of Criminal Law* (London: Stevens)

Joanne Conaghan and Wade Mansell; Tort

Allen,D. K., Bourne, C. J. and Holyoak, J. H. (eds) (1979) *Accident Compensation After Pearson* (London: Sweet & Maxwell)

Brazier, M. (1988, 8th edn) *Street on Torts* (London: Butterworths)

Cane, P. (1987, 4th edn) *Atiyah's Accidents, Compensation and the Law* (London: Weidenfeld & Nicolson)

Harris, D. et al. (1984) *Compensation and Support for Illness and Injury* (Oxford: Clarendon)

Horwitz, M. (1977) *The Transfomation of American Law* (London: Harvard University Press)

Cmnd 7054 (1978) *Report of the Royal Commission on Civil Liability and Compensation for Personal Injury* (London: HMSO)

Rogers, W.V.H. (1989) *Winfield and Jolowicz on Tort.* (London: Sweet & Maxwell)

White, G.E. (1985) *Torts Law in America: An Intellectual History* (Oxford: Oxford University Press)

Andy Clark, Kate Green and Nick Jackson: Property Law

Anderson, S. (1984) 'Land Law Texts and the Explanation of 1925', *Current Legal Problems*, pp. 63–83

Ball, M. (1983) *Housing Policy and Economic Power* (London: Methuen)

Ball, M. (1986) *Home Ownership: A Suitable Case for Reform* (London: Shelter)

Bohannan, P. (1964) 'Land, Land Tenure and Land Reform' in M. Herskovits and M. Harwitz (eds), *Economic Transition in Africa* (London: Routledge & Kegan Paul)

Bowles, S. and Gintis, H. (1986) *Democracy and Capitalism: Property, Community and the Contradiction of Modern Social Thought* (London: Routledge & Kegan Paul)

Cheshire, G.C. (1926) *The Modern Law of Real Property* (London: Butterworth)

Cotterrell, R. (1986) 'The Law of Property and Legal Theory' in W. Twining, *Legal Theory and Common Law* (Oxford: Blackwell)

Craig, P. (1986) 'The House that Jerry Built: Building Societies, the State and the Politics of Owner-Occupation', Housing Studies, vol. 1, part 1, pp. 87–108

Daunton, M.J. (1987) *A Property-Owning Democracy: Housing in Britain* (London: Faber)

Doling, J. et al. (1985) 'How Far Can Privatisation Go? Owner-Occupation and Mortgage Default', NatWest Bank *Quarterly Review*, August, pp. 42–52

Edelman, B. (1979) *Ownership of the Image* (London: Routledge & Kegan Paul)

Edgeworth, B. (1988) 'Post-Property?', *University of New South Wales Law Journal*, vol. 11, pp. 87–116

Ford, J. (1988) *The Indebted Society: Credit and Default in the 1980s* (London: Routledge)

Gough, T. (1982) *The Economics of Building Societies* (London: Macmillan)

Hirschon, R. (ed.) (1984) *Women and Property – Women as Property* (London: Croom Helm)

Law Commission (1986) 'Land Mortgages', working paper 99

Maddock, K. (1983) *Your Land is Our Land: Aboriginal Land Rights* (Ringwood, Victoria: Penguin)

Murray, R. (1987) 'Ownership Control and the Market', *New Left Review* vol. 164, pp. 87–112

National Consumer Council (1990) *Credit and Debt: The Consumer Interest* (London: HMSO)

Porter, V. (1989) 'The Copyright Designs and Patents Act 1988', *Journal of Law and Society*, vol. 16, pp. 340–51

Vincent-Jones, P. (1986) 'Private Property and Public Order: The Hippy Convoy and Criminal Trespass', *Journal of Law and Society* vol. 13, pp. 343–70

Ian Grigg-Spall, Paddy Ireland and Dave Kelly: Company Law

Clarke, S. (1982) *Marx, Marginalism and Modern Sociology* (London: Macmillan)

Gower, L.C.B. (1979, 4th edn) *Principles of Modern Company Law* (London: Stevens)

Harvey, D. (1982) *The Limits to Capital* (Oxford: Blackwell)

Harvey, D. (1989) *The Condition of Postmodernity* (Oxford: Blackwell)

Hilferding, R. (1981) *Finance Capital* (London: Routledge & Kegan Paul)

Holdsworth, W. (1937) *A History of English Law: Volume VII* (London: Methuen)

Ingham, G. (1984) *Capitalism Divided* (London: Macmillan)

Ireland, P., Grigg-Spall, I. and Kelly, D. (1987) 'The Conceptual Foundations of Modern Company Law' in P. Fitzpatrick and A. Hunt (eds), *Critical Legal Studies* (Oxford: Blackwell)

Klare, K. (1979) 'Law Making as Praxis', *Telos*, vol. 40 pp. 128–30

Koffler, J. (1979) 'Capital in Hell – Dante's Lesson on Usury', *Rutgers Law Review*, vol. 32 pp. 608–60

Landes, D.S. (1960) 'The Structure of Enterprise in the Nineteenth Century' in D. Landes (ed.) *The Rise of Capitalism* (New York: Macmillan)

Marx, K. (1972) Theories of Surplus Value, Part III (London: Lawrence and Wishart)

Marx, K. (1974a) *Capital: Volume I* (London: Lawrence & Wishart)

Marx, K. (1974b) *Capital: Volume III* (London: Lawrence & Wishart)

Reed, M.C. (1969) *Railways in the Victorian Economy* (Newton Abbott: David & Charles)

Sayer, D. (1979) *Marx's Method: Ideology, Science and Critique in Capital* (Hassocks: Harvester)

Scott, J. (1979) *Corporations, Classes and Capitalism* (London: Hutchinson)

Scott, J. (1986) *Capitalist Property and Financial Power* (Brighton: Harvester Press)

Scott, W.M. (1912, repr. 1951) *The Constitution and Finance of English and Irish Joint Stock Companies to 1720* (Cambridge: Cambridge University Press)

Simmel G. (1978) *The Philosophy of Money* (London: Routledge and Kegan Paul)

Strange, S. (1986) *Casino Capitalism* (Oxford: Blackwell)

Alastair Edie, Ian Grigg-Spall and Paddy Ireland: Labour Law

Abercrombie, N., Hill, S. and Turner, B. (1980) *The Dominant Ideology Thesis* (London: Allen & Unwin)

Bercusson, B. (1990) 'The European Community's Charter of Fundamental Social Rights of Workers', *Modern Law Review*, vol. 53, pp. 624–42

Cmnd 3888 (1969) *In Place of Strife* (London: HMSO)

Cohen, G.A. (1978) *Karl Marx's Theory of History* (Oxford: Oxford University Press)

Dicey, A.V. (1959) *An Introduction to the Study of the Law of the Constitution* (London: Macmillan)

Ewing, K. and Grubb, A. (1987) 'The Emergence of a New Labour Injunction', *Industrial Law Journal*, vol. 16, pp. 145–63

Ewing, K. (1988) Death of Labour Law', *Oxford Journal of Legal Studies*, vol. 8, pp. 293–300

Fine, B. (1984) *Democracy and the Rule of Law* (London: Pluto Press)

Fox, A. (1974) *Beyond Contract* (London: Faber)

Harvey, D. (1989) *The Condition of Postmodernity* (Oxford: Blackwell)

Hayek, F. (1944) *The Road to Serfdom* (London: Routledge)

Hendy, J. (1989) *Conservative Anti-Union Legislation*, London: Institute of Employment Rights

Hepple, R. (1986) *Labour Law and Industrial Relations in Great Britain* (Kingston-upon-Thames: Kluwer)

Kahn-Freund, O. (1972) *Labour and the Law* (London: Stevens)

Kinsey, R. (1979) 'Despotism and Legality' in B. Fine et al. (eds), *Capitalism and the Rule of Law* (London: Hutchinson)

Lazonick W., (1978) 'The Subjugation of Labour to Capital', *Radical Review of Political Economics*, vol. 10, pp. 1–31

Marx, K. (1970) *Capital: Volume I* (London: Lawrence & Wishart)

Renner, K. (1949) *The Institutions of Private Law and their Social Functions* (with an Introduction by O. Kahn-Freund) (London: Routledge & Kegan Paul)

Sayer, D. (1979) *Marx's Method* (Hassocks: Harvester)

Scruton, R. (1982) *Dictionary of Political Thought* (London: Macmillan)

Simon, D. (1954) 'Master and Servant' in J. Saville (ed.), *Democracy and the Labour Movement* (London: Lawrence & Wishart)

Wedderburn, W. (1987) 'From Here to Autonomy', *Industrial Law Journal*, vol. 16, pp. 1–20

Richard de Friend: Constitutional Law

Arblaster, A. (1984) *The Rise and Decline of Western Liberalism* (Oxford: Blackwell)

Cotterrell, R. and Bercussen, B. (eds) (1988) *Democracy and Social Justice* (Oxford: Blackwell)

Dummett, A. and Nicol, A. (1990) *Subjects, Citizens, Aliens and Others* (London: Weidenfeld & Nicolson)

Ewing, K.D. and Gearty, C. (1990) *Freedom Under Thatcher* (Oxford: Clarendon Press)

Graham, C. and Prosser, T. (eds) (1988) *Waiving the Rules: The Constitution Under Thatcherism* (Milton Keynes: Open University Press)

Griffiths, J. (1985, 3rd edn) *The Politics of the Judiciary* (Manchester: Manchester University Press)

Harden, I. and Lewis, N. (1986) The Noble Lie: *The British Constitution and the Rule of Law* (London: Hutchinson)

Hayek, F. (1960) *The Constitution of Liberty* (London: Routledge & Kegan Paul)

Scruton, R. (1984, 2nd edn) *The Meaning of Conservatism* (London: Macmillan)

Thomson, A. (1991) 'Taking the Right Seriously: The Case of F.A. Hayek' in P. Fitzpatrick (ed.), *Dangerous Supplements* (London: Pluto Press)

Joanne Scott: European Law

Hartley, T. (1981) 'An Introduction to the Constitutional and Administrative Law of the European Community' in T. Hartley (ed.), *The Foundations of European Community Law* (Oxford: Clarendon Press)

Hindley, B. (1988) 'Dumping and the Far East Trade of the EC', *The World Economy* vol. 11, pp. 445–63

Petersmann, L. (1983a) 'Participation of the EC in the GATT: International Law and Community Law Aspects' in D. O'Keefe and R. Schermers (eds), *Mixed Agreements* (Deventer, The Netherlands: Kluwer)

Petersmann, L. (1983b) 'Application of GATT by the ECJ', *Common Market Law Review*, vol. 20, pp. 397–437

Raghavan, C. (1990) *Recolonization – GATT, the Uruquay Round and the Third World* (London: Zed Books)

Ravenhill, J. (1985) *Collective Clientelism: The Lomé Conventions and North–South Relations* (New York: Columbia University Press)

Snyder, F. (1987) 'New Directions in European Community Law' in P. Fitzpatrick and A. Hunt (eds), *Critical Legal Studies* (Oxford: Blackwell)

Spencer, M. (1990) *1992 and All That: Civil Liberties in the Balance* (London: The Civil Liberties Trust)

Ian Grigg-Spall and Paddy Ireland: Afterword

Arblaster, A. (1984) *The Rise and Decline of Western Liberalism* (Oxford: Blackwell)

Baudrillard, J. (1975) *The Mirror of Production* (St. Louis, Mo.: Telos Press)

Bell, D. (1976) *The Cultural Contradictions of Capitalism* (London: Heinemann)

Buchanan, A. (1982) *Marx and Justice: The Radical Critique of Liberalism* (Totowa, N.J.: Roman & Alan Held)

Carty, A. (1990) *Postmodern Law* (Edinburgh: Edinburgh University Press)

Corrigan, P. and Sayer, D. (1985) *The Great Arch: English State Formation as Cultural Revolution* (Oxford: Blackwell)

Ellis, B.E. (1991) *American Psycho* (London: Picador)

Fine, B. (1979) 'Struggles against Discipline', *Capital and Class*, vol. 7, pp. 75–89

Foucault, M. (1979) *Discipline and Punish* (Harmondsworth: Penguin)

Gabel, P. (1980) 'Reification in Legal Reasoning', *Research in Law and Sociology*, vol. 3, pp. 25–51 (Toronto: University Press)

Gilligan, C. (1982) *In a Different Voice* (Cambridge, Mass.: Harvard University Press)

Gorz, A. (1976) *The Division of Labour: The Labour Process and Class Struggle in Modern Capitalism* (Hassocks: Harvester Press)

Harvey, D. (1982) *The Limits to Capital* (Oxford: Blackwell)

Harvey, D. (1989a) *The Condition of Postmodernity* (Oxford: Blackwell)

Harvey, D. (1989b) *The Urban Experience* (Oxford: Blackwell)

Koffler, J. (1979) 'Capital in Hell – Dante's Lesson on Usury', *Rutgers Law Review*, vol. 32, pp. 608–60

Lazonick, W. (1978) 'The Subjection of Labour to Capital', *Radical Review of Political Economics*, vol. 10, pp. 1–31

Macfarlane, A. (1985) 'The Root of all Evil' in D. Parkin (ed.), T*he Anthropology of Evil* (Oxford: Oxford University Press)

Malcolmson, R. (1981) *Life and Labour in England, 1700–80* (London: Hutchinson)

Marcuse, H. (1970) *The Aesthetic Dimension: Towards a Critique of Marxist Aesthetics* (London: Macmillan)

Marglin, S. (1971) 'What do Bosses do? The Origins of Functions of Hierarchy in Capitalist Production', Discussion Paper no. 22, Harvard Institute of Economic Affairs

Marx, K. (1954) *Capital: Volume I* (London: Lawrence & Wishart)

Marx, K. (1976) *Capital:* Volume I (Harmondsworth: Penguin)

Marx, K. and Engels, F. (1952) *The Communist Manifesto* (Moscow)

Meszaros, I. (1989) *The Power of Ideology* (Hemel Hempstead: Harvester)

Nisbet, R. (1984) 'Uneasy Cousins' in G.W. Carey (ed.), *Freedom and Virtue* (Maryland: University Press of America)

O'Donovan, K. (1985) *Sexual Division* (London: Weidenfeld & Nicolson)

Pashukanis, E. (1983) *Law and Marxism* (London: Inklinks)

Pateman, C. (1988) *The Sexual Contract* (Cambridge: Polity Press)

Pilling, G. (1980) *Marx's Capital* (London: Routledge & Kegan Paul)

Pollard, S. (1963) 'Factory Discipline and the Industrial Revolution', *Economic History Review*, vol. 16, pp. 254–71

Rogers, W.V.H. (1979) *Winfield & Jolowicz on Tort* (London: Sweet & Maxwell)

Sayer, D. (1987) *The Violence of Abstraction: Analytical Foundations of Historical Materialism* (Oxford: Blackwell)

Scruton, R. (1984, 2nd edn) *The Meaning of Conservatism* (London: Macmillan)

Simmel, G. (1978) *The Philosophy of Money* (London: Routledge & Kegan Paul)

Taussig, M. (1980) *The Devil and Commodity Fetishism in South America* (Chapple Hill: University of North Carolina Press)

Thompson, E. P. (1967) 'Time, Work Discipline and Industrial Capitalism', *Past and Present*, vol. 38, pp. 56–97

Waldegrave, W. (1978) *The Binding of Leviathan: Conservatism and the Future* (London: Hamilton)

Chapter 3

Kim Economides and Ole Hansen: Critical Legal Practice

Abel, R.L. (1988) *The Legal Profession in England and Wales* (Oxford: Blackwell)

Bankowski, Z. and Mungham, G. (1976) *Images of Law* (London: Routledge & Kegan Paul)

Campbell, T. (1983) *The Left and the Rights: A Conceptual Analysis of the Idea of Socialist Rights* (London: Routledge & Kegan Paul)

Clarke, A. and Economides, K. (1989) 'The Poverty of Technology', paper for BILETA Conference

Clarke, A. and Economides, K. (1990) 'Technis and Praxis: Technological Innovation and Legal Practice in a Modern Society', *Yearbook of Law Computers and Technology*

Cotterrell, R. (1986) 'Critique and Law: The Problematic Legacy of the Frankfurt School', paper for Conference of Law and Society Association, Chicago

Economides, K. and Smallcombe, J. (1991) *Preparatory Skills Training for Trainee Solicitors* (London: Law Society)

Gabel, P. and Kennedy, D. (1984) 'Roll over Beethoven', *Stanford Law Review*, vol. 36, pp. 1–56

Garth, B.G. (1987) 'Independent Professional Power and the search for a Legal Ideology with a Progressive Bite', *Indiana Law Journal*, vol. 62, pp. 183–214

Geuss, R. (1981) *The Idea of a Critical Theory* (Cambridge: Cambridge University Press)

Hansen, O. (1990) 'Exempting Degrees: The Change of the Century', *New Law Journal*, vol. 140, pp. 1714–15

Hunt, A. (1990) 'Rights and Social Movements: Counter-Hegemonic Strategies', *Journal of Law and Society*, vol. 17, pp. 309–28

Kennedy, H. (1990) 'Towards a culture of rights', *Law Society's Gazette*, vol. 87/41, p. 2

Partington, M. (1988) 'Academic Lawyers and Legal Practice In Britain', *Journal of Law and Society*, vol. 15, no. 4, pp. 374–91

Raes, M. (1988) 'Habermas's Approach to Law', *Journal of Law and Society*, vol. 15, pp. 122–38

Scheingold, S. (1988) 'Radical Lawyers and Socialist Ideals', *Journal of Law and Society* vol.15, pp.122–136

Sedley, S. (1990) 'Law and State Power: A Time for Reconstruction' *Journal of Law and Society*, vol. 17, no. 2, pp. 234–41

Trubek, D. (1983) 'Complexity and Contradiction in the Legal Order', *Law and Society*, vol. 11, pp. 529–69

Trubek, D. (1984) 'Where the Action is: Critical Legal Studies and Empiricism', *Stanford Law Review*, vol. 36, pp. 575–623

Unger, R. (1983) 'The Critical Legal Studies Movement', *Harvard Law Review*, vol. 96, no. 3, pp. 563–675

John Fitzpatrick: Legal Practice and Socialist Practice

Bernstein, E. (1961) *Evolutionary Socialism* (New York: Schocken)

Blackburn, R. (1991) 'Fin de Siècle Socialism: After the Crash', *New Left Review*, no. 185, pp. 45–66

Freeman, M. (1988) 'Whose Freedom: Individual Rights and Class Politics', *Living Marxism*, no. 2, p. 7

Gramsci, A. (1971) *Selections from Prison Notebooks* (London: Lawrence & Wishart)

Held, D. (1991) 'Between State and Civil Society' in G. Andrews (ed.), *Citizenship* (London: Lawrence & Wishart)

Keane, J. (1988) *Democracy and Civil Society* (London: Verso)

Luxemburg, R. (1988) *Reform or Revolution* (New York: Pathfinder)

Marx, K. (1845) 'Draft Plan for a Work on the Modern State', quoted in I. Meszaros (1986) *Philosophy, Ideology and Social Science* (Hemel Hempstead: Wheatsheaf)

Marx, K. (1973a) *Grundrisse* (Harmondsworth: Penguin)

Marx, K. (1973b) *The German Ideology* (London: Lawrence & Wishart)

Marx, K. (1976) *Selected Works* (London: Lawrence & Wishart)

Marx, K. (1986) 'Draft Plan for Work on Modern State' in I. Meszaros, *Philosophy Ideology and Social Science* (Brighton: Wheatsheaf)

Marx, K. and Engels, F. (1968) *Selected Works* (London: Lawrence & Wishart)

Richards, F. (1990) 'Midnight in the Century', *Living Marxism*, vol. 26, December, pp. 34–8

Wood, E.M. (1986) *The Retreat from Class* (London: Verso)

Wood, E.M. (1988) 'Capitalism and Human Emancipation', *New Left Review*, no. 167, pp. 3–20

Wood, E.M. (1990) 'The Uses and Abuses of Civil Society in R. Miliband and L. Ranitch (eds), *Socialist Register – The Retreat of the Intellectuals*

John Fitzpatrick: Collective Working

Ritchie, J. (1991) 'Collectives, Hierarchies and Parity', paper for Law Centres' Federation General Meeting, 27 March 1991

Bill Bowring: Socialism, Liberation Struggkes

Babu, A. (1989) *The Struggle for Post-Union Africa* (London: Third World Library)

Brownlie, I. (1981) *Basic Documents on Human Rights* (Oxford: Clarendon Press)

Cassese, A. (ed.) (1979) *UN Law Fundamental Rights* (Holland: Sythoff)

Cassese, A. (1986) *International Law in a Divided World* (Oxford: Clarendon Press)

Crawford, J. (ed.) (1988) *The Rights of People* (Oxford: Clarendon Press)

Slovo, J. (1990) *Has Socialism Failed?* (London: Inklinks)

Stephens, M. (1989) *Enforcement of International Law in the Israeli-occupied Territories* (Ramallah, West Bank: Al-Haq)

Wilson, H. (1988) *International Law and the Use of Force by National Liberation Movements* (Oxford: Clarendon Press)

Contributors' Addresses

SAMMY ADELMAN, School of Law, University of Warwick, Coventry, England CV4 7AL

ANNE BOTTOMLEY, Rutherford College, The University, Canterbury, Kent, England CT2 7NX

BILL BOWRING, 4 Verulam Buildings, Grays Inn, London, England EC4A 1JY

RICHARD CARROLL, 42 Ulcombe Gardens, Canterbury, Kent CT2 7QZ

ANDY CLARK, School of Law, University of Warwick, Coventry, England CV4 7AL

JOANNE CONAGHAN, Eliot College, The University, Canterbury, Kent, England CT2 7NS

RICHARD DE FRIEND, Eliot College, The University, Canterbury, Kent, England CT2 7NS

COSTAS DOUZINAS, Faculty of Law, University of Lancaster, Lancaster, England LA1 4YW

KIM ECONOMIDES, University of Exeter, The Queen's Drive, Exeter, England EX4 4QJ

ALASTAIR EDIE, Law Department, Coventry Polytechnic, Priory Street, Coventry, England CV1 5FB

ROBERT FINE, Department of Sociology, University of Warwick, Coventry, England CV4 7AL

JOHN FITZPATRICK, Eliot College, The University, Canterbury, Kent, England CT2 7NS

PETER FITZPATRICK, Darwin College, The University, Canterbury, Kent, England CT2 7NY

KEN FOSTER, School of Law, University of Warwick, Coventry, England CV4 7AL

KATE GREEN, Law Department, East London Polytechnic, Longbridge Road, Dagenham, Essex, England RM8 2AS

IAN GRIGG-SPALL, Rutherford College, The University, Canterbury, Kent, England CT2 7NX

224

OLE HANSEN, South Bank Polytechnic, Borough Road, London, England SE1 0AA

PAUL HARRIS, Department of Law, New College of California, 50 Fell Street, San Francisco, California 94102, USA

ALAN HUNT, Law Department, Carleton University, Ottawa, Canada L16 5BG

PADDY IRELAND, Eliot College, The University, Canterbury, Kent, England CT2 7NS

NICK JACKSON, Rutherford College, The University, Canterbury, Kent, England CT2 7NX

DAVID KAIRYS, Temple University, 1719 N. Broad Street, Philadelphia, Pennsylvania 19122, USA

DAVID KELLY, Department of Law, Staffordshire Polytechnic, College Road, Stoke-on-Trent, Staffs, England ST4 2DE

DUNCAN KENNEDY, Harvard Law School, Cambridge, Mass. 02138, USA

WADE MANSELL, Eliot College, The University, Canterbury, Kent, England CT2 7NS

MICHAEL MANSFIELD QC, 14 Tooks Court, Cursitor Street, London, England EC4 1JY

KATE MARKUS, Brent Community Law Centre, 190 Willesden High Road, London, England NW10 2PB

ALAN NORRIE, School of Law, University of Warwick, Coventry, England CV4 7AL

SOL PICCIOTTO, School of Law, University of Warwick, Coventry, England CV4 7AL

MOLLIE ROOTS, Rutherford College, The University, Canterbury, Kent, England CT2 7NX

JOANNE SCOTT, Darwin College, The University, Canterbury, Kent, England CT2 7NY

ALAN THOMSON, Darwin College, The University, Canterbury, Kent, England CT2 7NY

RONNIE WARRINGTON, Faculty of Law, University of Lancaster, Lancaster, England LA1 4YW

DAVID WATKINSON, 2 Garden Court, Middle Temple, London, England EC4Y 9BL